# Resurrecting the Past: The California Mission Myth

Michelle M. Lorimer

GREAT OAK PRESS, PECHANGA, CALIFORNIA

A CIP catalog record for this book is available from the Library of Congress.

ISBN: 978-1-942279-01-3

Publisher: Great Oak Press, Pechanga, California

Printed in the United States of America

# Contents

# *Preface*

European colonization of the Americas brought enormous changes to the lives of indigenous peoples. But it was not a passive experience; Native communities had to wrestle with foreign forces who believed that indigenous cultures, religions, and societies were inferior to those of Europeans. The Spanish endeavored to subjugate indigenous peoples, strip them of their cultures, and force them into accepting a new way of life at the bottom of the newly imposed social and economic order.

Spain's empire, in decline in late eighteenth century, established missions, presidios, and pueblos in Alta California in an attempt to replicate aspects of Spanish society in its northern territory. Following their traditional model, the Spanish moved aggressively to incorporate Native peoples into this system and control their lives. This was accomplished through coerced labor or forced bondage and prohibition of indigenous languages, spiritual beliefs, and traditional societal and family structures. In place of these indigenous ways of life, the Spanish imposed European social structures, customs, and Catholicism on Native people at their settlements. However, Native peoples resisted this colonization, consistently finding ways to circumvent the eradication of their cultures. Through this struggle—though much was lost and great pain felt—the Spanish never fully erased the cultures of Native Californian communities on whose land they laid claim and established their missions.

Although arguably the mission system may have failed, regional boosters at the turn of the twentieth century worked to promote a romanticized version of mission history that neglected the lived experiences of Native peoples. As a result, the greatest legacy of the Spanish missions in popular culture is a narrative that more closely reflects the views of people who worked diligently to preserve the colonial sites in the late nineteenth and early twentieth centuries. The history emphasized by Euro-American promoters, preservationists, and church leaders who worked to rebuild the missions necessarily pushed the lived experiences of Native Californians into the shadows of the historical record.

The epigraph at the outset of each chapter provides insight into the powerful mission myth developed by popular writers and regional boosters of Southern

California. Although the myth of the romantic mission era is still alive and well at many of these historic sites throughout the state, the voices of Native Californians provide a striking counternarrative that offers significant insight into both the lived experiences of Native Californians and the continued impact of colonial systems on Native peoples today.

# *Acknowledgments*

Researching this book has led me on many adventures. At its core it began as a public history project with a focus on Native Californian experiences and the Spanish California missions. Locating sources of information took me beyond the archives and historical records left by foreign explorers and tourists of California. In fact, I traveled throughout California many times to meet with Native peoples and visit missions. Through this I amassed a personal collection of sources for this project after, inevitably, stepping into the shoes of a mission tourist. I would like to thank the many Native people, docents, and mission staff from across the state who shared their time and interpretation of mission history with me. Many members of my extended family also helped me accumulate material for this project, as they thoughtfully shared with me pamphlets, souvenirs, postcards, and books from contemporary Spanish historical sites. The story told in many of these writings and objects exemplifies the perpetuation of the mission myth in popular culture today, and it reinforces the need to reexamine history in California from Native perspectives.

With the encouragement of my dissertation advisor Clifford Trafzer, I strove to explore why Native experiences are often silent at many contemporary mission sites and in popular California histories more generally. I owe a great debt of gratitude to Cliff for guiding me through this journey with his scholarship as my example. I am truly grateful for his mentorship and friendship. While studying at University of California, Riverside, I also benefited from the advice of members of my doctoral committee including Rebecca "Monte" Kugel, Catherine Gudis, Larry Burgess, and Yolanda Moses. At the same time, Steven Hackel sparked my interest in California mission history. Beyond UCR, I am thankful to George Phillips and Edward Castillo for their valuable insight and comments on drafts of this project. Brenda Buller-Focht, Andrew Shaler, Sherrie Dennehy, Susan Wood, and other friends, family, and colleagues have helped improve this book through listening and reading portions. Moreover, the stories told each year by many Native peoples at the California Indian Conference continues to reaffirm that more accurate discussions of mission history in popular culture must be acknowledged to facilitate healing and a more inclusive understanding of the past. To Julia Bogany, Gregg Castro, and the many other Native people who have shared knowledge with me, I am eternally grateful.

The California Center for Native Nations and the Rupert Costo Fellowship at UCR generously supported me through much of the early stages of this work. While in graduate school, the Anne Siebert Academic Scholarship and the Old Towne Preservation Association helped fund my research dealing with historic preservation in chapters 2 and 3. I also owe a debt of gratitude to the staff at the Huntington Library for their help and support. As a fellow at the Huntington, I had the pleasure of exploring the Library's rare books, manuscripts, and photo collections dealing with the missions and tourism. The images used in this book are but a small selection of the hundreds of excellent photographs and ephemera dealing with the missions in the Huntington's vast collections.

During the years that I have devoted to this research, my family has been my rock. Their interest and support of my work has kept me motivated through trying times. My parents and siblings have accompanied me on visits to missions from San Diego to San Francisco, and beyond. And my parents, Tom and Patty, spent many other days watching my young son while I worked on drafts of this project. As I explored the impact of the mission myth, Mike and Maureen Lorimer graciously shared their insight into the mission debate as educators actively engaged in teacher education and at elementary schools. I am forever grateful to the Dennehy, Acosta, Chittenden, Lorimer, Wos, Mattson, and Stonerock families for being reliable constants in my life. Most of all, I am forever grateful to my husband Chris for his encouragement, support, and for being my travel companion while on this journey. His presence, and that of our son Christopher, has made my life richer. It is to them that I dedicate this work.

# *Introduction*

Touring through the Spanish California missions today, many visitors learn about the early history of the state. Contemporary mission sites are graced with beautifully manicured gardens, tiled courtyards, fountains, large stone sculptures, and covered alcoves in which visitors can enjoy the relaxing environment created by mission stewards. The exhibitions in mission museums highlight the lives and accomplishments of Spanish Franciscan missionaries, especially Father President Junípero Serra, who pioneered these "civilizing" institutions. The exhibitions display religious relics, including oversized Bibles and hymnals, the vestments worn by Spanish priests, and crucifixes, rosaries, clocks, and candleholders.

These objects represent the Spanish colonial history of contemporary mission sites. However, they overshadow the roles and accomplishments of the Native Californians who overwhelmingly populated and labored at missions in the late eighteenth and early nineteenth centuries. Many historical representations of California missions today neglect to acknowledge such vital components of Native life at the missions, including Native labor, resistance, sustenance, disease, punishment, and death. At the same time, they generalize or oversimplify the histories of Native peoples in the region and their connection to the land. Thus underneath the charming façade maintained at many contemporary mission sites is a more tumultuous history that, if told, would reflect poorly on the constructed "Spanish fantasy past" and mission myth in California.[1]

## A Romanticized History

The presentation of the past at California missions today reflects a romanticized history carefully contrived by Euro-American writers and promoters at the turn of the twentieth century. The popular publications of Charles Fletcher Lummis, John Steven McGroarty, George Wharton James, and many others commemorated the Spanish legacy in Southern California at a time when the region's population began to swell. They ignored the historical perspectives of Native Californians and highlighted histories that masked Native contributions in the development of the region. Encouraged further by the idyllic description of Spanish California's landscape found in Helen

Hunt Jackson's popular novel *Ramona: A Story* (1884), promoters used the missions, in ruins by the late 1800s, as symbols of a dramatized early California history to attract new residents to the state, as well as tourists and their money. These popular portrayals became so engrained in the minds of Americans that, for many, California's history only began with Spanish contact. The stereotypical representations of Native Californians as "barbarous, ferocious, and ignorant" found in European and American historical writings helped silence Native voices in their history and popular culture well into the twentieth century.[2]

Few popular writers and scholars in the early twentieth century included the rich histories and cultures of Native Californians in their descriptions of the history of the region. By contrast, many scholars have examined the impacts and contributions of the Spanish in North America, beginning with Hubert Howe Bancroft and Herbert Eugene Bolton.[3] Bancroft and a number of his contemporaries argued that the Spanish era was a "Golden Age" in the history of California.[4] These scholars applauded the establishment of Spanish mission institutions and venerated the Franciscan padres for "civilizing" Native Californians. This perspective lasted well into the twentieth century until pioneering scholars such as Francis Jennings and Gary Nash refocused the historical lens to view European settlement from a distinctly *Native* perspective. They countered the European "civility" versus Native "savagery" dichotomy that pervaded academia in the early twentieth century, especially as it was related to American expansion west. New generations of scholars in the late twentieth century increasingly used archeological evidence and Native sources to demonstrate that indigenous peoples had developed sophisticated societies, cultures, and economies over the span of thousands of years before European colonization began in the sixteenth century.[5] Others described how Native peoples had negotiated the varied structures of colonialism instituted by foreign powers in order to exercise control over their own lives.[6]

**Reexamining California History**

In recent decades, scholars of California history have begun to draw on indigenous sources to reexamine the impacts of Euro-American contact and settlement from Native perspectives. These scholars have revealed how Euro-American settlement devastated Native Californian communities in many ways. Foreigners introduced deadly diseases, invasive plant and animal species, violent settler populations, and culturally destructive social institutions, such as the Spanish missions, to the California landscape. Unlike the reports of "vanishing" or increasingly "extinct" Native communities popularized in books and newspapers in the early twentieth century, scholars today demonstrate how Native Californians both adapted to and resisted a variety of the changes brought by foreigners.[7] Although Native Californians witnessed a demographic collapse that saw their numbers sharply fall from more than 310,000 in the 1770s to less than 30,000 by 1870, Native Californian communities managed to survive.[8] By mitigating the impact of changes brought by Euro-American influences, the Native peoples of California safeguarded the survival of their communities.[9]

In recent years, popular venues such as the Smithsonian Institution's National Museum of the American Indian (NMAI) have worked tirelessly to demonstrate that Native communities continue to exist and thrive throughout the Americas.[10] Cutting-edge institutions such as the NMAI provide Native perspectives on the effects of European contact and colonization that counter the Eurocentric narratives common in popular culture. In California, the counternarratives provided by Native communities and new generations of scholars informed by Indian peoples demonstrate that Native people did not passively submit to the Spanish. Rather, Native Californians reacted to colonization in a variety of ways and strove to find opportunities to preserve their lives and cultures in the face of extremely destructive foreign forces.[11] Despite this shift on the national level, many California mission sites do not include Native perspectives on life during the Spanish and Mexican eras. They continue to promote sanitized and romanticized presentations of the mission period that paint the Spanish as benevolent forces in the lives of Native Californians—a perspective that many Native Californians vehemently challenge.[12]

A majority of the contemporary mission sites owned and operated by the Catholic Church echo the perspectives of outdated historical narratives popular in the early twentieth century. The exhibition spaces in many mission museums are heavily object-based and have minimal interpretation of Native experiences. Many of these current presentations neglect to include realistic depictions of the lives of the thousands of Native Californians who lived and died at the missions. They also do not describe the way in which Native people found avenues of control within these colonial institutions and actively resisted the Spanish in a variety of forms into the 1830s. In short, visitors to these historical sites encounter skewed and biased representations of California history that ignore Native perspectives and the negative components of Spanish colonization.

One publication sold at a mission site argues that "it is difficult to picture early California more than 200 years ago when the wild, uninhabited miles of our Western land knew only the occasional footsteps of . . . Indian tribes."[13] In reality, Native peoples made the California landscape their home for thousands of years before the Kumeyaay, in what is now southern San Diego County, first came into contact with Spanish sailors under Juan Rodríguez Cabrillo in 1542. Indeed, Native peoples in California significantly outnumbered these newcomers, and the foreign population did not surpass Native Californians until 1849, when waves of foreigners, and many Euro-Americans, flooded into California during the gold rush. Before Euro-American contact, indigenous populations flourished with the natural diversity provided by the California landscape.[14]

Native communities such as the Salinan, Ohlone, Miwok, Maidu, and Yurok populated (and continue to live in) the areas that surround the great redwood forests of today's Northern California and along the rocky coastline. In today's Southern California, indigenous communities such as the Chumash, Gabrielino-Tongva, Ajachemen, Luiseño, and Kumeyaay thrived along the Pacific coastline that supplied abundant food for hundreds of coastal Indian villages. They traveled up to 60 nautical miles to San Nicholas Island in plank canoes to reach the villages and trade sites they established on the Channel Islands. In fact, they had great knowledge and impressive skills using these ocean-going vessels. The Gabrielino-Tongva and Serrano in what is now called the Los Angeles basin and San Bernardino Valley, respectively, built intricate trade networks that helped transport valuable goods to distant villages. Likewise, the desert Cahuilla, Chemehuevi, Mohave, Halchidhoma, and Quechan populated the vast deserts that stretched out to the Colorado River. For thousands of years, then, Native Californians developed complex societies that transformed the heritage of the region and enshrined the landscape with intrinsic meaning at culturally significant sites.[15]

The largest number of Native peoples north of the Rio Grande lived in the area now commonly known as California. These people did not view themselves as "California Indians," nor did they share a common culture, language, or religion. In reality, Native Californians lived in communities that reflected the extreme diversity of the California landscape. The various groups in California spoke over a hundred different dialects, and the cultures, religions, traditions, and subsistence strategies of Native Californian communities specifically reflected the climates and resources available in their particular regions. For example, the ocean played an important role in the lives of the Chumash people in the Santa Barbara region, but was less significant to the desert Cahuilla. The Chumash benefited from a balanced coastal climate and rich natural environment that helped them develop into one of the largest Native communities in California. Although Native Californians more sparsely settled the deserts and high mountains, populations boomed among the Chumash, the Yokuts in the San Joaquin Valley, and

4

the Gabrielino-Tongva in the greater Los Angeles area.[16]

The experiences Native Californians had, and continue to have, with the landscape shaped and informed many of their sociocultural interactions. The beliefs and traditions of indigenous communities reflect the diversity of the California landscape. Meanwhile, the extremely diverse Native communities in California trace their histories back to the time of creation. Tribal songs, stories, and histories include common themes about the unity of the natural and supernatural worlds, the power of the creator and animal spirits, and the interdependence between humans and nature. These themes are also visible in cave and rock art throughout California. For example, scholars believe that Chumash shamans painted cave walls to influence supernatural forces to intervene in human affairs. Native Californian creation stories—communicated orally through countless generations—tell of the formation of the earth by the Creator. These narratives document the trials of the first people, and they imbue the landscape with meaning through the lessons learned by early ancestors at the site of important events.[17] For instance, the Serrano in Southern California, like many other Native peoples, passed their tribal histories down through generations orally in stories and songs. They chart their presence in the San Bernardino Mountains region to the beginning of time when the Creator, Kokiitach, lived and died in the pine tree forest that surrounds modern-day Big Bear Lake. Kokiitach died just east of the lake, and the first people buried his remains at A'atsava, in Bear Valley. The Serrano refer to the area as Kutainan. An abundance of food emerged out of Kokiiach's remains that nourished descendants of the Serrano people. They believe that their ancestors grieved for a long time following Kokiiach's death, "so long in fact that they 'turned into pines' and their bones became scattered as pine nuts" in the valley.[18] They also believe that the lands where Kokiitach lived, died, and was buried, as well as the surrounding pine trees, are very important. The Serrano did not alter the landscape to imbue it with deep meaning, and yet the Bear Valley and Big Bear Lake areas are considered extremely significant sites in Serrano tribal history.

Religious and cultural traditions influenced the interactions of Native Californians with people and the land, and they framed their experiences with foreigners. Many of the Spanish and Euro-Americans, for example, did not value the religious and cultural traditions of Native Californians, and many even viewed indigenous people as inferior and animal-like subhumans.[19] In reducing Native communities to life at the Spanish missions and in reservations during the American era, foreigners failed to recognize the sociopolitical sovereignty of Native Californian communities.

Locally, Native Californians organized themselves into lineages and clans.

Although some peoples held connections to their larger community through shared language, culture, and territory, most daily activity occurred at the village level. Defined boundaries separated the larger cultural groups. The territory of a single group could span 50 to several hundred square miles, depending on its location and available resources. Groups located on some of the most naturally rich land often had larger populations. For example, the Gabrielino-Tongva, estimated by scholars to number more than 5,000 divided into twenty-eight tribelets, occupied 1,500 square miles, including the San Gabriel Valley, the Los Angeles basin, the Santa Ana plain and mountains, and the western portions of the San Bernardino Valley. In such prosperous regions, indigenous people developed complex religions, cultures, and trade connections with other tribes hundreds of miles away.[20]

Most of the California landscape provided Native people with an abundance of wild plants, grains, and animals. Native Californians had extensive knowledge of the natural world around them, and they used this knowledge to develop successful subsistence strategies that focused primarily on hunting and harvesting. Because of the natural abundance, Native people throughout most of California did not need to develop complex or highly organized agriculture. However, they expertly harvested the land and managed the natural environment. For example, some planted small gardens, burned local vegetation to encourage new growth, and spread seeds near their villages. Many groups, especially in coastal, valley, and foothill areas, also harvested acorns, a nutrient-rich food that was relatively nonperishable when stored in its shell. Entire communities assembled to harvest acorns, and Native women processed them into an edible meal.[21] Because of the abundance of resources in many areas of California, many tribal groups were able to trade their surplus food and raw materials with other communities. Despite territorial boundaries between groups, inland people were able to acquire shells, soapstone, and other goods from the coast. At the same time, coastal people were able to access antelope skin shirts, red ochre, bighorn pelts, and other goods from inland and desert groups.[22]

Beginning in the late eighteenth century, Spanish and Euro-American settlers who valued sedentary farming viewed Native Californians as "less civilized" than agriculturalists such as the Pueblos in modern-day New Mexico. These newcomers frequently discriminated against Native Californians, referring to them as "primitive" and dirty "diggers"—a word that conjured images of ignorant, undeveloped people who aimlessly wandered the countryside and used sticks to dig for roots as food.[23] The newcomers discounted Native land ownership and land management techniques, noting in their travel journals that Native Californians "appeared the most miserable of the human race having nothing to subsit [*sic*] on (nor any clothing) except grass seeds, grasshoppers, etc."[24] Foreign travelers and explorers inaccurately concluded that Native Californians did not develop the land because they were "stupid" and "ignorant." Euro-Americans unfamiliar with Native Californians mistook these erroneous and degrading statements as facts that would endure into the twentieth century.[25]

Euro-Americans also misunderstood Native labor strategies. Labor roles among Native Californian communities were generally very structured, but they did not follow the strict daily routines common in Euro-American cultures. Native men and women each performed different tasks and served particular functions in society. Women typically remained near villages to gather plants and hunt small animals. They prepared the food, watched over the children, and made clothing, among other things. Men hunted and played active roles as political and religious leaders. They also interacted with other tribal leaders in intertribal trade and diplomacy. Occasionally, women crossed into male spheres. For example, some women, such as Toypurina among the Gabrielino-Tongva, became shamans and political leaders in their own right. This gendered division became problematic, however, after Spanish colonization.[26]

Cultural misunderstandings and conflicting beliefs about the structure of daily labor routines caused tension between Native Californians and the Spanish. For example, the Spanish compelled indigenous men at the missions to farm and harvest crops—work that traditionally fell within a woman's sphere. Moreover, Europeans and Euro-Americans did not acknowledge the developed trade network and seasonal work routine of Native peoples. They deemed Native Californians stupid and "lazy" because the land was not "improved" with permanent buildings common in Europe and the United States in the nineteenth century.[27]

Throughout the nineteenth and twentieth centuries, newcomers created a history for California that excluded Native people as active participants in this past. Yet in his seminal work *The Invasion of America: Indians, Colonialism, and the Cant of Conquest* (1975), Jennings argued that "in examining the American past, an ethnohistorian finds, not the triumph of civilization over savagery, but an acculturation of Europeans and Indians that was marked by the interchange or diffusion of cultural traits" in a society now dominated by Euro-Americans.[28] However, early popular histories of California often excluded Native perspectives, and instead placed great emphasis on stories of the Euro-American dominant culture.

Frequently, indigenous people in California saw foreigners usurp the figurative and literal landscape from Native control for personal gain. Although some

Native Californians maintained access to their lands, others faced discrimination and biased American laws that restricted their access to their ancestral homelands. As Euro-Americans staked claim to Native lands, they painted indigenous peoples as barriers to social and cultural progress. Historical writings depicted Native peoples in a separate space, as outsiders, who must change or give way to the wave of "civilization" that spread north from New Spain in the late eighteenth century and west from the United States after the 1840s. Notions that Native peoples and their cultures teetered on the verge of extinction permeated popular writings in the late nineteenth and early twentieth centuries.[29] According to historian James J. Rawls, many Americans viewed the extinction of Native peoples as inevitable over time, and many Americans in California in the 1850s helped hasten the process by engaging in extermination campaigns.[30] Extreme discrimination and violence against Native Californians further helped to silence their voices in popular culture.

Meanwhile, many of the emerging museums and public interpretive sites in the late eighteenth and nineteenth centuries reflected these negative stereotypes about indigenous peoples. Exhibitions and public presentations focused on romanticized or nostalgic depictions of Native peoples. Curators and site stewards sought to preserve components of cultures that they deemed "vanishing." They did so by amassing collections of Native basketry, pottery, rugs, clothing, sacred objects, and human remains rather than acknowledging the perseverance and cultural adaptation of many Native peoples.[31] Their patrons and audiences later applied the myth of the vanishing Indian to the world around them. What historic sites and museums failed to address was the contemporary Native communities who were wrestling with poverty, the loss of their ancestral homelands, widespread discrimination, and active efforts to control their lives. These realistic themes simply did not fit into the romantic, idyllic image of historic sites such as the Spanish missions in California that promoters and local boosters sought to popularize.

The history promoted by boosters such as Lummis and McGroarty in the early twentieth century focused on dramatic representations of the mission era—centered on the benevolent work of Spanish priests and the celebration of mission ruins. Boosters pushed Native Californians into the periphery of this constructed narrative, despite the central role of indigenous peoples in building, populating, sustaining, and expanding the missions. Following this tradition, many contemporary mission museums continue to present unhistorical representations of the past. Interpreters at these sites frequently overlook themes such as Native labor, resistance, disease, Spanish-inflicted punishments, violence, and death. They glorify the Spanish priests, de-emphasize Native people, and minimize the impact of Spanish colonization on Native Californian populations. Scholars in the late twentieth century provided more accurate and detailed analyses of early California history. However, popular representations of mission history do not adequately reflect scholarly knowledge about the role of Native Californians within the mission system. Although some contemporary sites work to present more balanced and honest representations of the past, sanitized and romanticized narratives remain the most prominent in popular culture today.

This work is aimed primarily at the representation of Native Californians at contemporary California mission sites. Chapter 1 is an overview of Spanish colonization, the establishment of the mission system, and the impact of these systems on Native Californian peoples. It reveals that popular stories of the Spanish era in California long reflected an idealized mission period that minimized the importance of Native people—a legacy still present in popular culture. Chapter 2 examines the development and popularization of mission mythology by regional promoters in Southern California such as Lummis and McGroarty and enthusiasts of Jackson's novel *Ramona*. To claim California history as their own, Euro-American migrants in Southern California in the late 1880s took hold of the Spanish legacy and created an idealized narrative that built connections between the mission ruins and a shared European heritage in the area.

Exclusion and misrepresentation of Native people became a common facet of historical narratives in California in the early twentieth century. Chapter 3 tackles the misrepresentation of Native people in museums during that period and the exclusion of Native experiences in movements to preserve the California missions. Through the preservation of Spanish sites in California, many people began to understand Spanish colonization as the beginning of *any* history in the region. Americans did not recognize Native historical sites on the landscape as important, if they even recognized their existence at all. The creation of unhistorical and biased interpretations of California's early history contributed to the continued misrepresentation of Native Californians at contemporary mission sites in the state. Chapters 4, 5, and 6 turn to specific examples of the ways in which mission museums continue to represent Native experiences within the dramatized histories of Spanish California. By examining the unglamorous but realistic components of mission life, including labor, resistance, death, disease, and punishment, these chapters demonstrate that many mission sites focus on their own religious and institutional histories, minimize Native perspectives, and promote distorted perceptions of the past.

Scholars in the twenty-first century are using historical records and Native testimonies to extract more accurate historical narratives. However, many California missions continue in the footsteps of *Ramona* enthusiasts and regional boosters who viewed Spanish California as an idyllic period and the missions as symbols of that bygone era. Some mission sites, especially a small few operated by the state of California, are trying to mend the unrealistic depiction of Spanish history common in popular venues. Chapter 7 examines the interpretations at the sites that focus more heavily on Native perspectives and their perception of the mission experience. Their presentation of history displays a more balanced portrait of early California that emphasizes the lived experiences of indigenous populations instead of simply celebrating the lives and labors of Franciscan priests and Spanish explorers.

Introduction

## Notes

1. Carey McWilliams coined the phrase "Spanish fantasy past" in *North from Mexico: The Spanish-Speaking People of the United States* (New York: Praeger, 1948).
2. Clifford E. Trafzer, *As Long as the Grass Shall Grow and Rivers Flow: A History of Native Americans* (Fort Worth, TX: Harcourt College Publishers, 2000), 54.
3. Hubert Howe Bancroft, *History of California*, 6 vols. (San Francisco: The History Company, 1884–1890); Herbert Eugene Bolton, *The Spanish Borderlands: A Chronicle of Old Florida and the Southwest* (New Haven, CT: Yale University Press, 1921); David J. Weber, *The Spanish Frontier in North America* (New Haven, CT: Yale University Press, 1992); John L. Kessell, *Spain in the Southwest* (Norman: University of Oklahoma Press, 2002).
4. Albert L. Hurtado, "Fantasy Heritage: California's Historical Identities and the Professional Empire of Herbert E. Bolton," in *Alta California: Peoples in Motion, Identities in Formation, 1769–1850,* ed. Steven W. Hackel (Berkeley: University of California Press, published for the Huntington-USC Institute on California and the West, 2010), 201–203.
5. Francis Jennings, *The Invasion of America: Indians, Colonialism, and the Cant of Conquest* (Chapel Hill: University of North Carolina Press, 1975); Gary B. Nash, *Red, White, and Black: The People of Early North America* (Englewood, NJ: Prentice-Hall, 1974); Edward H. Spicer, *Cycles of Conquest: The Impact of Spain, Mexico, and the United States on the Indians of the Southwest, 1533–1960* (Tucson: University of Arizona Press, 1962).
6. Lee Panich and Tsim Schneider, eds., *Indigenous Landscapes and Spanish Missions: New Perspectives from Archeology and Ethnohistory* (Tucson: University of Arizona Press, 2014), 5–22.
7. Ibid.; Richard L. Carrico, *Strangers in a Stolen Land: Indians of San Diego County from Prehistory to the New Deal* (San Diego: Sunbelt Publications, 2008), 1–49; Steven W. Hackel, *Children of Coyote, Missionaries of Saint Francis: Indian-Spanish Relations in Colonial California, 1769–1850* (Chapel Hill: University of North Carolina Press, 2005), 1–123; James J. Rawls, *Indians of California: The Changing Image* (Norman: University of Oklahoma Press, 1984), 1–65, 240–271; James A. Sandos, *Converting California: Indians and Franciscans in the Missions* (New Haven, CT: Yale University Press, 2004), 1–68, 154–184; George Harwood Phillips, *Vineyards and Vaqueros: Indian Labor and the Economic Expansion of Southern California, 1771–1877* (Norman: University of Oklahoma Press, 2010), 15–158; George Harwood Phillips, *Chiefs and Challengers: Indian Resistance and Cooperation in Southern California*, 2d ed. (Norman: University of Oklahoma Press, 2014), 3–146.
8. Some scholars and Native Californians including Jack Norton and Florence Shipek estimated that the pre-contact population was as high as 1 million people. This study uses Sherburne Cook's moderate estimate of 310,000, but recognizes that as many as 1 million Native people may have lived in California at the time of contact. Clifford E. Trafzer and Joel Hyer, eds., *"Exterminate Them!": Written Accounts*

11

*of the Murder, Rape, and Enslavement of Native Americans during the California Gold Rush* (East Lansing: Michigan State University Press, 1999), xiv; Russell Thornton, *American Indian Holocaust and Survival: A Population History since 1492* (Norman: University of Oklahoma Press, 1987), 109; Sherburne F. Cook, *The Conflict between the California Indian and White Civilization* (1943; repr., Berkeley: University of California Press, 1976), 3–194, 399–445; Jack Norton, *Genocide in Northwestern California: When Our Worlds Cried* (San Francisco: Indian Historian Press, 1979).

9. Native Californians contribute their stories and histories to publications that emphasize cultural continuity. Malcolm Margolin, ed., *The Way We Lived: California Indian Stories, Songs, and Reminiscences* (Berkeley: Heyday Books and California Historical Society, 1993), 6–9; Rawls, *Indians of California*, 171.

10. The National Museum of the American Indian (NMAI) opened its doors to the public in September 2004 after over a decade of planning and construction. Many aspects of this museum, including its structural appearance, layout of the exhibition space, and style of its displays, reflect input from Native leaders and community members. Furthermore, Native people such as W. Richard West Jr. (Cheyenne), the founding director of the NMAI, hold vital positions in the administration of the museum. Duane Blue Spruce, ed., *Spirit of a Native Place: Building the National Museum of the American Indian* (Washington, DC: Smithsonian Institution, in association with National Geographic, 2004).

11. Margolin, ed., *The Way We Lived*, 139–211.

12. Many Native Californians voiced their opposition to the romanticized perspective of California mission history at a symposium that addressed the canonization of Father Junípero Serra. It was held at the University of California, Riverside, in March 2015.

13. Val Ramon, *Mission San Gabriel Arcángel: Commemorative Edition* (Yucaipa, CA: Photografx Worldwide, 2008), 4.

14. Sherburne Cook used mission records and anthropological sources to conservatively estimate the Native Californian population at approximately 135,000. Cook focused on the decline of the Native Californian populations after contact. He calculated the pre-contact population to provide a baseline for his study of population decline. Cook revised his calculations of Native Californian populations several times, and eventually concluded that Native Californians numbered approximately 310,000 by the late 1770s. Cook, *Conflict between the California Indian and White Civilization*, 3–194, 399–445; Hackel, *Children of Coyote*, 1–22; Albert L. Hurtado, *Indian Survival on the California Frontier* (New Haven, CT: Yale University Press, 1988), 2–3; Rawls, *Indians of California*, 6.

15. See the discussion of Native understandings of the landscape in chapter 3 of this study.

16. William S. Simmons, "Indian Peoples of California," *California History* 76 (summer-fall 1997): 48–77.

17. Ibid.

18. Clifford E. Trafzer, *The People of San Manuel* (Patton, CA: San Manuel Band of

Mission Indians, 2002), 16–20.

19. Rawls, *Indians of California*, 26–65.

20. William McCawley, *The First Angelinos: The Gabrielino Indians of Los Angeles* (Banning, CA: Malki Museum Press, 1996), 23–27.

21. They ground the acorn meat into a fine powder and then leached out the bitter tannins by soaking the powder in water. Native people used the remaining acorn meal to make a variety of foods. Helen McCarthy, "Managing Oaks and the Acorn Crop," in *Before the Wilderness: Environmental Management by Native Californians*, ed. Thomas C. Blackburn and Kat Anderson (Menlo Park, CA: Ballena Press, 1993), 213–228.

22. Simmons, "Indian Peoples of California," 48–77; McCawley, *First Angelinos*, 115–140.

23. Allen Lonnberg, "The Digger Indian Stereotype in California," *Journal of California and Great Basin Anthropology* 3 (1981): 215–223.

24. Jedediah Smith, as quoted in Rawls, *Indians of California*, 49.

25. Rawls, *Indians of California*, 48–52.

26. Lowell J. Bean and Thomas F. King, eds., *'Antap: California Indian Political and Economic Organization* (Ramona, CA: Ballena Press, 1974), 26; McCawley, *First Angelinos*, 143–185.

27. Rawls, *Indians of California*, 28–60; Hackel, *Children of Coyote*, 280–281.

28. Jennings, *Invasion of America*, 13.

29. Trafzer and Hyer, *"Exterminate Them!"* 14–30; Rawls, *Indians of California*, 171–201.

30. Rawls, *Indians of California*, 171–177.

31. Moira G. Simpson, *Making Representations: Museums in the Post-Colonial Era* (New York: Routledge, 2001), 35–36.

# 1

# *The California Missions and Spanish Colonization*

It was then [in that fateful year of 1769] that Destiny marked South-ern California for its own, ordaining the fig and the vine to make soft the desert wastes, lemon and orange bloom for the upland slopes, herds on a thousand hills, living waters to make green the sun-browned land; and at last . . . the tangible, bright reality of thrice seven times seven golden cities that now throb with the tides of commerce and the tread of countless feet. . . . Glamorous as Southern California is to him who looks back upon its history and traditions through the glow of Time's white mist.
—John Steven McGroarty, *History of Southern California* (1914)

Contemporary missions remain in a suspended state in popular culture and California history. Early promoters of Southern California created a mythical history for Euro-Americans based on the physical ruins of old missions and illusory history torn from the pages of Helen Hunt Jackson's *Ramona*.[1] These romanticized interpretations venerated the lives of Spanish missionaries and exalted the missions as benevolent "civilizing" institutions. However, this mythic past has overshadowed the true history of Spanish California and the crucial role missions played as components of larger Spanish colonial interests in Alta California and the Spanish borderlands from the sixteenth to nineteenth centuries.[2] The mission myth also masked the overwhelmingly negative impact Spanish colonization had on Native Californians. An ex-amination of historical scholarship on Spanish colonization and the role of mission institutions will provide much needed background for understanding a more accurate history of the California missions and their lasting legacy on Native communities.

## Spanish Colonization

Native Californians, especially those in coastal areas, experienced dramatic changes to their ways of life when Spanish foreigners first stepped foot in the region in the sixteenth century. Spanish explorers who arrived in the Americas in the late fifteenth and early sixteenth centuries brought with them notions of militant Christianity influenced by the Reconquista, the Catholic reconquest of Spain from the Islamic Moors. Explorers such as Juan Ponce de León, who led the first European expedition to Florida in the early sixteenth century, came to the Americas as experienced veterans of the Reconquista.[3] Many of the predacious young soldiers that accompanied these expeditions, known as *conquistadores*, became infamous for their brutality.

The battle to reconquer Spain from the Moors developed over seven hundred years. During that time, soldiers achieved high status in Spanish society. The combined effort of the Catholic Church and Spanish state to conquer the Moors and expand beyond the Iberian Peninsula informed the Spanish policy later used to colonize the Americas. Historian of the American Southwest David J. Weber articulated in *The Spanish Frontier in North America* that "Spaniards had evoked the values of the reconquest and gained valuable experience in conquering infidels and colonizing overseas territory."[4] To this end, the Spanish "refined their fighting skills" and altered their modes of conquest to best suit the conditions and peoples they encountered in the Caribbean as well as in South, Central, and North America.[5] While the Catholic Spaniards worked to reconquer the Iberian Peninsula, indigenous people in the Americas were living complex lives with developed societies, cultures, economies, and religions. They were unprepared for the disease and violence brought by these ethnocentric Spanish parties.

Weber regarded the actions of Spaniards in the Americas as an "extension of the Reconquista—a moral crusade to spread Spanish culture and Catholicism to pagans."[6] They viewed the simultaneous founding of the Americas and the end of the Reconquista in 1492 as a sign of God's support for their "righteous" efforts to spread Spanish culture and Catholicism around the world. Spaniards utilized this divine recognition to justify colonization and domination over other people, especially non-Christians. To this end, the Spanish pope Alexander VI granted Spain dominion over the New World in 1493 to convert pagan—non-Christian—inhabitants.[7] This decree meant nothing to Native peoples in the Americas, but signaled centuries of Spanish settlement efforts and forced conversion policies that threatened the lives and cultures of hundreds of thousands of indigenous peoples.

Accordingly, the Spanish developed the *requerimiento* in 1513 that commanded Native peoples to "acknowledge the [Catholic] Church as the ruler and superior of the whole world."[8] The requerimiento stipulated that the Spanish would treat Native people well as long as they agreed to its demands. However, it declared war against those who did not comply, threatening to turn children and women into slaves, and it made clear that the Spanish had the right to "do to [Native people] all the harm and damage that we can."[9] For example, under Francisco Vásquez de Coronado, the Spanish invaded Zuni Pueblo in modern-day New Mexico as well as other communities noncompliant with the requerimiento. The conquistadors destroyed Zuni villages, allowed their animals to feast on indigenous crops, and stole all they wanted from the Zuni.[10] Coronado's expedition continued traveling to present-day Kansas, engaging indigenous peoples along the way and claiming the vast domain for Spain. Although he did not explore Alta California, Coronado was a role model for others who came later.

Along with the spread of religion and territorial gain, a main goal of Spanish colonization was to enrich the Spanish crown through productive ventures in the Caribbean and the Americas, especially silver and gold mines. The crown encouraged militant entrepreneurs, known as *adelantados*, to risk their personal fortunes to expand the borders of the Catholic Spanish empire. Adelantados operated under the assurance that the Spanish crown would provide them with titles of nobility, land, wealth, and power over conquered territory if their endeavors succeeded. These conquerors amassed small armies to man expeditions to the "New World"—soldiers who looked to "serve God, country, and themselves at the same time."[11] This emphasis on wealth achieved through religious and territorial conquest harked back to the conquest-oriented ideologies of the Reconquista, first expressed in the Americas by means of the brutal subjugation of the peoples of the Caribbean Islands and Central and South America.[12] Countless Native people lost their lives to the relentless labor regimens under Spanish overseers. Centuries later, Spanish soldiers in the Americas continued to maintain a similar sense of conquest entwined with motivations of personal gain, as demonstrated in accounts provided by Spanish missionaries and explorers.[13] Native people along the California coast encountered these attitudes under Spanish colonization in the late eighteenth century.

The voyage of Christopher Columbus in 1492 was a watershed historical event that marked the beginning of both European exploration and resettlement in the Americas. It also marked the beginning of the extensive social, political, economic, and demographic devastation of indigenous communities. Native peoples faced some of the most devastating changes brought by the Spanish, including illness, violence, and subjugation in what scholars term the first "Columbian encounters" from the sixteenth to eighteenth centuries.[14] As noted, the Spanish commonly used the power of the requerimiento to abuse Native people in many of the first colonized territories.[15]

As historical archeologist Kathleen A. Deagan observed, the Spanish ideally sought to settle in regions that "contained land and resources with a high and profitable yield, preferably of gold or silver, and a sizable stable population to use as a controlled and enslaved labor force."[16] This process of exploiting Native populations for their labor, along with violence and the introduction of European diseases, quickly decimated indigenous populations in the Caribbean by 1520.[17] With a vanishing Native labor pool, the foreigners were forced to revise their treatment of indigenous people in future encounters.

These failed labor practices early on weighed heavily on Spanish polices in the Americas and pressured the Spanish crown to reconsider its treatment of indigenous populations. Revised policies proclaimed that Native people had souls and therefore could not be enslaved. To control indigenous labor, the Spanish government established the *encomienda* system in 1503. As a part of this process, the Spanish attempted to relocate indigenous people to consolidated regions to Christianize them and utilize Native labor more effectively—a process known as *reducción*. Under the encomienda system, the Spanish government required Native peoples to "exchange" labor for instruction in Christianity. However, the system failed in many regions because Native resistance made its enforcement difficult, and so the Spanish discontinued the policy in 1549.[18] Later, a form of encomienda reemerged in New Spain (Mexico) and in Spanish borderland institutions such as the California missions in the eighteenth and nineteenth centuries. Spanish soldiers used Native convict labor to construct buildings, and missionaries contracted out Native laborers to military garrisons.[19] As members of the mission community, the Spanish also compelled Native people to "trade" instruction in Catholicism for their labor. Contemporary mission sites neglect to address the brutality of early Spanish exploration and their exploitation of Native laborers.

Spanish settlements in the geographically, ecologically, and culturally diverse regions of Central and South America assumed a form similar to that of Spanish colonies in the Caribbean.[20] Scholars point to Columbus's fourth voyage in 1502 as the beginning of sustained Spanish contact with Native people in Central America. However, the conquest of the Yucatán Peninsula and greater regions of Mesoamerica faced strong armed resistance by groups such as the Mayans. The Spanish eventually claimed control over much of Central America after decades of violence and as European diseases weakened the ability of Native people to effectively revolt against Spanish military might. The Spanish instituted the encomienda system in Central America, especially along its densely populated Pacific Rim that also contained fertile land and natural resources. They forced indigenous people to mine for gold until they depleted resources, and they exacted tributary payments of material goods. The Spanish also participated in a lucrative indigenous slave trade that exported human chattel to less populated but naturally rich regions in eastern Central America, such as the mines in Zacatecas, Mexico.[21]

Beginning with Herbert Eugene Bolton in the 1920s, historians of Spanish America traced Spanish exploration and colonization in the Americas from the West Indies in the 1520s. Thereafter, the Spanish developed settlements in South America in places such as modern-day Peru and Bolivia. Mining centers in these territories brought great wealth to explorers and the Spanish crown in the late sixteenth century, but overwhelming labor regimens, disease, and Spanish violence again devastated Native populations. The Spanish also created settlements in Central America during the mid- to late sixteenth century in present-day Mexico City. The city, built directly on top of the Aztec capital, Tenochtitlán, became the "metropolis of European life and culture in all North America," a distinction it maintained until the late eighteenth century.[22] Bolton observed that the Spaniards exploited Native people for labor in large and extremely profitable mining operations for gold, and especially silver, in Central and South America. Mining towns such as Zacatecas, Durango, and Monterrey grew to become some of the largest provinces in Mexico when mining, commerce, and Spanish settlement expanded extensively in the region into the eighteenth century.[23] Again, Native people suffered greatly at the expense of Spanish expansion and the search for wealth.

The Spanish also established political and religious institutions in Central America as early as 1520. During the course of the sixteenth century, missionaries and Spanish explorers expanded the territory of New Spain northward. Many Native people fled the intruding Spaniards, but others grudgingly submitted in hopes of finding protection from the foreign diseases and the Spanish soldiers who attacked Native communities. Exploratory voyages led by Francis Drake (1578–1579), Francisco Gali (1584), and Sebastián Vizcaíno (1602) continued into the early seventeenth century to survey the natural resources and map the geography of much of the Pacific coastline of North America.[24] Explorers did not find the large amounts of silver or gold in North America they had seen in Central America, nor did they discover the mythic interoceanic Strait of Anián that many believed bisected the American continent and connected the Pacific to the Atlantic Ocean. Hubert Howe Bancroft described this strait as the "strait separating the Mexican regions from Asia. This strait at first was between South America and the Asiatic main; but was pushed constantly northward by exploration, and was to be found always just beyond the highest latitude visited."[25] Explorers and cartographers perpetuated a number of myths as they distorted the location of California in their writings. They depicted California close to the North Pole, as an island, or as an exaggerated peninsula.

As time went on, the Spanish ventured farther north into Baja California, Sonora, Alta California, and modern-day New Mexico.[26] Exploratory expeditions along the Pacific Coast continued for a while, but the Spanish paid few visits to the region until nearly two centuries later when international events spurred increased interest in the region that became the American West. Native people on the Pacific Coast of the American continent scarcely encountered Spaniards, and when they did it was usually only in emergencies when sailors became ill or when Spanish explorers desperately needed provisions.[27] In parts of Central America and the American Southwest, such as New Mexico, the Spanish established new settlements using indigenous laborers. Spanish conquistadors became infamous in European society for their abusive behavior and excessive cruelty toward Native people, documented in 1552 by Dominican friar Bartolomé de las Casas in *Brevísima Relación de la Destrucción de las Indias* (A Brief Account of the Destruction of the Indies).[28] Spanish leaders influenced by enlightenment ideologies of the eighteenth century called for more humane treatment of Native peoples. They were determined to dispel the "black legend" of Spanish brutality that tarnished the integrity of the nation's colonizers in popular European culture.[29]

Despite the ideals of reformers in Europe, some Spanish colonies far removed from centers of Spanish society continued to use Native people as forced laborers and subjected them to violent punishments for not conforming to Hispanic customs. However, Weber argued that some Spaniards, especially in the eighteenth century, prided themselves on their proper treatment of indigenous peoples.[30] Historians in the late nineteenth century were often highly critical of the Spanish for their mistreatment of Native people— documented and graphically illustrated in historical records. Bancroft, a distinguished pioneer of California history writing in the late nineteenth century, critically discussed Spanish soldiers in his multivolume tome *History of California*. Although he condemned soldiers, Bancroft was more generous in his descriptions of the missionaries who accompanied many expeditions, especially those in Alta California. Bancroft and some of his contemporaries argued that the Spanish era was actually a "Golden Age" of California history.[31] Promoters and popular writers of California history, including Bancroft and Charles Fletcher Lummis, revised the prevalent "black legend" of Spanish history in the Americas, replacing brutal Spanish conquistadors with more benign Franciscan missionaries who worked to bring "civilization" to a "wild" land.[32] The black legend of Spanish colonization demonized Spanish colonizers as extremely cruel toward Native peoples specifically and non-Catholics in general. Lummis took a "white legend" perspective that focused on the positive aspects of Spanish colonization. As writers focused on Spanish history, Native peoples faded into the periphery of popular narratives.

Working to promote California history, Bancroft compiled and documented the stories of many of the people who contributed to the history of the region, including Spanish explorers. Bancroft described how, after nearly two centuries of naval voyages to Alta California, the Spanish began exploring the region again in the late eighteenth century when Spanish officials learned of a growing Russian presence in the Pacific Northwest.[33] Meanwhile, the inspector general of New Spain, José de Gálvez, taking a "defensive expansionism" approach, decided to use Alta California as a strategic buffer zone between New Spain and the growing interests of other imperial nations. To strengthen New Spain's military presence, Gálvez proposed establishing a chain of presidios, or military forts, throughout the northernmost regions of New Spain. Spanish officials also sent Franciscan missionaries to assist in expansion of the Spanish domain and subjugation of Native peoples. In 1769, under Father President Junípero Serra, the Spanish established a series of missions in Alta California.[34]

Similar to the narratives constructed by Bancroft and Lummis, many contemporary interpreters of Spanish history in California begin their discussion of California with the arrival of the "Sacred expedition" led by Serra and Gaspar de Portolá, governor of Baja California. They ignore the centuries of Native and Spanish history that preceded the creation of mission institutions, removing them from their historical perspective. A thorough understanding of the social, economic, and political goals of Spanish officials in eighteenth-century California helps accurately place the Alta California missions in their proper historical context.

Scholars in the twentieth century increasingly focused on the influence of Spanish, Mexican, and American interactions with Native peoples in the American Southwest. For example, Edward H. Spicer in *Cycles of Conquest: The Impact of Spain, Mexico, and the United States on the Indians of the Southwest, 1533–1960,* detailed the long history of "conquest" of specific Native communities in the Spanish borderlands and American Southwest. In doing so, Spicer examined the ways in which Spanish, Mexican, and Euro-American officials and institutions labored to "civilize" Native peoples in the region in the context of cultural change. He looked past contemporary national boundaries, as Bolton did, to examine the cultural impact of foreigners who "worked in accordance with plans concerning what they wanted the Indians to become as well as in fulfillment of their own special interests."

Specifically, Spicer examined the "Spanish Program," beginning with notions the Spanish held about Native people before contact—notions learned from the European concept of the "barbarian."[35]

Spanish understandings of the contrast between European "civility" and indigenous "barbarism" influenced successive Spanish policies in the Americas. These policies sought to construct components of civilized life that the Spanish believed Native people lacked, such as proper Christian religion, sociopolitical organizations, and the "civilized decencies" of European cultures.[36] Thus civil and religious officials embarked on an effort to "civilize" the many Native communities they encountered in the Americas, as most Spaniards did not recognize the highly developed cultures, religions, and traditions of indigenous peoples. The administrative government in New Spain looked to the plans of Roman colonies and idealized notions of church communities to create centers for Native peoples.[37]

The Spanish used two distinct approaches during the era of "Conquest of Culture" in New Spain; they compelled Native people to either join religious mission complexes or become residents and laborers at mining towns. These two systems were in conflict, however, because Jesuit missionaries in the seventeenth century were structuring Native populations into a cohesive political and socioeconomic unit around the church. And yet many indigenous people worked for wages under Spanish employers in mines outside of these religious communities.[38] Eventually, these two systems merged in the California missions: the priests theoretically held complete temporal control over Native peoples as childlike wards, leading indigenous converts both spiritually and in their duties as laborers.

## Role of Mission Communities

Romantic interpretations of mission history inherently ignored the struggle of Native people to navigate the new Spanish institutions and indigenous perceptions of the changes under way. For example, the introduction to the contemporary educational series *The Missions: California's Heritage* noted that "it took a great deal of time for some Indian tribes to understand the new way of life a mission offered, even though the Native Americans always had food and shelter when they became mission Indians."[39] In the briefest way possible, the author summarized the varied experiences of Native people in the mission system. She contended that Native Californians struggled to accept the regimented way of life offered at the mission because it "was an enormous change from the less organized Indian life before the missions came."[40] This brief statement discounts the countless factors that brought

Native people into the missions, including destruction of traditional food sources by European animals, malnutrition, starvation, the diseases that ravaged Native communities, and violence—all introduced by the Spanish. It also discounts Native ways of life, connections to their homeland, and kinship bonds. Furthermore, the author asserted that difficulty accepting order was the primary obstacle Native people faced in the missions rather than the inherent complications of assimilating to a completely new way of life that coincided with attempts to destroy their cultures and societies.

Some early mission communities allowed Native people to maintain certain aspects of their traditional ways of life, although missionaries introduced new concepts and behaviors over time. Generally, missionaries structured their religious communities into social units and attempted to create atmospheres most suitable for "intensive efforts to change features of Indian behavior."[41] However, the regulations introduced varied throughout New Spain because mission officials tailored communities to the lifestyles and customs of local indigenous populations. For example, mission officials altered their tactics when they worked among nomadic and sedentary groups; this issue arose in New Mexico among the sedentary Pueblo and mobile Apache communities. When working with more nomadic groups, mission officials felt it necessary to completely reorient Native lifestyles. Generally, missionaries sought to construct compact and sedentary Native communities around the Spanish Catholic Church. They thought it necessary to create villages, or *reducciones*, to localize congregations that the missionaries could then control and "civilize." The churches were to serve as places of worship and instruction of proper "civilized" Christian and Spanish customs.[42] This was a dramatic change for Native communities that moved regularly to access different food resources. In the Southwest, the Spanish struggled to force nomadic groups into missions, but many Native people were able to avoid reducciones, especially after gaining access to Spanish horses in the late seventeenth century. Sedentary indigenous communities did not require reducciones in the same way. Both Jesuit and Franciscan padres constructed churches as the first component of a newly developed mission site. However, Native people in sedentary villages did not fully shed their religious beliefs and customs to accept Spanish Catholicism. For example, many Pueblo people fought Spanish domination and over time incorporated underground religious sites, known as *kivas*, within the missions established by the Spanish.[43]

As key components of Spanish expansion in the Americas, mission settlements also developed ranches, farms, aqueducts, and other important facilities that allowed these sites to contribute economically to New Spain. Spanish missionaries introduced cattle, sheep, horses, and other foreign animals, as well as European crops into mission complexes. Indians served as almost all of the labor required at mission institutions. Indeed, structured work regimens became a daily part of life for baptized Native people, known as *neophytes*, within the missions.[44] As noted, however, this shift was often difficult for Native peoples. Coupled with conflicting cultural beliefs, tension developed between indigenous people and the Spanish foreigners. Many Native people fled from the coastal region of California to the interior to escape Spanish attempts to control their bodies and minds.

Along with constructing the mission and presidio buildings, neophytes also tended the fields and livestock. The padres and other skilled instructors introduced the indigenous converts to new crafts such as blacksmithing, masonry, carpentry, and weaving as a part of their labor regimens. Introducing work regimens into the lives of converts restructured the daily routine of Native peoples. Along with reducciones, structured labor routines served to inhibit indigenous peoples from practicing outward expressions of their cultures.[45]

Mission complexes, especially those in Alta California in the late eighteenth century, became economically independent units through the creation of localized settlements around the church. To maintain a self-sufficient economy, mission officials strictly supervised Native people and enforced the regimented daily routines under the threat of physical punishments such as whippings. Scholars have debated the amount of force padres and soldiers used to keep Native people at the missions, and they disagree about whether indigenous people were slaves to the mission system.[46] Today, Native voices are increasingly informing such scholarly discussions of Spanish America.

The polemical debate over the impact of missionization in California began in the late nineteenth and early twentieth centuries. Scholars such as Bancroft and Sherburne F. Cook argued that the Spanish excessively mistreated Native peoples. Moreover, scholars used demographic studies to demonstrate that contact with the Spanish exposed indigenous people to European diseases that caused significant declines in Native populations. Franciscan scholars such as Zephyrin Engelhardt responded to these allegations by providing a more positive portrayal of mission history. However, Engelhardt focused heavily on the institutional history of the missions and missionaries in Alta California rather than their impact on Native peoples. This debate gained momentum into the 1980s with growing calls to canonize Serra. Scholars in the late twentieth century increasingly readdressed Spanish mission history to extract more varied perspectives than those provided by Engelhardt and his successor, Francis F. Guest.[47]

Regardless of their position, scholars agree that the establishment of the first two mission settlements in Alta California, one in the north at Monterey

Bay and the other in San Diego, proved to be a difficult task for the Spanish. Gálvez planned two land expeditions and three sea expeditions to travel from La Paz, Baja California, to Alta California. According to the plan, the five expeditions would meet in San Diego, where they would reorganize and divide. One group would stay in San Diego and the other company would continue north to Monterey to establish the second mission and the capital of Alta California. As planned, the ships *San Carlos, San Antonio,* and *San José* set sail on three separate sea expeditions to San Diego from La Paz, but poor weather and strong winds delayed the ships and contributed to significant onboard illness for the sailors.[48] Thus the sailors who arrived in San Diego were sick and weak. Native people watched the foreigners cautiously, but also provided them with some food and supplies while the Spanish initially reciprocated with trade goods, beads, and cloth.[49]

The first Spanish land expedition, made up of twenty-five soldiers, a priest, and forty-two Native converts used as peons, encountered the weary sailors on May 14, 1769. This expedition, led by Capt. Fernando Rivera y Moncada and accompanied by Father Juan Crespí, arrived in San Diego shortly before the appearance of the second land expedition in late June to early July of the same year. Serra, a number of soldiers, and several neophytes accompanied the second expedition, led by Portolá.[50] Several indigenous communities saw the expeditions as they crossed through Native territories, but because the foreigners continued to move and did not settle, they met little active resistance before reaching San Diego.

Many members of the second overland party arrived in San Diego comparatively healthy, despite food and water shortages on the journey.[51] Portolá, Crespí, Father Francisco Gomez, and a majority of the party soon disembarked for Monterey. Serra and nearly a dozen others remained in San Diego to establish the presidio and Mission San Diego, originally located near the Kumeyaay village of Cosoy, and found today at Presidio Hill in San Diego.[52] The Kumeyaay did not openly accept the Spanish settlements in their territory. In fact, they attacked the Spanish several times and refused to join the mission for many years. Even after many Kumeyaay joined the mission fold, a large number of Kumeyaay dissatisfied with the Spanish staged a large-scale revolt that destroyed Mission San Diego in 1775, which is described in Chapter 5.[53]

The various motivations for Spanish exploration and colonization of the Americas changed over time as European expansionist interests in the Americas grew. The Spanish originally launched explorations into the Americas during the late sixteenth century in search of wealth, but their motives shifted to settlement over the next two centuries. As European powers vied for control of the American continent in the eighteenth century, the Spanish began to utilize defensive expansion techniques to secure more territories and protect their northern borders. Scholars have analyzed the use of defensive expansion in what Bolton first termed the "Spanish Borderlands."[54] The borderlands existed as a buffer region between the vast empire constructed by Spain in Central and South America "between the Rio Grande and Buenos Aries," and the remainder of the American continent colonized by France, Great Britain, and Russia.[55]

Bolton, who published "Defensive Spanish Exploration and the Significance of Borderlands" in 1930, argued that his contemporaries analyzed the history of the United States from a perspective that did not venture below the U.S.-Mexico border. Because of this limited perspective, scholars concluded that the Spanish failed in their colonization of the American Southwest. According to Bolton, these scholars neglected to recognize the role of the Spanish borderlands within the context of the larger Spanish empire in Central and South America. Bolton contended that Spain actually did succeed in its colonization plans. The Spanish effectively established settlements in the borderlands regions to create a buffer zone between the greater empire of New Spain and the growing colonial presence of other European powers in the area.[56]

Bolton believed this misunderstanding existed because most Euro-American historians viewed the history of the continent from a Turnerian frontier perspective, wherein "civilization" moved westward from the English colonies. Beginning in 1893 with Fredrick Jackson Turner's "The Significance of the Frontier in American History," historians have debated the qualities imbued in the United States as a nation produced by its frontier experiences. In doing so, they have increasingly emphasized the importance of the "frontier," or borderlands, in American history. Turner argued that the movement of frontiersmen westward into "wilderness" was a process that created the American spirit and a unique national identity. Analyses of the American West that followed Turner generally ignored ethnic minorities such as African Americans and Hispanics. They only referenced Native peoples in discussions of their "primitive" nature, violence, or their lifeways fading into the past with the advancement of the American frontier. Turner's "frontier thesis" spawned a movement of idealized histories of the American West, but also was highly criticized for its imprecise, overly simplistic, and exclusionist portrayal of the region.[57]

Throughout his career, Bolton labored to revise the common narrative of Anglo-centric American history that emerged in the late nineteenth century. He worked to help scholars and the general public alike understand the important role the Spanish played in the history of the United States by training junior scholars and publishing textbooks for California students of all ages. In doing so, Bolton nurtured the romanticized depictions of Spanish America first fostered by writers in the late nineteenth and early twentieth centuries such as Bancroft and Lummis.[58] At the same time, he frequently ignored the experiences of Native communities and the impacts of the Spanish on their ways of life.

The expedition commanded by Portolá and accompanied by Serra described earlier established the first mission in Alta California under Serra and marked the beginning of Spanish military occupation at Monterey under Portolá. Life changed drastically for the Native peoples who remained in these areas. Many coastal Native communities felt the pressure of the Spanish cross and crown, whereas Native peoples living in the interior of California maintained their ways of life for many more generations. Meanwhile, Spanish officials created a chain of mission complexes between Monterey and San Diego to claim Alta California for Spain, and in 1774 Juan Bautista de Anza led an expedition north from Mexico that established a land route from Sonora to California. For a time, this land route connected outposts of northern New Spain in New Mexico, Arizona, and Colorado with Alta California as a defensive strategy against other European powers and Native nations that threatened Spanish settlements, such as the Apache and Comanche.[59]

Bolton argued that presidios and missions were developed as key institutions in the Spanish plan to create "defensive outposts" along its northern border. The fortification and population of presidios varied greatly, depending on the concentration of Spaniards, indigenous peoples, and other Europeans in the region. Generally, presidios protected surrounding settlements, sent scouts and detachments on expeditions, engaged hostile indigenous people in skirmishes, and protected the region from foreign trespassers. Bolton also highlighted the important role of missions—describing them as "*par excellence* [as] a frontier institution."[60] For him, missions were civilizing influences in Native communities that the Spanish created to "save souls and spread Spanish civilization among the heathen."[61] But many Native Californians viewed the missions as oppressive spaces that restricted their movement and worked to eradicate their traditions, cultures, and languages.

The Spanish crown created mission institutions to be self-sufficient and provided minimal funding for Alta California outposts after their establishment. This situation forced missions to heavily recruit Native people for free labor. Similar to the plight of presidios, missions in parts of the Spanish borderlands that faced the highest risk of foreign intrusion received the most financial support and resources. Spanish padres, constantly in need of more money, but seeing their requests for funds rejected, sometimes spread rumors of looming imperial aggression to secure future funding. Native people at less prosperous missions frequently suffered the shortfalls of poor harvests and few material products, while soldiers and priests usually took the same shares year after year. Along with missions and presidios, the Spanish established civil settlements near mission complexes in the borderlands to demonstrate their "control," however futile, over the region.[62]

Spanish control over the borderlands region did not extend far into the nineteenth century. Following a series of international events, Spain eventually lost control of its territory in the Caribbean, Florida, Texas, Georgia, and Louisiana. Those events included British expansion into the Caribbean, Spain's involvement in the Seven Years' War (1756–1763), the American Revolution, and Euro-American expansion west. After the Louisiana Purchase of 1803, the United States further threatened Spanish settlements in portions of Florida and Texas. Moreover, the first two decades of the nineteenth century witnessed several wars for independence against Spain in many Spanish-American colonies, including Mexico. In addition, powerful Native nations in the Southwest, such as the Comanche, weakened Spanish influence over the region.[63]

Also during this time, French-Canadian and Euro-American explorers became increasingly intrigued by the Spanish Borderlands as an "abiding place of Romance." Bolton noted that efforts by the Spanish to create a buffer zone between northern New Spain and the remainder of North America sparked the interest of Europeans and Euro-Americans in exploring the region and discovering the mythical land Spain wanted to protect from the rest of the world. Foreign traders, including Americans, also helped to supplement the Alta California colonies with goods, while Spain virtually ignored the outposts in the early nineteenth century during wars of independence in their other colonies. The products that Native laborers produced at the missions became more important as these trade outlets grew. Increasing numbers of foreigners proved to be a reliable source of goods, but also settled in the area and married into elite Spanish California families. Over time, this presence eroded Hispanic control of the region.[64]

At the same time, romanticized stories of "dark-eyed señoritas" emerged in popular publications and lured adventurous young American men west.[65] Euro-Americans pushed into the "uninhabited" regions between U.S. and Spanish territories. Trappers and traders, however, also quickly settled *within* Spanish borderlands and other territories in Florida, New Mexico, Texas, and Alta California, increasingly settling on Native lands. This caused tensions and wars between Euro-Americans and indigenous communities, who fought to protect their lifeways and maintain control of their ancestral homelands. American migrants who traveled to Texas in the 1820s and California in the 1840s found already established Euro-American towns.[66] They, too, used indigenous people as inexpensive laborers. Many Native peoples accepted these roles as a way to make a living in a quickly changing world, but Euro-American encroachment undermined their traditional economies and left them largely unsustainable.

## The End of the Mission Era

After Mexican independence, the new liberal government sought to dispel symbols of conservative Spanish control from the newly free nation that was struggling with political instability. As a part of this effort, civil officials emancipated neophytes from the missions and whittled away the missions' control over vast tracts of land in Alta California. As word of emancipation spread, many Native peoples left the missions. The new government withdrew much of the power of the Franciscan padres in the late 1820s and eventually confiscated livestock and resources from the mission stores. The Mexican government also legislated for dismemberment of the entire mission system in 1833, a process known as secularization that was put into practice in 1834. The government hoped to open more land to Mexican citizens and entice people from Mexico to move north into the Alta California frontier. The mission buildings became parish churches, and most of the mission lands moved into private hands. Many Native people took the skills they learned at the missions and applied them to new jobs on private ranchos. Some neophytes received small plots, while hundreds of thousands of acres became available to the public and quickly transferred to a relatively small number of elite families.[67]

These Spanish-speaking families in California, known as *Californios*, created large ranches using livestock primarily from the disbanded missions. Similar to early Spanish settlements, Native people again became the main labor force, but religious instruction was no longer a priority in a secularized California. For the most part, Native people from the missions became the low-wage laborers for *ranchos,* or moved to growing towns such as Los Angeles to find work. A class of highly skilled Native horsemen, known as *vaqueros*, also emerged from the missions and rancho economies. Americans that moved into California in the 1840s and 1850s viewed many Native peoples as sad victims of Californio abuses and denigrated equally Spanish and Mexican control of the region. Others, such as John C. Frémont, described impressive Native horsemen who spoke, dressed, and rode like the Spanish but had "an Indian face."[68] Americans disparaged the "lazy" Mexicans for forcing Native people to maintain the land and used this as partial justification for settling California for the United States.

Within a generation, Spain lost control of its American colonies, the Alta California missions deteriorated into ruins, and Euro-American migrants increasingly settled in the region. The U.S.-Mexican War and the Treaty of Guadalupe Hidalgo formally turned California, and much of the West, into an American possession. The California gold rush, in full swing by the summer of 1849, brought hundreds of thousands of newcomers to the area—a majority of whom were young Euro-American men. By September 1850, Congress had admitted California as the thirty-first state in the Union. Incoming settlers that once looked down on the Hispanic period of the region began to reimagine it as a simpler time. According to Weber, "in the 1880s, Anglo Americans began to appreciate and exaggerate what they had previously disdained."[69] The mission ruins became symbols of California's newly celebrated Spanish legacy, and American interpretations of the Spanish past silenced Native experiences at the sites.

Even though Spain lost control of its American territories in the early nineteenth century, historians and writers who romanticized the Spanish heritage in the Americas often pointed to the undeniable marks the Spanish left on their former colonies.[70] For example, Bolton pointed to the Spanish names of states such as Florida, Nevada, Colorado, and California, as well as several towns and rivers with Spanish names that hark back to a time when Spain controlled the region. Architecture "from Georgia to San Francisco" also reflected a common Spanish past in the modern American South and West on view in cathedrals in New Orleans and mission ruins across California. Popular mission and pueblo architecture in the American Southwest embodies a physical continuation of the Spanish past—just as contemporary adoptions of Spanish history, culture, and folklore represent the "old Spanish days."[71] Conversely, Euro-Americans unaware of Native history have to look much deeper at the landscape to see indigenous sites that have not been publicized by regional promoters. These local boosters chose to focus heavily on dramatizing the Spanish past—in part to entice more Americans to settle in the region—which is a focus of Chapter 2.

As noted, Lummis, Bolton, and Bancroft supported the romanticized depiction of Spanish California in their writings.[72] Although Bolton based his argument on a Spanish perspective to demonstrate the *success* of the Spanish in the Americas, he did not delve deeper into other aspects of Spanish colonization in the region. Bolton also generally ignored the important roles Native people played in the Spanish borderlands. However, other contemporary scholars such as George Harwood Phillips, Jack D. Forbes, Pekka

Hämäläinen, and Juliana Barr, by conducting studies of indigenous peoples in California and the Southwest, were able to demonstrate that Native peoples played a crucial role, through raids and attacks, in maintaining this region as Spanish borderlands. For example, Hämäläinen argued that Spaniards and Euro-Americans had to confront the powerful Comanche "Empire" in order to settle within the Spanish borderlands—a task at which the Spanish failed and left for the United States to tackle. [73]

Another group of contemporary scholars has taken up Bolton's early focus, initiated in the 1920s, to highlight Spanish perspectives in American historiography. They are more interested in questioning historical documents and less inclined "than were the Boltonians to allow documents to speak for themselves, or to let the document define the question."[74] Scholars such as Spicer, Weber, John Kessell, Robert H. Jackson, Lisbeth Haas, and others pushed their analyses of Spanish conquest and the Spanish borderlands beyond the political boundaries delineated contemporarily by Mexico and the United States. Furthermore, these historians attempted to include Native people as primary actors in the history of the Spanish borderlands, a void left by Bolton and his supporters.[75] In the late twentieth century, Weber, Jackson, Edward D. Castillo, James A. Sandos, Steven W. Hackel, and many others explored Spanish colonial history from more critical and complicated perspectives. Their work challenged traditional narratives of the "Spanish fantasy past" popularized in the late nineteenth and early twentieth centuries. Contemporary researchers also detailed the overwhelmingly negative impact of Spanish colonization on Native communities—including violence, disease, attacks on indigenous cultures, and the destruction of indigenous populations. Yet they also illustrated the many ways that Native peoples negotiated within foreign power structures to control their own lives. Despite the work of many scholars today, popular histories of the Spanish California missions continue to reflect the romanticized narratives created by regional promoters and boosters in the early twentieth century.

## Notes

1. David Hurst Thomas, "Harvesting Ramona's Garden: Life in California's Mythical Mission Past," in *Columbian Consequences*, Vol. 3, *The Spanish Borderlands in Pan-American Perspective*, ed. David Hurst Thomas (Washington, DC: Smithsonian Institution Press, 1991), 119–157; Dydia DeLyser, "Ramona Memories: Fiction, Tourist Practices, and Placing the Past in Southern California," *Annals of the Association of American Geographers* 93 (December 2003): 886–908.

2. The Spanish borderlands in the Americas include the Caribbean Islands, Florida, and the American Southwest. Herbert Eugene Bolton coined the term "Spanish Borderlands" in *The Spanish Borderlands: A Chronicle of Old Florida and the Southwest* (New Haven, CT: Yale University Press, 1921); David J. Weber, "The Idea of the Spanish Borderlands," in *Columbian Consequences*, Vol. 3, *The Spanish Borderlands in Pan-American Perspective*, ed. David Hurst Thomas (Washington, DC: Smithsonian Institution Press, 1991), 3–20.

3. John L. Kessell, *Spain in the Southwest* (Norman: University of Oklahoma Press, 2002), 3–5.

4. David J. Weber, *The Spanish Frontier in North America* (New Haven, CT: Yale University Press, 1992), 20; Clifford E. Trafzer, *As Long as the Grass Shall Grow and Rivers Flow: A History of Native Americans* (Fort Worth, TX: Harcourt College Publishers, 2000), 20–39. The Spanish Inquisition of 1481 was a military and religious movement led by Queen Isabel of Castile and King Fernando of Aragón—the "Catholic Monarchs." This movement, along with the Reconquista, created a sense of unity among many of the diverse territories of the Iberian Peninsula that formed Spain.

5. Weber, *Spanish Frontier in North America*, 19–21.

6. Ibid., 20.

7. Ibid., 21.

8. Ibid., 21–22.

9. Ibid., 22.

10. Ibid., 22–23.

11. Ibid., 23.

12. Kathleen A. Deagan, "Sixteenth-Century Spanish-American Colonization in the Southeastern United States and the Caribbean," in *Columbian Consequences*, Vol. 2, *Archaeological and Historical Perspectives on the Spanish Borderlands East*, ed. David Hurst Thomas (Washington, DC: Smithsonian Institution Press, 1990), 225–250.

13. Iris H. W. Engstrand, "Seekers of the 'Northern Mystery': European Exploration of California and the Pacific," in *Contested Eden: California before the Gold Rush*, ed. Ramon A. Gutierrez and Richard J. Orsi (Berkeley: University of California Press, 1998), 78–110.

14. David Hurst Thomas, ed., *Columbian Consequences*, 3 vols. (Washington, DC: Smithsonian Institution Press, 1989–1991); Alfred W. Crosby, *The Columbian Exchange: Biological and Cultural Consequences of 1492* (Westport, CT: Praeger, 2003).

15. Deagan, "Sixteenth-Century Spanish-American Colonization," 225–250.

16. Ibid., 228.

17. Ibid., 229.

18. Ibid., 228–229. Native people frequently resisted Spanish forces, and yet Spanish violence coupled with the ravages of foreign diseases on Native communities reduced the strength of their resistance.

19. Steven W. Hackel, *Children of Coyote, Missionaries of Saint Francis: Indian-Spanish Relations in Colonial California, 1769–1850* (Chapel Hill: University of North Carolina Press, 2005), 296–297.

20. Grant D. Jones and David M. Pendergast, "The Native Context of Colonialism in Southern Mesoamerica and Central America: An Overview," in *Columbian Consequences*, Vol. 3, *The Spanish Borderlands in Pan-American Perspective*, ed. David Hurst Thomas (Washington, DC: Smithsonian Institution Press, 1991), 161–185.

21. Ibid., 167–173; Peter Gerhard, *The Northern Frontier of New Spain*, rev. ed. (Norman: University of Oklahoma Press, 1993), 10–11.

22. Herbert Eugene Bolton, "Defensive Spanish Exploration and the Significance of Borderlands," in *Bolton and the Spanish Borderlands*, ed. John Francis Bannon (1930; repr., Norman: University of Oklahoma Press, 1964), 37.

23. Ibid., 37–39.

24. Hubert Howe Bancroft, *History of California,* Vol. 1, in *The Works of Hubert Howe Bancroft*, Vol. 18 (San Francisco: The History Company, 1886), 81–97.

25. Ibid., 97, 107.

26. Gerhard, *Northern Frontier of New Spain*, 10–26.

27. Engstrand, "Seekers of the 'Northern Mystery,'" 86–92.

28. The full translated title of the work by Las Casas is *A Brief Account of the Destruction of the Indies Or, a faithful Narrative of the Horrid and Unexampled Massacres, Butcheries, and all manner of Cruelties, that Hell and Malice could invent, committed by the Popish Spanish Party on the inhabitants of West-India, Together With the Devastations of several Kingdoms in America by Fire and Sword, for the space of Forty and Two Years, from the time of its first Discovery by them.*

29. David J. Weber, *Bárbaros: Spaniards and Their Savages in the Age of Enlightenment* (New Haven, CT: Yale University Press, 2005), 47–51.

30. Ibid., 49–51.

31. Albert L. Hurtado, "Fantasy Heritage: California's Historical Identities and the Professional Empire of Herbert E. Bolton," in *Alta California: Peoples in Motion, Identities in Formation, 1769–1850,* ed. Steven W. Hackel (Berkeley: University of California Press, published for the Huntington–USC Institute on California and the West, 2010), 201–203.

32. Ibid., 197–214.

33. The Russians also forced Native people to work for them, trapping beavers.

34. Hackel, *Children of Coyote,* 40–42.

35. Edward H. Spicer, *Cycles of Conquest: The Impact of Spain, Mexico, and the United States on the Indians of the Southwest, 1533–1960* (Tucson: University of Arizona Press, 1962), 279.

36. Ibid., 282.

37. Ibid., 282–285; Dora P. Crouch, "Roman Models for Spanish Colonization," in *Columbian Consequences*, Vol. 3, *The Spanish Borderlands in Pan-American Perspective*, ed. David Hurst Thomas (Washington, DC: Smithsonian Institution Press, 1991), 21–35.

38. Spicer, *Cycles of Conquest*, 285–287.

39. Boulé, *Missions*, 7–8.

40. Ibid., 8.

41. Spicer, *Cycles of Conquest*, 294.

42. Ibid., 288–290.

43. John L. Kessell, *Kiva, Cross, and Crown: The Pecos Indians and New Mexico, 1540–1840* (Albuquerque: University of New Mexico Press, 1987), 29–229.

44. Spicer, *Cycles of Conquest*, 290–295.

45. Ibid., 294–295.

46. James A. Sandos, *Converting California: Indians and Franciscans in the Missions* (New Haven, CT: Yale University Press, 2004), 1–13; Hackel, *Children of Coyote*, 272–320; Robert H. Jackson and Edward D. Castillo, *Indians, Franciscans, and Spanish Colonization: The Impact of the Mission System on the California Indians* (Albuquerque: University of New Mexico Press, 1995), 73–140; Rupert Costo and Jeannette Henry Costo, eds., *The Missions of California: A Legacy of Genocide* (San Francisco: Indian Historian Press, 1987), 1–28.

47. Zephyrin Engelhardt, *The Missions and Missionaries of California*, 4 vols. (San Francisco: James H. Berry Company, 1908–1915); Hubert Howe Bancroft, *History of California*, 6 vols. (San Francisco: The History Company, 1884–1890); Sherburne F. Cook, *The Conflict between the California Indian and White Civilization* (1943; repr., Berkeley: University of California Press, 1976), 3–194; Francis F. Guest, "An Examination of the Thesis of S. F. Cook on the Forced Conversion of Indians in the California Missions," *Southern California Quarterly* 61 (1979): 1–77; David J. Weber, "Blood of Martyrs, Blood of Indians: Toward a More Balanced View of Spanish Missions in Seventeenth-Century North America," in *Columbian Consequences*, Vol. 2, *Archaeological and Historical Perspectives on the Spanish Borderlands East*, ed. David Hurst Thomas (Washington, DC: Smithsonian Institution Press, 1990), 429–448.

48. Hackel, *Children of Coyote*, 42–45.

49. Junípero Serra to Francisco Palóu, San Diego, July 3, 1769, in *Writings of Junípero Serra*, Vol. 1, ed. Antonine Tibesar (Washington, DC: Academy of American Franciscan History, 1955), 141–147. Hereafter referred to as Serra to Palóu, San Diego, July 3, 1769; P. Albert Lacson, "Making Friends and Converts: Cloth and Clothing in Early California History," *California History* 92 (spring 2015): 6-26.

50. Hackel, *Children of Coyote*, 42–45.

51. Francisco Palóu, "Juan Crespí to Francisco Palóu, San Diego, June 9, 1769," in *Historical Memoirs of New California*, Vol. 4, ed. and trans. Herbert Eugene Bolton (New York: Russell and Russell, 1926), 253–265.

52. Bancroft's discussion of Spanish exploration and colonization highlighted key points in the history of the Spanish in Alta California, but generally ignored Spanish involvement in the larger borderlands region. Bancroft also did not provide a detailed discussion of the political and economic motives of the Spanish government—a task outside the scope of Bancroft's main focus in *History of California*, 1: 137.

53. Sandos, *Converting California*, 55–68.

54. Bolton, "Defensive Spanish Exploration and the Significance of Borderlands," 1–42.

55. Ibid., 32.

56. Ibid., 32–33.

57. Fredrick Jackson Turner, "The Significance of the Frontier in American History," in *The Frontier in American History* (1920; repr., New York: Dover Publications, 1996), 1–38; Stephen Aron, "Lessons in Conquest: Towards a Greater Western History," *Pacific Historical Review* 63 (May 1994): 125–147. Turner originally presented his "frontier thesis" at a meeting in Chicago in 1893 at the time of the World's Columbian Exposition.

58. Hurtado, "Fantasy Heritage," 197–214.

59. Bolton, "Defensive Spanish Exploration and the Significance of Borderlands," 46–48; Pekka Hämäläinen, *The Comanche Empire* (New Haven, CT: Yale University Press, in association with the William P. Clements Center for Southwest Studies, Southern Methodist University, 2008), 141–291; Brian Delay, *War of a Thousand Deserts: Indian Raids and the U.S.-Mexican War* (New Haven, CT: Yale University Press, 2008), 1–60.

60. Bolton, "Defensive Spanish Exploration and the Significance of Borderlands," 49.

61. Ibid.

62. Ibid., 49–51.

63. Hämäläinen, *Comanche Empire*, 141–291; Delay, *War of a Thousand Deserts*, 1–60; Juliana Barr, *Peace Came in the Form of a Woman: Indians and Spaniards in the Texas Borderlands* (Chapel Hill: University of North Carolina Press, 2007), 1–25.

64. Bolton, "Defensive Spanish Exploration and the Significance of Borderlands," 56.

65. Ibid.

66. Ibid., 57–59.

67. Sandos, *Converting California*, 109–110.

68. Quoted in George Harwood Phillips, *Vineyards and Vaqueros: Indian Labor and the Economic Expansion of Southern California, 1771–1877* (Norman: University of Oklahoma Press, 2010), 219–220.

69. Weber, *Spanish Frontier in North America*, 343.

70. Ibid., 341–343.

71. Bolton, "Defensive Spanish Exploration and the Significance of Borderlands," 59–63.

72. John Francis Bannon, ed., *Bolton and the Spanish Borderlands* (1930; repr., Norman: University of Oklahoma Press, 1964), 3–64; Weber, *Spanish Frontier in North America*, 341–342.

73. Hämäläinen, *Comanche Empire*, 1-17, 141–291; Barr, *Peace Came in the Form of a Woman*, 1–25, 159–196; Jack D. Forbes, *Apache, Navaho, and Spaniard* (Norman: University of Oklahoma Press, 1971), 1–20.

74. David J. Weber, "The Spanish Borderlands: Historiography Redux," *History Teacher* 39 (November 2005): 43–56.

75. Lisbeth Haas examines the perspective of Pablo Tac in *Pablo Tac, Indigenous Scholar: Writings on Luiseño Language and Colonial History, c. 1840* (Berkeley: University of California Press, 2011), 3–39; and *Saints and Citizens: Indigenous Histories of Colonial Missions and Mexican California* (Berkeley: University of California Press, 2014).

# 2

# *Regional Promoters and the California Mission Myth*

But the Philistine—he of the shrieking auto club or the plethoric pocket-book—looked at the dashing coach, the type of California's early days, with but slight interest, and passed on to drop his golden coin in a musty curio shop, or to profane the sanctity of those majestic hills with the noisy snort of his motor car. . . . As for you who love Santa Barbara and have felt the spell of the passing day, revisit it quickly before the charm that won you is a thing of the past.
—Kathleen Lynch, "The Passing of Old Santa Barbara," *Out West* (1904)

Spanish colonization left a lasting legacy on Native communities throughout the Americas. Many interpretations of American history in the nineteenth century demonized the Spanish based on long-standing antagonisms between the Protestant Anglo and Catholic Spanish cultures. To claim California history as their own, Euro-American migrants in Southern California in the late 1880s took hold of the Spanish legacy and created an idealized narrative that built connections between the mission ruins and a shared European past. Regional boosters such as Charles Fletcher Lummis helped promote this history in magazines and travel journals circulated across the nation. Coupled with the romantic story and idyllic setting poetically depicted in Helen Hunt Jackson's watershed novel *Ramona* (1884) and John Steven McGroarty's *The Mission Play* (1911), Americans increasingly traveled to the region to experience the drama of Southern California firsthand. Developers, entrepreneurs, and local promoters, including McGroarty, successfully used the inherited Spanish mission history in Southern California to market a constructed past to these visitors. In creating this past, regional boosters used the idyllic descriptions of Spanish and Mexican California provided by Californios and brushed over the harsh realities of life that reflected poorly on this mythical history. These constructed narratives rarely included positive portrayals of Native peoples or ordinary Mexican-California citizens as central figures.[1]

The creation of a historical narrative offered a "usable history" for new American residents that supported a Golden Age of California, ignoring Native peoples and glorifying the accomplishments of the Spanish church. Proponents and residents of Southern California increasingly yearned for a history more applicable to their regional identity and one far removed from gold rush mythology dominant in Northern California. James Miller Guinn, cofounder of the Historical Society of Southern California (1883), argued that scholars of California and new residents should not focus solely on the gold rush as the origins of the new state's history. Rather, Guinn and some of his contemporaries contended that narratives of California must look further back to a more "relevant" and "noble" history.[2] Euro-Americans interested in revising the origin story of California did not consider the Native past a usable or relatable history. At the time, many Euro-Americans viewed Native Californians as vanishing remnants of an arcane time who would soon pass into extinction. In Southern California, the ruins of the Spanish missions, pueblos, presidios, and ranchos—with their crumbling adobe walls and cracked red tile roofs—stood as keen markers on the landscape that encompassed some of the earliest visible symbols of a European presence in the region.[3] Euro-Americans who moved to California from the east found a relatable history of colonization in the Spanish past, assisted by popular writings that further dramatized the California landscape.

## Helen Hunt Jackson

The late nineteenth century was a turning point for Los Angeles and Southern California. Promoters of the area had significantly more success drawing tourists to the region once the railroad companies laid tracks across the landscape.[4] At the same time, the influential writings of Helen Hunt Jackson, a New England activist and author, emerged as a key catalyst in the creation of the romantic Spanish heritage in Southern California. Jackson penned *A Century of Dishonor* in 1881 to illustrate the poor living conditions of Native peoples in California whose ancestors, the so-called Mission Indians, were associated with the Spanish missions.[5] However, this monograph did not put in motion the change she had hoped to see. To connect to a broader American audience, Jackson embarked on a mission to write a novel that resonated with people. Although she had intended for *Ramona* to further shed light on the deplorable conditions of Indian affairs in the United States (much like *Uncle Tom's Cabin* had done for African Americans in the late 1850s), the picturesque landscape and idyllic atmosphere of California's fading Spanish era painted by Jackson drew the bulk of readers' attention.[6]

Like many of her contemporaries, Jackson, who spent a great deal of time in California investigating the contemporary condition of Mission Indians, pointed to mission secularization as the culprit behind the displacement of indigenous people.[7] Many popular writers at the time also blamed Mexican secularization policies for the high rates of malnutrition, disease, and mortality found in many Native communities in the mid-nineteenth century. She argued that Mexican governors and administrators of California stole all they could from the missions, even though the secularization law called for officials to turn over mission lands to Native peoples. According to Jackson, Mexican landowners forced Native Californians "to work far harder than before," while failing to provide them with adequate food. Mexican leaders hired Native people "out in gangs to work in towns or on farms, under masters who regarded them simply as beasts of burden."[8] This type of work regimen originated at the Spanish California missions, and it continued into the Mexican and American eras to varying degrees.[9] Following deceitful negotiations, the U.S. government forced many Native Californians onto secluded reservations where they struggled to survive. The government frequently failed to provide adequate supplies and food, and greedy Indian agents stole from reservation stores as well.[10]

In response to her visits to California, Jackson argued that "a more pitiable sight has not been seen on earth than the spectacle of this great body of helpless, dependent creatures, suddenly deprived of their teachers and protectors" following the end of the mission system.[11] Jackson viewed the missions as a protective force in the lives of Native peoples. But she did not look back to the beginning of Spanish colonization and the establishment of the mission system as the origin of the devastation she previously described. Rather, Jackson viewed the Franciscan priests with great reverence. She recounted the stories told to her about Native Californians waiting each Sunday at the missions "in long procession, to get their weekly gifts. Each one received something,—a handkerchief, dress, trinket, or money."[12] In her writings, Jackson depicted the missions as places of relief for Native peoples, contrasting the seemingly benign Spanish institutions with the brutality of Euro-American settlement that continued to threaten Native Californian communities during her visits to the region in the late nineteenth century.[13]

Indeed, Jackson viewed the Spanish and Mexican eras as the halcyon days for Native Californians, before American swindlers moved in to usurp Native claims to the land. Euro-Americans' admiration of the "Spanish fantasy past" offered respite from their present problems and deepened their growing nostalgia for Spanish California history.[14] In fact, Jackson described her hope to write *Ramona* as "a novel, in which will be set forth some Indian experiences in a way to move people's hearts."[15] But unbeknownst to Jackson, her poetic description of California's landscape and the tragic love story central to the novel pulled on more heartstrings than the underlying call to improve the living conditions of Mission Indians.[16] In the decades following Jackson's death in August 1885, Euro-Americans poured into California and further encroached on the land rights of the earlier inhabitants.

Euro-Americans adopted California's Spanish history for themselves through *Ramona*—marking the beginning of a relatable "American" history in the region that tended to silence Native experiences. Yet the story of *Ramona* did not easily lend itself to American appropriation. In the novel, Ramona, a beautiful Scots-Indian woman, falls in love with Alessandro, a Native laborer and son of the village chief who is leader of the sheep shearers at the Moreno rancho where Ramona lives. Ramona's guardian, Señora Moreno, a member of the landed Mexican-Californio elite, disapproves of Ramona's relationship with an Indian man. But despite Señora Moreno's objections, Ramona and Alessandro secretly marry and run away together. All does not go well, however. The waves of land-hungry and often violent American settlers force the couple to move, time and time again. Tragedy and poverty follow Ramona and Alessandro throughout their life together—a life tragically sullied by discriminatory emigrants and an American legal system unsympathetic to the criminal acts perpetrated against Native peoples.

Alessandro and Ramona, like many Native people of the time, attempt to distance themselves from the discrimination. They build a secluded and very modest home in the foothills of the local mountains. Like many other Native Californians struggling to coexist in a hostile California in the nineteenth century, Alessandro travels into town to find day work for minimal wages. But despite their best efforts, Alessandro and Ramona fall victim to the violence inflicted by foreigners. In the end, a Euro-American settler accuses Alessandro of stealing his horse and murders him in front of Ramona—just steps outside of their home. Because Alessandro is an indigenous man accused of horse thievery and the only witness is Ramona, a half-Indian woman, the discriminatory California courts do not prosecute Alessandro's murderer.[17] Inspired by true events, *Ramona* illustrated some of the many injustices Native people routinely faced in California and vilified the encroaching flood of Euro-American settlers in the region. And yet ironically, *Ramona* tourism encouraged some of the largest waves of Euro-Americans to travel to Southern California. Combined with a housing boom, the population of Southern California skyrocketed at the turn of the twentieth century. For example, Los Angeles grew by over 200,000 people from the late 1880s to 1910—expanding the number of residents sixfold from only two decades previously. Also during that time, Los Angeles grew to be a markedly American town.[18] Americans had pushed Native people largely into the periphery and onto reservations.

The *Ramona* tourists traveled from the East Coast and Midwest on the newly completed railroad lines. In conjunction with a railroad fare war that significantly dropped prices to less than two dollars for travelers interested in visiting Southern California, local entrepreneurs were quick to erect sites proclaiming to be the actual location of significant events torn from the pages of *Ramona*. Tourists came, with books in hand, to see places such as Ramona's home, her marriage site, and Alessandro's grave, while some even traveled to meet the "real" Ramona. Although these tourists collected postcards and purchased souvenir spoons inscribed with Ramona's name, comparatively few joined Jackson in advocating improvements in Indian affairs. Meanwhile, many wealthy Euro-Americans from the East who sought a warmer place to retire moved to Southern California and contributed to the growing population that understood the area through the eyes of Jackson's poetic language. To many tourists and future residents of California, the actual history of California became nearly lost in the romanticized stories presented by boosters and displayed in *Ramona*.[19]

The glorification of Ramona did not end at the turn of the twentieth century. For example, the small town of Hemet, California, located in the San Jacinto Valley, created the *Ramona Pageant* in 1923. In his adaptation of *Ramona,* playwright Garnet Holme highlighted the "jovial" atmosphere of Hispanic California, including several Spanish and Mexican dances. The Automobile Club of Southern California, *Los Angeles Times*, Motor Transit Company, and Pacific Electric Railway Company helped promote the pageant to tourists in the 1920s and early 1930s. The *Ramona Pageant* drew thousands of tourists to the secluded city for its annual production—an event that has lasted over ninety years. Also in the 1930s, Jackson's novel *Ramona* sparked several films starring leading Hollywood actors including Loretta Young and Don Ameche who brought the romanticized story of Hispanic California to the big screen. But as Dydia DeLyser observed in *Ramona Memories: Tourism and the Shaping of Southern California* (2005), "what remains to be seen is whether the pageant will hold continued appeal to those [today] for whom the phenomenon of Ramona is not a part of their daily consciousness but rather hidden deep beneath the surface of the region's identity, representation, and social memory."[20] In the early twentieth century, though, *Ramona* was still an active part of the Southern California zeitgeist.

## Charles Fletcher Lummis

Into this atmosphere of historical myth making and romance walked Charles Fletcher Lummis, who was hired by the *Los Angeles Times* in 1884. Lummis remains one of the most prominent and influential boosters in

California history and the greater Southwest. Using the *Times* to promote the region, publisher Harrison Gray Otis advertised land developments and tourist attractions targeted to *Ramona* enthusiasts under the guise of "real" news bulletins. As DeLyser has observed, Otis, Lummis, and others not only promoted a romanticized image of the Spanish past, but also "embraced this glowing new social memory."[21] Lummis adopted the Spanish heritage of the Southwest and became its biggest proponent in popular culture. His work as a civic leader, magazine editor, author, museum founder, and letter writer at the turn of the twentieth century helped to reshape the image of Spanish America in the popular American mindset.[22]

Before scholars such as Herbert Eugene Bolton, John Francis Bannon, and David J. Weber analyzed the importance of the Spanish influence in North America, histories of the United States focused on triumphalist Anglocentric narratives.[23] In the early twentieth century, many Euro-American historians viewed the Spanish influence as peripheral; English and French influences had much greater importance and power in shaping the history of the American continent, they believed.[24] Although he was not a trained historian, Lummis worked to reorient the general perspective of Spanish colonial history in popular American society, especially as anti-Spanish sentiment grew in the years leading up to the Spanish-American War (1898).[25] Fueled by a disregard for the New England sensibilities into which he was born into, Lummis moved to the Southwest and eventually made it his life's mission to remove the tarnish of the popular Spanish "black legend" in which many Euro-Americans still believed at the time.[26] Late in life, Lummis articulated his feelings, noting that he felt at home in the Southwest, or what he termed "Spanish America." Although Lummis was born a "Puritan," he argued that "my whole imagination and sympathy and feeling were Latin. That is, essentially Spanish." Growing up in the home of a strict Methodist preacher, Lummis escaped what he called "the repressive influence of my birthplace" to find in the Southwest that "the generous and bubbling boyish impulses which had been considerably frosted in New England were, after all, my birthright."[27] He romanticized the Southwest in his personal life and in his public writings. Lummis also dramatized contemporary Native peoples—recording songs and stories, taking photographs, and buying countless objects from the diverse communities he encountered. These objects made up the founding collection for the Southwest Museum in Los Angeles, California.

Lummis was an intelligent, eccentric character who pioneered the cultural history of the American Southwest.[28] He attended Harvard University but never graduated; he enjoyed physical exertion more than attending class and failed to pass some of his final exams his senior year.[29] Rejection by Harvard, a bulwark among eastern institutions, gave Lummis a chance to explore opportunities on different shores.[30] As a man of extremes, Lummis exhausted himself on several occasions and had a stroke while in his twenties. He took several jobs working for newspapers as both a writer and editor, but eventually petitioned Otis for a contract job to document his cross-country trek by foot from Cincinnati to Los Angeles (2,200 miles) for the *Los Angeles Times*. Lummis left his post as editor of the *Scioto Gazette* in Cincinnati after contracting malaria. He was drawn to California for its health benefits and pursued the walking campaign in part to help regain his strength.[31]

Early in his career, Lummis observed, described, photographed, and collected objects from the people he met along his "tramp across the continent," including many Native communities in the Southwest. While Lummis chose to walk to California, Euro-Americans followed the railroads and moved West at ever-increasing rates in the late nineteenth and early twentieth centuries. In many cases, these settlers used violence, intimidation, and a biased California legal system to push indigenous peoples off of their lands and into peripheral areas of society. Like Jackson, Lummis lamented the mistreatment of Native communities by Euro-American migrants and worked to publicize these injustices.[32] However, Lummis's colorful early writings focused more exclusively on describing and romanticizing Native cultures than critically examining the impact of Spanish and American colonization. As noted by historian Sherry Smith, Lummis did not approach the history of the Southwest and California through an unbiased lens. Instead, he romanticized both Native and Spanish history, but when describing instances of conflict between the two groups, such as the Pueblo Revolt, Lummis inevitably focused on Spanish heroism that had sown "civilization" in the Southwest.[33] In fact, the California mission ruins that stood as contested sites of repression for many Native Californians played an important role in Lummis's promotion of a more romantic Spanish past in California and the Southwest.

The many negative realities of Spanish contact with indigenous peoples did not fit into the "white legend" of Spanish colonization that Lummis worked to promote wherein Spanish padres were benevolent colonizers that brought European standards of "civilization" to California. In fact, he did not seem to reconcile the two for much of his career. Instead, Lummis treated Spanish colonization and contemporary Native affairs as unrelated experiences. Meanwhile, "Don Carlos," as Lummis became known, developed a deep appreciation for the cultures he observed during his journeys through the Southwest. And as a writer, observer, collector, and appreciator of Native cultures, he increasingly viewed the role of the American government in Indian affairs with hostility—especially when it concerned issues such as off-reservation boarding schools and land rights disputes.[34]

Overall, Lummis was a complicated figure who advocated Indian rights but continued to promote a greatly romanticized and exaggerated history of Spanish California and the Southwest. He sought to lure tourists to California with his promotional writings, and yet he and other philanthropists also worked as advocates for Mission Indians who often encountered deceitful Euro-Americans who intruded on Native lands. Lummis used his relationship with President Theodore Roosevelt (they were classmates at Harvard) to help reform Indian rights policies through the newly formed Sequoya League.[35] But at the same time he increasingly grasped onto the California missions as symbols of the Spanish America he adored.[36] The California missions, in ruins by the early twentieth century, stood as relics of a less complicated life that Lummis and other antimodern easterners began to yearn for in the face of quickly spreading urbanization. As historian William Cronon observed, American longing for a less complex, frontier, life "inevitably implied ambivalence, if not downright hostility, toward modernity and all that it represented. If one saw the wild lands of the frontier as freer, truer, and more natural. . . then one was also more inclined to see the cities and factories of urban-industrial civilization as confining, false, and artificial."[37] The Spanish-California landscape and the seemingly unchanging lives of Native peoples reminded Euro-Americans of a simpler time filled with ever-fleeting glimpses of leisure. Boosters promoted this historically false perspective, but many Americans nonetheless consumed the dramatic tales.[38]

Lummis worked constantly to promote Southern California as a desirable destination to people across the country. Mirrored by the efforts of the Los Angeles Chamber of Commerce, "based on the proposition that what the country most needs to insure its material prosperity is more people to develop its resources," regional boosters sought to bring people, especially new residents, into Southern California. They hoped that new residents would bring in more businesses to help the region develop.[39] They ignored the toll of new residents on already strained Native Californian populations. To Lummis, the development of Southern California could not have been done without paying tribute to the labors of the Spanish. He observed that "Southern California is not only the new Eden of the Saxon home-seeker, but part, and type, of Spanish America; the scene where American energy has wrought miracles."[40] To help draw people into Southern California, Lummis amplified his promotional efforts. He became an editor and main contributor to the regional magazine the *Land of Sunshine* and continually depicted California and the Southwest as a dramatic haven for Easterners and Midwesterners in need of refuge.[41]

Lummis, at 36 years old, was introduced as the new editor of the *Land of Sunshine* in December 1894. The introductory article listed Lummis's achievements and publications to date. Included was *The Spanish Pioneers*, "which presents for the first time, in popular form, the conclusions of modern science concerning the conquest and colonization of North and South America."[42] Lummis's writings were so complimentary of the Spanish that the Royal Academy of Spain gave him a formal compliment and notice of gratitude. His first article, "The Spanish-American Face," plays to this theme of "modern science" as applied to Spanish conquest and colonization.[43] It also displayed his bias for Spanish culture, religion, and aesthetics while ignoring the negative impact of Spanish colonization on Native peoples.

Lummis's inaugural article was in step with his positive promotion of Spanish colonization in the Americas. He argued that "to the thoughtful student few side-lights in history are more striking than this vital individuality of the Spanish."[44] He proclaimed that the Spanish-American face was the most beautiful. Travelers could see this face in any location that the Spanish colonized because, unlike the English, "there is no land in which he[a Spaniard] ever sat down which does not to this day bear in its very marrow the heritage of his religion, his language and his social creed. His *marca* is upon the faces, the laws, the very landscape."[45] Lummis noted that indigenous people in the Americas commonly learned to speak Spanish, practiced Catholicism, and intermarried with the Spanish. By contrast, the English colonizer "has never impressed his language or his religion upon the peoples he has overrun." Lummis observed that "something of his [the Englishman's] face goes into the half-breeds he begets but will not father; but even his physical impress is much less marked than in the case of his Latin predecessor."[46] In each instance, Lummis essentially argued that Spanish colonization efforts were more effective and benevolent than the English efforts because Spanish colonizers, after generations in the Americas, left a more permanent mark on the people and the landscape and incorporated Native peoples into their developing societies.

Lummis did not remove Spanish colonization from its religious roots; instead, he used religion as a catalyst to elevate the virtue of Spanish heritage. He argued that "to no woman on earth is religion a more vital, ever-present, all-pervading actuality. . . . Even when outcast, no woman of Spanish blood falls or can fall to the outer vileness which haunts the purlieus of every English-speaking great city." Because Spanish women were so devoted to their religion and "social conservatism," they "contribute[d] fewer recruits to the outcast ranks than any other civilized woman."[47] In his article, Lummis openly promoted Spanish America as exceedingly moral, culturally rich, and idyllic. He contested the notion that former Spanish territories were somehow backward outposts or less civilized than regions colonized by the English—a common sentiment held by many Euro-Americans in the East.[48] Lummis emphasized the centuries-old culture and religious traditions visible on the landscape and on the faces of people in Spanish America. In doing so, he set the stage for years of promoting the romance and gallantry of Spanish colonization in the Southwest in his publications, while minimizing discussions of the negative impact of Spanish colonization on Native peoples. He used the magazine in which this article appeared as the pulpit from which he promoted Spanish America to people in the Northeast and Midwest, where the Los Angeles Chamber of Commerce distributed thousands of copies of Lummis's publications.[49]

Similarly, George Wharton James, a contemporary of Lummis who wrote about and promoted California and the Southwest, highlighted the noble intentions of the Spanish padres in California. He asserted that many people recognize that Franciscan priests at the missions treated Native peoples as children in a patriarchal system. However, James noted that Native people continued to thrive within the missions and that "few [people] question that the Indians were happy under this system and concede that they made wonderful progress in the so-called arts of civilization. From crude savagery they were lifted by the training of their fathers into usefulness and productiveness."[50] Like Jackson, James attributed the decline of Native Californian populations to mission secularization and the rapid Americanization of California in the late nineteenth century.[51]

As noted, Americans drawn to California by glorified depictions of the region increasingly infringed on the rights of Native Californians. Lummis considered Native people, especially Mission Indians, to be an important yet disconnected part of the legacy of Spanish mission history that he worked to save and popularize. Recognizing the inevitability of ever-increasing Euro-American settlement, Lummis spearheaded the development of the Sequoya League under the headline "To Make Better Indians."[52] Echoing the efforts of Jackson before them, members of the league wanted to help improve the lives of Native peoples. They viewed economics as the primary source of change, arguing that "the Sequoya League stands for a revival of the honest old work, and for giving the maker of a $50 basket (for instance) something of the $40 profit that now goes to the middle-man—but without raising the price."[53] In this way, they sought to improve the living conditions of Native communities in California by making transactions more equitable. Members of the league also criticized the Indian education system established by the U.S. government that promoted training in generally low-paying vocations such as blacksmith, carpenter, and laundress. Native people could make a better living, the argument went, if they participated in the local economy, stayed with their families on reservations, learned traditional crafts, and sold collectible items to Euro-American tourists. Lummis, for his part, supported

Native economies by purchasing (and collecting as an amateur archeologist) countless objects from indigenous communities throughout the Americas.[54]

As the mouthpiece of the Sequoya League, Lummis criticized the U.S. Office of Indian Affairs for maintaining poor conditions on Indian reservations. Writing in 1905, Lummis claimed that the condition of former Mission Indians declined over the last forty years under American supervision.[55] Despite departmental failures, he praised California residents for stepping in to supply food, grain for planting, and clothing for the six hundred "Mission Indians" of the Campo reservations while they waited for the federal government to improve conditions. He criticized the Indian Office for failing to supply local Native peoples with the resources to support themselves and for "squandering" the nearly $25,000 from the Warner's Ranch settlement earmarked for the Cupeño, who had been evicted by Americans and relocated from their ancestral homeland.[56] The league thus focused on improving the contemporary conditions of the Mission Indians that the federal government was neglecting. To make his criticisms poignantly clear, Lummis placed in the *Sequoya League Bulletin* excerpts from "Reports of the Commissioner of Indian Affairs, Agent of the Mission Indians," dating back to 1880. These excerpts illustrated that the agents and commissioner were well aware of the deplorable conditions of the Mission Indians in San Diego County, but neglected to improve their situation. According to Lummis, Native peoples had been "driven from their fertile valleys to worthless desert camping grounds which have been made into 'Reservations.'"[57]

Lummis's criticisms of the contemporary circumstances of the Mission Indians in the early twentieth century placed full blame on the negligence of the U.S. government. Although much blame did rest with the federal government, Lummis and many of his contemporaries did not extend their critical gaze further back to seek the genesis of the struggles of Native communities impacted by the Spanish. In his quest to dispel negative depictions of Spanish colonization, Lummis and others often painted the Spanish as benevolent colonizers who worked to uplift indigenous peoples. He did not recognize the many components of the mission system that strained Native communities, nor did he acknowledge the resistance exerted by Native Californians against the oppressive Spanish systems. Straining forces included forced assimilation, stringent labor regimens, violence, extreme punishments, and the deadly diseases that disseminated Native communities.

In working to promote Spanish California, Lummis spearheaded a campaign to help preserve the crumbling mission ruins. After creating the Landmarks Club, Lummis and other philanthropists raised thousands of dollars to help repair the disintegrating structures at, among other places, Mission San Juan

Capistrano and Mission San Fernando. They also sought to restore El Camino Real ("the King's Highway"), which connected the missions.[58] To combat Euro-American Protestant disinterest in the Catholic structures, Lummis promoted the missions as relics of California's European past. He asked readers to help save the missions "not for the Church but for Humanity."[59] Lummis's work to elevate the missions as landmarks of California's earliest history ultimately succeeded in attracting the hearts and minds of travelers to the region. For example, Mai Richie Reed, the daughter of a successful and wealthy tailor and clothing dealer in Philadelphia, absorbed the works of many writers and photographers of California and the Southwest, including George Wharton James, who wrote about the beauty of the California and Southwest landscape, the romance of the missions, and Native cultures and basketry. Reed also read John Van Dyke's and Lummis's writings on the Southwest and California—all of which "depicted an exotic world as far removed from the norms and constraints of eastern society as the surface of the moon."[60] In April 1907, Reed traveled with friends aboard the California Limited passenger train to the Southwest to view the places described so vividly by these writers. The following year, she again traveled to the Southwest, but also toured California's missions, documenting her travels in a diary and scrapbook.[61] Other regional boosters also grabbed hold of mission history as a catalyst for encouraging travel to California and entertaining tourists once they arrived.

## John Steven McGroarty

A contemporary of Lummis, playwright, author, and poet John McGroarty equally idolized and promoted the Spanish past in California. He worked as a writer for the *Los Angeles Times,* and in 1911 he published a comprehensive history of California entitled *California: Its History and Romance.* Just as many other boosters of early California, McGroarty's history of the state begins with the first presence of Europeans and ignores centuries of Native history in the process. He pointed to San Diego's long history in which the city "looks back on a past that stretches nearly four hundred years into the now dim and misty pathways of civilization," as if San Diego had just emerged from the ocean mere centuries before American colonization. Like Bolton and Lummis, McGroarty built connections between Spanish America and the English colonies, finding the Spanish heritage richer and more appealing. He compared Spanish culture in the Southwest to the romance of the founding of the United States, noting that "her tiled rooftrees and Christian shrines received the salutes of the booming tides before the Declaration of Independence was signed and before Betsy Ross wove from summer rainbows and wintery stars the miracle of 'Old Glory.'"[62] Boosters, including McGroarty, Lummis, and Frank A. Miller of the famous Mission Inn in Riverside, California, used newspapers, literature, poetry, theater arts, and architecture as venues to popularize early California history at the local and national levels.[63] However, they continued to minimize the historical experiences of Native Californians in their popular narratives and the lasting legacies of colonization on Native communities.

McGroarty, whom Kevin Starr described as a "genial journalist and a dreamy poet," spent four decades working as a regional writer for the *Los Angeles Times,* but he is most well known for writing and producing the *Mission Play.*[64] Indeed, McGroarty's work in promoting manufactured histories of the West was recognized far and wide. President Herbert Hoover even sent McGroarty a telegram congratulating him on the 3,000th performance of the *Mission Play,* commenting on McGroarty's ability to "so vividly [re-create] the atmosphere of California's romantic early history."[65]

McGroarty's *Mission Play* helped to develop a sense of shared history for Southern Californians in the early twentieth century. Overwhelmed by demand, the *Mission Play* was extended nine weeks beyond its anticipated run (of only one week) and set national records for consecutive shows performed.[66] Between 1912 and the early 1930s, nearly 2.5 million people witnessed the booster perspective of California's dramatic history through McGroarty's eyes.[67] The four-and-a-half hour production cost over $1.5 million and, as noted, was performed over 3,000 times. McGroarty promoted the play as a historical dramatization of California's history, but he minimized the narratives of Native Californians and Mexican residents of the region, essentially "whitewashing" California's history to fit the narratives of wealthy Euro-American playgoers and tourists.[68] According to historian William Deverell, over time the *Mission Play* became a mainstay of Southern California history, wherein "regional culture would canonize the play as Southern California history itself, come back to life exactly where all assumed it had begun, under the stars at the San Gabriel Mission, that ancient engine of civilization."[69] Like Jackson's *Ramona* and the writings of Lummis in the *Land of Sunshine/ Out West* magazine, the *Mission Play* blurred the lines between history and romantic dramatization.

The millions of patrons eager to see the *Mission Play* mistook the spectacle that McGroarty produced for the stage as a true portrayal of regional history. For example, Gracia L. Fernández, a teacher and leader of the Spanish Club at New Utrecht High School in Brooklyn, New York, visited Mission San Gabriel in 1918 with a group of students. She arranged for the students to view the *Mission Play* in an attempt to awaken in them "a genuine interest in the literature and institutions of the peoples of Spain and Spanish America with whom destiny has linked the United States for future cooperation."[70]

She noted that "in Southern California the traditions of Spanish life richly exist. One afternoon we visited the mission of San Gabriel near Los Angeles and witnessed a performance of the Mission Play of California, the dramatic portrayal of the early history of California by the poet McGroarty. Between acts the audience promenades in an enclosed circular walk outside the theater. . . . The chapel bell brings the audience back to the next act."[71] Like many others, the New Utrecht Spanish Club viewed history of California through the eyes of McGroarty and his romanticized portrayals of the period. Their "genuine" experience with Spanish California history was mediated through the lenses of promoters and regional boosters interested in creating a more idyllic presentation of the past.

Because of the overwhelming popularity of the *Mission Play*, McGroarty successfully advocated construction of a new building to house the audiences that quickly outgrew the original structure built for the play. With underwriting from wealthy railroad magnate Henry E. Huntington and the overarching Mission Playhouse Association, McGroarty oversaw construction of the Mission Playhouse designed by popular architect Arthur B. Benton, the original designer of Miller's renowned Mission Inn.[72] Located within a short walking distance of Mission San Gabriel Arcángel, the Mission Playhouse cost the consortium $750,000 and provided enough space for 1,450 patrons and the 300 cast and staff members required for the production.[73]

Fittingly, the playhouse was in the Mission Revival style, creating the impression that the patrons viewed the *Mission Play* within the walls of an actual mission. Mission Revival architecture boomed in Southern California in the late nineteenth and early twentieth centuries. Local boosters helped popularize the architectural style in romanticized portrayals of the mission era. The physical construction of the Mission Playhouse embodied the "almost organic connection between the old Spanish land and the American people who now possessed it."[74] The façade of the playhouse was fashioned after McGroarty's favorite mission, Mission San Antonio de Padua, "one of the most beautiful and important of the Mission establishments . . . that has been sadly neglected and is only infrequently visited."[75] The new Playhouse opened on March 5, 1927, to a gala that cost $100 per ticket, or nearly $1,350 today, with numerous wealthy Los Angeles boosters and leaders in attendance.[76]

The Mission Playhouse quickly became known as a place to see and "a place to be seen." Local leaders, socialites, and clergy members gathered to witness the dramatic *Mission Play* in a building that also included interior amenities such as luxurious seats and large chandeliers replicated after those found on Spanish galleons.[77] Patrons paid between $1 and $2 for tickets to see how "the story of race, the story of ethnicity, the story of California: all could be played out on stage in San Gabriel in perfect adherence to truth," where playgoers displayed a "willingness to suspend disbelief, to mis-remember everything about the dark ground of the region's even recent past."[78] Thus Euro-American boosters and playgoers participated in the construction of California's history that focused on European and American domination while marginalizing the historical experiences of Native peoples.

The *Mission Play* depicted an extremely romanticized version of California history. It began with the founding of the Franciscan mission system and concluded in the American era. The play virtually ignored the violence and abuse of Native people at the hands of Spanish soldiers and missionaries. The *Mission Play* also bypassed the Mexican period nearly completely. It ends with the missions in ruins during the late nineteenth century, and it points to the Mexican government as the agent that caused their downfall. As patrons enveloped themselves in the idealized "Spanish fantasy past," they helped Lummis, McGroarty, and the Mission Playhouse Association further the construction of a sanitized regional history and mission mythology that called for the preservation of mission ruins.[79] Indeed, in the final scenes of the play a Native *vaquero* named Ubaldo and Señora Yorba discuss the future of the California missions as they bid farewell to Mission San Juan Capistrano. The señora suggests that, as Euro-Americans build cities in California and make the state "the wonder of the world, so also will they think, sometime, of these holy places where the padres toiled and builded [*sic*] too. . . . Though we may not see it, Ubaldo . . . maybe in God's good time the Mission bells will ring again their old, sweet music."[80]

According to McGroarty, during the mission era California was a "sheer Utopia."[81] He idolized the Franciscan missionaries whose "magical hands" labored to "take an idle race and put it to work—a useless race that they made useful in the world, a naked race and they clothed it, a hungry race and they fed it, a heathen race that they lifted up into the great white glory of God."[82] The playwright presented Spanish missionaries as the founders and saviors of California—a land "wasted" by "idle" indigenous peoples. He misrepresented Native cultures that were complex and thriving before Spanish colonization as stagnant, "naked," and "hungry." And he portrayed the mission era as a time of plenty, when missionaries taught Native peoples to speak Spanish so they could "finally" communicate with other indigenous communities as well as the Spanish priests. According to McGroarty, the Spanish also taught Native people how to make the land useful. Thus the Spanish "civilized" both the landscape and indigenous peoples in California.

McGroarty believed there was "a great deal of mis-information concerning

50

the collapse of this great [Spanish] dream."[83] Booster publications, including McGroarty's *Mission Memories*, supported an independent understanding of California's development apart from the Anglocentric founding of the American colonies in the East.[84] Like Jackson and James, he ignored the rapid Americanization of California following the gold rush and pointed to the Mexican period and secularization as the downfall of the Spanish mission system. Although his interpretation is correct in the most basic sense, he overly simplified the political construction of the mission system. McGroarty ignored the structural foundation of the missions established by the Spanish crown, which stipulated that the priests would turn the land over to Hispanicized neophytes after ten years. McGroarty was also partially correct in his assessment that Native peoples lost control of the landscape with the partition of mission lands by the Mexican government.[85] McGroarty's writings in 1929 were not in-depth studies of California's history; rather, he wrote as a regional booster who mythologized the past to bring more tourism to the region and create a larger audience for the *Mission Play*.

As for the Mexican government's "black deed" of secularizing the missions, McGroarty argued that it occurred because Mexicans envied the wealth Native peoples accumulated from the prosperous mission system. The Mexican government wanted the rich land for itself, and so members of the Mexican California government "drove the Indians away, took the missions into its own hands without warrant or the slightest semblance of justice," sold the land to the highest bidders, and "pocketed the spoils."[86] In his writings of California history, McGroarty abridged and generalized the secularization policies of the Mexican-California government. He correlated the ruinous vestiges of the California missions with the visibly poor condition of Native Californian populations in the late nineteenth century.

As dreamed by Señora Yorba, promoters and local developers did turn their gaze on the California missions as sites in need of salvation. Wealthy Euro-American tourists enjoyed visiting mission sites in the early twentieth century that stood as relics of the mythical Spanish past. Conversely, these same people were not interested in incorporating Native and Mexican history or Spanish-speaking residents into developing regional narratives. Euro-Americans felt comfortable proliferating California's Spanish history that harked back to familiar European origins, but they minimized the roles of Native people and Mexicans in developing the region.[87] Thus McGroarty's ignorance of the Mexican period in the *Mission Play* illustrated the developing racial hierarchies in popular culture that placed Euro-Americans at the top. This cultural bias amplified the European components of California's early history in popular depictions of the period and contributed to unhistorical representation of the past in California.

51

Many boosters in the early twentieth century likened Southern California to Italy and the Mediterranean. McGroarty pointed to ancient Rome and Greece and noted that "every civilization is builded [*sic*] on the ruins of the civilization that preceded it."[88] Similarly, McGroarty argued that the "civilization" built by Euro-Americans in California in the late nineteenth and early twentieth centuries emerged from the foundation established by Spanish missionaries a century earlier. But he ignored the fact that Native peoples had built these silos of civilization in the region. He viewed mission tourism as an important expansion of civilization in California. For McGroarty, the missions were places where visitors could see the "glamorous tale, full of beauty and color and the grace of God." He argued that California still maintained its beauty and romance and that, although "the Missions are in ruin, one can still sense what glory and splendor once was theirs."[89]

As booster narratives that dramatized the Spanish period grew in popularity, new generations of writers in the early twentieth century romanticized the Spanish and Mexican eras further "by sentimentalizing them on the one hand, and sanitizing their accounts on the other hand."[90] By revising the past, Euro-American boosters and residents were able to promote Southern California as "a 'whiter' alternative to the polyglot congestion of the modern [early twentieth century] city."[91] Discrimination and racism influenced scholars and popular writers to sanitize history and virtually exclude both Native and Mexican populations from their "whitewashed" narratives.[92] McGroarty credited Spanish missionaries with providing Native Californians with the tools needed for continued survival. But he ignored the fact that Native people successfully survived in California for thousands of years before the Spanish arrived, as well as the reality that Spanish contact caused the death of many thousands of Native Californians.

McGroarty began the *Mission Play* with Native people simply fading into the background as the Spanish took center-stage. That said, there was some truth in the distortion of history presented by McGroarty. For example, European-imported animals grazed on indigenous California plants and decimated Native foods. Furthermore, Spanish soldiers and missionaries introduced European diseases such as syphilis, gonorrhea, smallpox, and cholera to the region. These types of disease caused extremely low birth rates and death among Native peoples.[93] However, McGroarty did not suggest in the *Mission Play* that Native people fell out of the historical narrative because of starvation, disease, violence, and death. Likewise, Euro-American abuse of Native Californians is a central theme in Helen Hunt Jackson's *Ramona*. Yet Jackson placed blame on the greed and violence brought by American emigrants and ignored the negative legacy of Spanish colonization on the socioeconomic well-being of Native populations. Time and time again, the dramatic and romantic depictions of California's Spanish mission heritage by Jackson, Lummis, McGroarty, and others—whether intentional or not— silenced Native experiences in popular narratives.[94]

Later, McGroarty did acknowledge the presence of indigenous peoples, but he did not attempt to understand Native people at the time of, or before, Spanish contact. He provided simplistic and patronizing vignettes of the lives and living conditions of Native Californians. For example, McGroarty claimed that Native people "had no houses or tepees and were accustomed in the severe weather of winter to cover their bodies with mud in order to keep out the cold." He further claimed that "very few of the California Indians occupied a plane of civilization higher than that of beasts when the white men first found them."[95] By publicizing these types of stereotypes, McGroarty established Spanish missionaries as saviors who introduced humanity into the lives of the archaic indigenous people in California.

Moreover, McGroarty's decision to begin the *Mission Play* with the Spanish arrival in California seems fitting because he had long insisted that indigenous people before Spanish contact were "lazy and indolent" beings who "had no names for themselves, no traditions, and no religion."[96] According to McGroarty, Native people were essentially a *tabula rasa* for the missionaries, who transformed Native peoples from "beasts" into "skilled artisans, husbandmen, painters, craftsmen and musicians."[97] McGroarty degraded Native people to glorify the actions of the Spanish missionaries. His unhistorical narrative ignored the labors and sacrifices of thousands of indigenous peoples at the California missions.

As described here, the dramatic and romantic depictions of California's Spanish mission heritage by Jackson, Lummis, McGroarty and others frequently silenced or misrepresented Native experiences in the stories told in popular venues. The long legacy of boosterism in California is still present on the landscape, where conserved and preserved mission sites overwhelmingly maintain the narratives established by boosters in the early twentieth century. Native people remain misunderstood and pushed into the periphery at many contemporary missions. Because of their popularity and the absence of a counternarrative, romanticized booster histories persist as the prevalent narrative of California history into the twenty-first century.

**Notes**

1. William Deverell specifically addresses the erasure of Mexican people from Southern California history in the early twentieth century. See William Deverell, *Whitewashed Adobe: The Rise of Los Angeles and the Remaking of Its Mexican Past* (Berkeley: University of California Press, 2005), 11–48.

2. James Miller Guinn, *A History of California and an Extended History of Los Angeles and Environs: Also Containing Biographies of Well-known Citizens of the Past and Present* (Los Angeles: Historic Records Company, 1915), v–vi, 33–66.

3. Ibid., 156. According to historian Glen Gendzel ("Pioneers and Padres: Competing Mythologies in Northern and Southern California, 1850-1930," *Western Historical Quarterly* 32: 55-79) in their effort to revise the history of the state scholars based in Los Angeles essentially launched a smear campaign against the "pioneers" and gold rush history that many people in the north worshipped. Moreover, Guinn described the argonauts as ignorant and greedy swindlers. He noted that the "conglomerate elements of society found the Land of Gold practically without law, and the vicious among them were not long in making it a land without order" (Guinn, *History of California,* 185).

4. Paul F. Allen, "Tourists in Southern California, 1875–1903" (master's thesis, Claremont Colleges, Claremont, California, 1940), 7–27, 38–51. Allen included a discussion of popular railroad trips, tourist attractions, and excursions in his now dated yet relevant analysis of tourism in Southern California.

5. Helen Hunt Jackson, *A Century of Dishonor: A Sketch of the United States Government's Dealings with Some of the Indian Tribes* (New York: Harper and Brothers, 1881).

6. Kevin Starr, *Inventing the Dream: California through the Progressive Era* (New York: Oxford University Press, 1985), 54–63.

7. George Harwood Phillips, *Chiefs and Challengers: Indian Resistance and Cooperation in Southern California*, 2d ed. (Norman: University of Oklahoma Press, 2014), 237–255.

8. Helen Hunt Jackson, *Glimpses of California and the Missions* (Boston: Little, Brown, 1907), 76–77.

9. Disease, violence, and outright genocide campaigns during the 1850s and 1860s severely reduced Native populations to some 17,000 by 1900. Americans turned to foreign laborers such as the Chinese, Japanese, and Mexican migrants to fill this void.

10. Clifford E. Trafzer, *As Long as the Grass Shall Grow and Rivers Flow: A History of Native Americans* (Fort Worth, TX: Harcourt College Publishers, 2000), 198–199.

11. Jackson, *Glimpses of California and the Missions,* 76–77.

12. Ibid., 92.

13. Dydia DeLyser, *Ramona Memories: Tourism and the Shaping of Southern California* (Minneapolis: University of Minnesota Press, 2005), 6–11.

14. Starr, *Inventing the Dream,* 54–55.

15. DeLyser, *Ramona Memories,* 10.

16. Ibid., 14–16.

17. Helen Hunt Jackson, *Ramona: A Story* (Boston: Roberts Brothers, 1884), 1–490; DeLyser, *Ramona Memories,* 10–11, 225. Originally published in the weekly *Christian Union* as a serial between May and November 1884.

18. Starr, *Inventing the Dream,* 62–65.

19. DeLyser, *Ramona Memories,* 31–58.

20. Ibid., 137–149; 149.

21. Ibid., 44–45.

22. Ibid., 45–48. Lummis undertook extensive letter-writing campaigns throughout his professional life, urging prominent Californians such as John Muir and Frank Miller to donate to the Landmarks Club or renew their subscriptions to his magazines.

23. John Francis Bannon, *The Spanish Borderlands Frontier, 1513–1821* (Albuquerque: University of New Mexico Press, 1974), 1–7.

24. As mentioned earlier, Bolton countered this common narrative and developed the Spanish borderlands school of studies in the early twentieth century. He argued that most scholars incorrectly believed that the Spanish failed in their conquest of North America. As he saw it, other historians mistook "the tail for the dog." For a more complete discussion of Bolton and the Spanish borderlands, see James A. Sandos, "From 'Boltonlands' to 'Weberlands': The Borderlands Enter American History," *American Quarterly* 46 (December 1994): 595–604; Herbert Eugene Bolton, "Defensive Spanish Exploration and the Significance of Borderlands," in *Bolton and the Spanish Borderlands,* ed. John Francis Bannon (1930; repr. Norman: University of Oklahoma Press, 1964), 32–64.

25. Mark Thompson, *American Character: The Curious Life of Charles Fletcher Lummis and the Rediscovery of the Southwest* (New York: Arcade Publishing, 2001), 294.

26. David J. Weber addressed American sentiments toward the Catholic Spanish in *The Spanish Frontier in North America* (New Haven, CT: Yale University Press, 1992), 335–343.

27. Charles Lummis, as quoted in Lawrence Culver, *The Frontier of Leisure: Southern California and the Shaping of Modern America* (New York: Oxford University Press, 2010), 32.

28. Starr, *Inventing the Dream,* 82–83.

29. Thompson, *American Character,* 5–18.

30. Sherry L. Smith, *Reimagining Indians: Native Americans through Anglo Eyes, 1880–1940* (New York: Oxford University Press, 2000), 121.

31. Starr, *Inventing the Dream,* 75–77.

32. Phoebe S. Kropp, *California Vieja: Culture and Memory in a Modern American Place* (Berkeley: University of California Press, 2006), 94–95; DeLyser, *Ramona Memories,* 46–47.

33. Smith, *Reimagining Indians,* 129–131. After nearly a century of contact with the Spanish many Pueblo peoples in present day New Mexico, under the leadership of Popé from San Juan pueblo, joined together in revolt in 1680. They attacked Spanish mission sites, priests, and killed more than 400 Spaniards in a rebellion against missionization, religious suppression, and Spanish political authority. This

successful revolt drove out the Spanish and allowed the Pueblo peoples to regain semblances of autonomy for nearly a decade. The Spanish began their official re-conquest of the area in 1692, using brutal force in their attempts to subdue Native peoples in the region.

34. Ibid., 134–135. Lummis first became active in the debate over compulsory ed-ucation for Native students, specifically Pueblo people, in off-reservation boarding schools. He argued that the federal government should locate schools *within* Native communities. He specifically voiced concern about the destruction of Native cul-tures and familial ties following the forced removal of students to the off-reservation schools. Lummis aimed much of his condemnation at Richard Pratt, the founder of Carlisle Indian School, the first off-reservation boarding school for Native children, in Carlisle, Pennsylvania. Like much of his writing, Lummis's gut response to the problems he observed in the boarding school system included more criticism than any active policy.

35. Thompson, *American Character*, 213–243.

36. Lummis neglected to recognize that, like American Indian boarding schools, the Spanish missions often broke apart Native families and removed children from their parents. Lummis and other boosters ignored Native perspectives of life in Spanish California. When analyzed critically, Lummis's criticism of the contemporary American treatment of Native peoples and simultaneous praise of the Spanish past is intrinsically contradictory.

37. William Cronon, "The Trouble with Wilderness; or, Getting Back to the Wrong Nature," in *Uncommon Ground: Rethinking the Human Place in Nature*, ed. William Cronon (New York: Norton, 1996): 69–90, 77.

38. Culver, *Frontier of Leisure*, 33–35.

39. D. Fellman, "A Unique Institution," *Land of Sunshine* 2 (January 1895): 31–33. The Los Angeles Chamber of Commerce did not act alone. San Bernardino, River-side, Orange, San Diego, and Ventura Counties all contributed to the exhibitions and promotional efforts undertaken by the Los Angeles Chamber of Commerce in efforts to lure more residents to Southern California.

40. Charles F. Lummis, "Land of Sunshine," *Land of Sunshine* 2 (January1895): 34.

41. Edwin R. Bingham, *Charles F. Lummis: Editor of the Southwest* (San Marino, CA: Huntington Library Publications, 1955), 134–186.

42. C. D. Willard, "The New Editor," *Land of Sunshine* 2 (December 1894): 12.

43. Charles F. Lummis, "The Spanish-American Face," *Land of Sunshine* 2 (January 1895): 21–22.

44. Ibid., 21.

45. Ibid.

46. Ibid.

47. Ibid., 22.

48. Deverell, *Whitewashed Adobe*, 11–48.

49. Culver, *Frontier of Leisure*, 36–37.

50. George Wharton James, *In and Out of the Old Missions of California* (Boston:

Little, Brown, 1906), 295.

51. Ibid., 294–296; Smith, *Reimagining Indians*, 158–159.

52. Charles Lummis, "Foundation of the Los Angeles Council," *Out West* 20 (June 1904): 549–557.

53. Ibid., 557.

54. Bingham, *Charles F. Lummis*, 116–118.

55. Charles Lummis, "Sequoya League, Second Bulletin, 'The Relief of Campo (1905),'" 9-12, Charles F. Lummis Manuscript Collection, Sequoya League Series, Campo Indian Relief Subseries, Braun Research Library, Autry National Center, Los Angeles.

56. Ibid., 3–7; Steven M. Karr, "The Warner's Ranch Indian Removal: Cultural Adaptation, Accommodation, and Continuity," special issue, *California History* 86 (2009): 24–43,82–84.

57. Charles Lummis, "Sequoya League, Third Bulletin, 'Getting Results,'" 2, Charles F. Lummis Manuscript Collection, Sequoya League Series, Campo Indian Relief Subseries, Braun Research Library, Autry National Center, Los Angeles. For more on the Sequoya League and Lummis's involvement in the Warner's Ranch eviction, see Karr, "Warner's Ranch Indian Removal," 24–43; Thompson, *American Character*, 220–243; Bingham, *Charles F. Lummis*, 118–133.

58. Today, mission bell markers along Highway 101 serve as landmarks for El Camino Real. Bingham, *Charles F. Lummis*, 103–111.

59. Thompson, *American Character*, 184–186.

60. Erik Berg, "'The Roads Are for the Timid': The Western Adventures and Romance of Mai Richie Reed," *Journal of Arizona History* 52 (spring 2011): 7.

61. Mai Richie Reed, *Mai Richie Reed Diaries, 1907–1908*, unpublished diaries, Huntington Library, San Marino, CA.

62. John S. McGroarty, *California: Its History and Romance* (Los Angeles: Grafton Publishing Company, 1911), 8.

63. Riverside Daily Press, "Vision of Frank A. Miller Became Reality in World's Famed Mission Inn; Long Cherished Dream Came True," *Riverside Daily Press*, June 15, 1935. For more on Miller and the Sherman Institute, see Nathan Gonzales, "Riverside, Tourism, and the Indian: Frank A. Miller and the Creation of Sherman Institute," *Southern California Quarterly* 84 (2002): 194–221. Along with other notable boosters of his time, including Lummis, Miller, an active supporter of the Southern California tourist industry, advocated the restoration of California mission sites. Miller also actively pushed for the preservation of the romanticized Spanish past in California through his renowned Mission Inn. Inspired by his relationship with local Native peoples and his fascination with old mission bells, Miller constructed the Mission Inn as a place that represented the "romance and ideals and charm of the mission period."

64. Starr, *Inventing the Dream*, 87.

65. President Herbert Hoover, "56 Message on the 3,000th Performance of the Mission Play. February 18, 1930," American Reference Library—Primary Source

Documents (January 2001), MasterFILE Premier, EBSCOhost.

66. Deverell, *Whitewashed Adobe*, 215–217.

67. Ibid.

68. Ibid.

69. Ibid., 209.

70. Gracia L. Fernández, "Club Work in the Elementary Year in High School," *Hispania* 1 (December 1918): 239.

71. Ibid., 235–239.

72. Deverell, *Whitewashed Adobe*, 209–211. Miller played a significant role in the creation of *The Mission Play.* He advocated for a drama, similar to the Passion Play, to document California's early romantic history. A friend recommended McGroarty to Miller, who gave McGroarty a desk at the Mission Inn to write the drama.

73. Starr, *Inventing the Dream*, 88.

74. Kropp, *California Vieja*, 167–168.

75. John S. McGroarty, *Mission Memories* (Los Angeles: Neuner Corporation, 1929), 20.

76. Deverell, *Whitewashed Adobe*, 245.

77. Ibid., 244–245.

78. Ibid., 217.

79. Ibid., 219–222.

80. "Program of the Mission Play," as quoted in Chelsea K. Vaughn, "The Joining of Historical Pageantry and the Spanish Fantasy Past: The Meeting of Señora Josefa Yorba and Lucretia del Valle," *Journal of San Diego History* 57 (2011): 213–235 Edna E. Kimbro and Julia G. Costello, *The California Missions: History, Art, and Preservation* (Los Angeles: Getty Conservation Institute, 2009), 60.

81. McGroarty, *Mission Memories*, 8.

82. Ibid., 7–8.

83. Ibid., 11.

84. Deverell, *Whitewashed Adobe*, 1–15.

85. McGroarty, *Mission Memories*, 11–12.

86. Ibid., 12.

87. Kropp, *California Vieja*, 25–30.

88. McGroarty, *Mission Memories*, 14.

89. Ibid., 15.

90. Sucheng Chan, "A People of Exceptional Character: Ethnic Diversity, Nativism, and Racism in the California Gold Rush," special issue, *California History* 79 (2000): 44–85.

91. Eric Avila, *Popular Culture in the Age of White Flight: Fear and Fantasy in Suburban Los Angeles* (Berkeley: University of California Press, 2004), 23. Deverell focused on the "whitewashing" of California's Mexican past, but the same concept could be applied to the silencing of Native Californians in the late nineteenth and early twentieth centuries. Deverell, *Whitewashed Adobe*, 1–10, 207–249.

92. Rawls, *Indians of California*, 205–217; Deverell, *Whitewashed Adobe*, 12–14.

93. Jackson and Castillo, *Indians, Franciscans, and Spanish Colonization*, 31–72.
94. Lummis did not see eye to eye with McGroarty's depiction of Native people and misrepresentation of some events. For example, in a letter to McGroarty, Lummis chastised the playwright for including "frightful anachronisms," specifically pointing out that "Father Serra didn't teach the California Indians to weave dam [*sic*] bad Navajo blankets!" Deverell, *Whitewashed Adobe*, 229.
95. McGroarty, *California*, 42.
96. Ibid., 42–43.
97. Ibid., 45.

# 3

# Land, Preservation, and Representations of Native Californians in Popular Culture

> It is in the Mission ruins that we must delve to find the beginning of
> Southern California's greatness.
> —John Steven McGroarty, *History of Southern California* (1914)

Representations of Native peoples at contemporary California mission sites reflects both the romanticized narrative constructed by boosters in the early twentieth century and older traditions in museum representations that frequently failed to present indigenous people as active participants in their own history. While a shift to provide active Native voices is present in many museum exhibitions today, this has not been adopted at most contemporary mission sites. There are many factors dating back to the late nineteenth century that contribute to the continued marginalization of Native voices in California's popular mission history, including tendencies for museums to collect and "display" uninterrupted indigenous objects as curiosities or relics of the past, the Spanish-centered legacy popularized by early mission promoters and preservationists, and discrimination against Native Californians in Euro-American society tied with Native efforts to protect and preserve their sites from predatory collectors. Because of these many factors, the outdated narratives at mission museums continues to reflect histories constructed in the early twentieth century rather than Native centered exhibitions that would work to dispel the mission myth.

The social memory constructed both physically and figuratively around the Spanish California missions constituted "the only sizable and concrete examples of California's claim to antiquity" for many Euro-Americans in the late nineteenth and early twentieth centuries.[1] However, these Spanish sites did not symbolize California's earliest history for Native peoples whose ancestors occupied vast areas of present day California for thousands of years before European contact. In fact, many Native peoples had and continue to have deep connections to their tribal histories and homelands through oral traditions, songs, and ceremonies. Yet many Euro-Americans in California in the late nineteenth century viewed Native Californians in a specific context, as "vanishing" peoples whose cultures and lifeways would inevitably give way in the face of advancing "civilization."[2] Euro-Americans at the time did not recognize Native historic or cultural sites as important, if they recognized their existence at all. In fact, many collectors and tourists who did know about Native sites desecrated these places by removing and collecting objects—both sacred and ordinary—and even gathered human remains as souvenirs. To actively protect important aspects of their cultures, histories, and sacred sites, many Native communities kept this information secret from opportunistic outsiders. While this helped protect Native sites, it also worked with the "vanishing Indian" stereotype to hide their histories from being included in wider narratives, in museums and at popular mission sites. Together with Euro-American discrimination against Native Californians and the marginalization of Native voices by boosters who worked to preserve and rebuild Spanish sites, the mission ruins and romanticized histories of Spanish colonization became the dominant narrative of the region's early history.

## Marginalizing Native Experiences

Early Euro-American settlers in California viewed Native Californians, and missionized Native peoples particularly, as victims of Mexican neglect and abuse following mission secularization. They believed that "lazy" Californios exploited indigenous people as an inexpensive labor force, while Euro-Americans simultaneously sought to gain control of Native laborers for themselves. After tens of thousands of Americans flooded into the state during the gold rush of the late 1840s to 1850s, Euro-Americans and Native peoples frequently clashed. Americans who sought to "strike it rich" in California began to see the indigenous peoples who occupied some of the most mineral-rich land and productive pastures as barriers to settlement and "obstacles to be *eliminated*."[3] In the state's early years California legislators passed predatory laws that allowed for the near enslavement of Native people, especially children, and vicious militiamen embarked on genocidal campaigns in northern California to exterminate entire Native communities. Accordingly, the dominant image of Native Californians in popular culture during the late nineteenth and early twentieth centuries reflected the societal roles Americans wanted indigenous peoples to play. Believing that Native peoples were already a vanishing race, Euro-Americans justified removing them to secluded reservations for "protection." Euro-Americans applauded themselves for "defending" Native people but ignored the basic wants and needs of those they claimed to have saved.[4] Instead, many Euro-American philanthropists and reformers worked to Americanize Native peoples while collecting their material objects as symbols of fading indigenous cultures. Many Native peoples maintained control of their histories by providing misinformation to collectors and anthropologists to protect themselves and their important sites from these cultural predators.[5]

In the early twentieth century, Native Californians viewed themselves and their environment in stark contrast to the constructed history promoted by boosters. For example, Euro-Americans such as Charles Fletcher Lummis sought to save local sites by bringing in tourists and, more important, the money that accompanied these visitors. By contrast, many Native communities in Southern California sought to preserve powerful or sacred sites by limiting access and restricting knowledge of the areas, even among members of their own communities. Many Native people also viewed the mission ruins, then and today, as physical reminders of Spanish-imposed efforts to alter and destroy their communities. Thus many Native peoples shunned the missions and concealed significant tribal sites to both protect and heal their communities.

Although many Euro-Americans at the turn of the twentieth century did not view Native history as worthwhile and believed that indigenous peoples would soon vanish into extinction, Native people persevered and many of their cultures continue into the present. With roots in popular stories from the early twentieth century such as *Ramona*, the *Mission Play*, and writings in promotional magazines, the current inaccurate representations of Native Californian cultures and mission history stem from the long legacy of popular dramatizations of California's past. They also reflect common national trends in museum exhibitions since the nineteenth century that failed to accurately represent Native peoples. Within the shadow cast by the romanticized portrayals of the past are the more accurate origins of the region, which have been passed on in the narratives told by Native Californians. Contemporary efforts by Native communities to prove that "we are still here," in conjunction with vigorous scholarship that focuses on Native experiences in historical encounters with European colonizers, have contributed to revisions of some of the fictionalized narratives that proliferated during the twentieth century.[6] More and more, Native people in contemporary society are exercising their united voices to force changes in popular representations of their communities.

## Museums and Missions

Contemporary museums occupy an important niche in society as spaces reserved for exhibition, education, commemoration, recreation, and discussion. Although the specific mission statement for every museum differs, the current notion that museums are spaces used to educate and engage the public is a basic principle at most of these sites. Many museums accept this task and attempt to provide well-rounded exhibitions to fulfill visitor expectations. Occasionally, museums with inherent agendas misrepresent history to the communities they serve by either omitting historical information or shaping their presentations to fit their social, cultural, religious, or political views. Michael Kelleher has argued that people today visit historic sites more than ever before. But a lack of serious conversation about sites can result in the creation of "synthetic" spaces that visitors mistakenly assume are authentic and accurate representations of the past.[7] Privately owned but publically patroned institutions such as the contemporary California mission sites overwhelmingly present biased narratives and constructed histories that masks the complex impact of Spanish colonization on Native peoples. Instead, many of these sites focus on the religious culture of the missions through sanitized discussions of Spanish priests and mission landscapes.[8]

The California mission museums are not alone in their misrepresentation of indigenous people. A long line of local, state, and national public history sites distorted the historical experiences of Native peoples for generations. When addressing issues of representation at modern California mission museum sites and absence Native voices, it is important to understand the history of Native representation in popular culture at Euro-American museums. Although other institutions have worked greatly to bring Native voices to the center of their exhibitions, many contemporary mission sites continue to provide an overwhelmingly one-sided historical perspective of Spanish colonization that was first popularized in the late nineteenth century.[9]

Throughout the twentieth century, museums and interpretation centers across the country commonly ignored or misrepresented indigenous peoples. The late nineteenth to early twentieth century marked a time when the federal government legislated for removal of Native peoples from tribal homelands and established the reservation system to move them off desirable land and away from growing Euro-American populations. These federal policies helped shape the minds of many throughout the United States by placing Native people outside of the national narrative—both figuratively and literally. Many Euro-Americans disregarded the basic human rights of Native people and violated their trust to acquire desirable land, property, and collected valuable objects that symbolized their "vanishing" cultures.

At the same time, philanthropic reformers worked to eradicate indigenous cultures and "civilize" Native people to prevent what many perceived to be their impending extinction.[10]

Accordingly, museums and public interpretive sites in the twentieth century represented Native cultures as static—rooted solidly in the past. Moira G. Simpson in *Making Representations: Museums in the Post-Colonial Era* argued that presumptions that Native cultures teetered on the verge of extinction influenced these inaccurate representations. Many times, museums contributed to this false belief by depicting Native peoples and their cultures as either nearly extinct or completely unchanged over the last century. Simpson noted that the nature of curation—to display an object in its "pure form with an emphasis upon traditional values and styles, and authentic artefacts [*sic*] and practices"—inherently excluded a discussion of cultural continuity and change among Native communities. The European and American influences that infiltrated Native communities and the cultural continuance of indigenous peoples, did not translate into exhibitions at many museums.[11]

Emphasizing "traditional" Native cultures, scholars in the emerging field of anthropology in the early twentieth century contributed to the erroneous belief that Native people had vanished. For example, renowned cultural anthropologist Alfred Kroeber believed that only indigenous cultures untouched by Euro-Americans could be "authentic." Some anthropologists did not recognize the centuries of organic cultural change that occurred in seemingly untouched Native communities since Europeans first built settlements on the American continent.[12] Like many of the articles in booster publications, exhibitions and public presentations focused on romanticized or nostalgic depictions of Native people that underscored their ability to "live in harmony with nature." Thus museums displayed "exotic" ethnographic material in purely *historical* contexts without any further inclusion of contemporary indigenous objects that demonstrated cultural endurance, adaptation, and survival.[13]

Collectors and non-Native curators greatly controlled public understanding of indigenous people during the turn of the twentieth century. Collectors in the late nineteenth century had a variety of motives for acquiring Native objects, few of which considered the interests or perspectives of indigenous peoples. For example, the federal government mandated the collection of indigenous human remains for scientific study. Skull collectors desecrated Native gravesites throughout the United States and took their remains from recent battlefields. At the same time, museums accumulated and exhibited the overwhelming surplus of these skeletons that government officials acquired. They converted these collections into curiosities and tourist attractions.[14]

Collections amassed by wealthy Euro-Americans also eventually found their way to prominent museums. Many early collectors, including Lummis, focused on representing idealized and romanticized portrayals of Native peoples.[15] Museums perpetuated the myth of the vanishing Indian to their patrons and audiences, who then applied this knowledge to the world around them. Indigenous anthropologist Sonya Atalay articulated the issues associated with absent Native voices in museum exhibitions, noting that "prior to European colonization, communities were able to act as stewards over their own cultural resources and history—examining, remembering, teaching, learning, and protecting their own heritage," yet when European colonization began in the Americas these newcomers "began to exercise their curiosity over the materials beneath their feet in the 'New World.' While disease, quests for land, warfare, and forced religion were decimating Native people and disrupting their daily lives and practices, antiquarians and anthropologists were gathering the remains of the dead and dying. . . for study and placement in museums around the world."[16]

Indeed, collecting the remains of Native peoples became a profitable venture because of the high demand from researchers and museums. For example, physical anthropologists at the Smithsonian, American Museum of Natural History, and Chicago Field Museum of Natural History studied the remains of indigenous peoples, but also exhibited their skeletons and sacred objects on public view.[17] These displays continued for generations with little changing in the ways museums represented Native peoples. Many academics similarly represented Native peoples and their cultures as relics of the past.[18]

Historically, anthropologists came into contact with Native peoples under colonialist controls. Within this skewed perspective, many of these scholars deemed indigenous cultures and people as "primitive." This perspective permeated representations of indigenous cultures in popular venues and museum exhibitions. Similar to many Euro-American collectors in the early twentieth century, anthropologists felt the need to teach society as a whole about Native communities and *preserve* aspects of indigenous cultures.[19] These scholars viewed contemporary Native people who had acculturated to any degree to be detached from their cultural heritage. Conversely, Euro-Americans also perceived those who refused to assimilate as "primitive" relics of the past. By ignoring the transformation of Native peoples in a modernizing world, museum staff and anthropologists focused on depictions of indigenous people from the eighteenth and nineteenth centuries that illustrated the decline of Native cultures and populations. This narrative easily translated into constructed histories of the California missions, wherein Native peoples left behind their undeveloped ways of life to accept the gift of civilization brought by Spanish missionaries.

James J. Rawls observed in the early 1990s that "the popular image of the mission remains generally—if unthinkably—romantic."[20] Still today, local dioceses of the Catholic Church control nineteen of the twenty-one missions today. These site stewards and curators control museum collections and exhibits that continue to focus on venerating the missionaries rather than interpreting the lives and influences of Native people at the missions to any detailed extent. Despite the polarized academic debate over the California mission system, mission exhibitions provide little information about the controversial roles of the Spanish padres and soldiers and the mistreatment of Native people—topics that would not flatter the mission institutions. They do not engage in complicated discussions about forced assimilation, of the attempted destruction of indigenous cultures and religions, stringent labor regimens, disease, and punishments, and provide ambiguous information about resistance efforts against the Spanish. These romanticized presentations continue the cycle of misinformation and poor representation of Native peoples at important interpretive sites in California.

Despite the changing culture in other modern museums such as the National Museum of the American Indian, which seek to spread understanding of indigenous peoples, many mission sites have not adapted to this shift. They exist in limbo as generally private religious institutions that overwhelmingly serve public audiences, especially the thousands of fourth-grade school children who visit the missions each year as they learn about California history. Restored and reconstructed mission sites today owe much of their existence to the work of local promoters and preservationists during the early twentieth century who helped construct the mission myth. These promoters laid the groundwork for the heavily biased exhibitions commonly seen at mission museums today.

**Renovation of Mission Sites**

After mission secularization in the 1830s and the U.S. annexation of California in 1848, many defunct mission sites quickly fell into decay. Beginning in the late 1880s, following forty years of neglect, Southern California boosters such as Lummis and civic groups influenced by *Ramona* enthusiasts advocated a romantic revival of the historic sites. Promoters of regional history used *Ramona* mythology and a benign depiction of Spanish colonizers to draw tourists and settlers into California. Native people were almost never found in these representations. Moreover, popular understandings of Native peoples and their interactions with the land became increasingly obscure as Euro-Americans continued to remove indigenous peoples from their lands.[21] As symbols of the dramatic Spanish past, mission preservation and restoration efforts claimed California for Euro-Americans and continued to relegate indigenous history to the periphery. As direct benefactors of this constructed history, many contemporary mission museums continue to reflect this idealized past.

Euro-American settlers flocked to many of the same regions in which the Spanish constructed many of their mission sites, in desirable areas with fertile lands and adequate water supplies. Over the course of the twentieth century, bustling towns and cities became a common feature in California, spreading along the coast, from San Diego to the San Francisco Bay area. In many instances, these growing towns overwhelmed the once-dominant presence of the missions, making the early Spanish settlements one aspect of the historical beginnings of popular tourist locations such as San Diego's beaches, Los Angeles, San Francisco, and Santa Barbara. The commerce and crowd of local city businesses encircled the old Spanish missions. By the mid-twentieth century, most mission landscapes no longer resembled their rural beginnings. Moreover, efforts to preserve the Spanish sites focused heavily on attracting tourist dollars.[22]

In this context, the California missions were veiled indicators of Native dispossession. Boosters and mission interpreters in the twentieth century hailed them as the first sites of "civilization" on the "wild" California land-scape. For example, the author of a short book about Mission San Diego created for schoolchildren noted that "on the west coast of our continent . . . there could be found only untamed land inhabited by Native Americans, or Indians. Although European explorers had sailed up and down the coast in their ships, no one but American Indians had explored the length of this land on foot."[23] According to this premise, Native people were only explorers of the land, presumably because they did not irrigate, farm, and claim their territory with permanent structures in a way that many Europeans thought acceptable. However, with the Serra-Portolá expedition of 1769 "to this wild land came a group of adventurous men from New Spain" who tamed the wilderness.[24] It is this romantic ideal of the first vestiges of civilization in a wild land that early promoters sought to preserve at Spanish mission sites. Focusing on the hardships the Spanish missionaries, soldiers, and settlers endured in the untamed wilderness, the narratives highlighted the noblest intentions of the early Spanish explorers. This focus transformed the Cal-ifornia landscape from what many in the late nineteenth century saw as a backward Mexican territory to a western Plymouth Rock—a place where the people of the region emerged out of darkness and were guided into the light of European civilization by Spanish priests.

Efforts to save vestiges of this dramatic beginning emerged in preservation campaigns for the crumbling California mission ruins in the 1890s. A secular group led by Los Angeles City librarian Tessa L. Kelso spearheaded the campaign to preserve the sites under the Association for the Preservation of the Missions. Kelso promoted her cause through displays of the crumbling Spanish ruins at the library, organized trips to the missions, and popular magazine articles.[25] Other local associations similarly advocated mission preservation, including the Pasadena Loan Association, which sought the "preservation of the Spanish past in the American Present . . . [and] reviving, for practical travel, the old Spanish King's Highway."[26] The Native Sons of the Golden West and the Historic Landmarks Committee also established goals to identify and preserve historic sites such as the California missions. The movement to preserve the missions did not draw mass attention until Lummis took up the cause "to conserve the missions and other historic landmarks of Southern California" with the founding of the Landmarks Club in 1895.[27] Kelso became a board member of the club and provided the $100 coffers from her defunct association to the new group. However, Lummis was the one who stepped forward as the central spokesperson for California mission preservation. He persistently raised funds and promoted the ambitious goals of the Landmarks Club.[28]

Lummis used the *Land of Sunshine* magazine, which became *Out West* in 1901, to increase the number of paying club members; the annual subscription fee was $1. He also conducted a stringent letter-writing campaign to promote mission conservation to donors, including renowned California conservationist John Muir and wealthy philanthropist Phoebe Apperson Hearst.[29] Preservationists did not petition Native people to support their projects. Lummis simply appealed to his Euro-American readership to become due-paying members, arguing that "no man or woman who cares a dollar's worth to keep the United States from being the only civilized country in the world which lets its only ruins disappear, is barred from membership."[30] He succeeded in raising enough funds to start work at the missions, choosing Mission San Juan Capistrano as the first site to receive the club's attention as "one of the choicest architectural bits among all the Missions."[31] Specifically, Lummis referred to the kitchen at the mission.

Lummis believed that "the only ruins worthy of name [in the United States] are all in the Southwest. The missions of Southern California, though least ancient of these monuments of the past, are architecturally the finest and the only practically accessible to the average traveler." He argued that, "after two generations of average neglect," the missions were in such dire need of preservation that they would cease to exist if local residents did not undertake preservation efforts immediately.[32] Today, the State of California's Office of Historic Preservation salutes the Landmarks Club as the first organization in California to officially recognize historic sites. Beginning with Mission San Juan Capistrano, the Landmarks Club worked to replace the roofs and stabilize the adobe structures of deteriorating missions at a cost of between $1,500 and $2,000 at each site. Although Lummis and the Landmarks Club encouraged tourists to visit mission ruins, he also condemned the vandalism of "boys or tourists of little shame," who took roof tiles and bricks from the sites.[33]

Indeed, like at many known Native sites, tourists and collectors removed relics from the mission ruins. But unlike at Native burial sites, gravediggers rarely scavenged and wrought havoc on mission cemeteries.[34] Still, not all mission cemeteries have been left untouched because several mission preservation and restoration projects have disturbed these sacred grounds. For example, Angelo Cassanova, who became parish priest at Mission San Carlos Borroméo de Carmelo in 1862, undertook restoration efforts at the Monterey mission. Part of the restoration included uncovering the graves of prominent missionaries, including Father President Junípero Serra, his successor, Fermin Francisco de Lasuén, as well as Juan Crespí. Because the mission church had fallen into disuse for roughly twenty years and the roof had collapsed, Cassanova felt compelled to assess the burial sites and evaluate the remains of the priests. Hundreds of tourists from nearby towns flocked to the mission on July 3, 1882, to see the tombs of the padres. Cassanova and his crew documented the condition of the graves and reburied the tombs with more secure stone slabs. According to Franciscan scholar Zephyrin Engelhardt, Mission San Carlos owed its initial restoration to Cassanova's "untiring zeal and the sympathy of many benefactors."[35]

Franciscan priests, along with boosters of Spanish mission history and local Catholic leadership, embarked on preservation efforts at several other California missions, including Missions San Luis Rey and Santa Barbara. Secular groups such as the Historic Landmarks League in conjunction with wealthy newspaperman William Randolph Hearst also worked to protect California missions in the early twentieth century. The league purchased Mission San Francisco de Solano in Sonoma, and eventually turned the property over to the state of California, forming what is now Sonoma State Park. Native people were not given a voice in the preservation projects of the California missions, despite the heavy toll paid by their ancestors who built and populated these sites.

Tourism to the missions grew dramatically in the early twentieth century with the popularization of mission conservation, preservation, and restoration efforts together with the rise of the automobile culture in Southern California. The myth of the California missions became ever more engrained in early history of the region as the missions became popular destinations for vacationing tourists to the Golden State.[36] Soon mission bell markers placed by the El Camino Real Association lined Highway 101 marking where the padres reportedly traveled on the path that once connected the missions. The bells as well as the increasingly preserved California mission ruins continued to claim the landscape with Hispanic symbols of California's proclaimed antiquity.[37]

Mission preservation efforts did not end in the early decades of the twentieth century. Instead, restoration and especially reconstruction continued in large part in the 1930s under President Franklin D. Roosevelt's New Deal initiatives. Historic preservation legislation at the state and national levels also helped advocates register and preserve Spanish heritage sites in California. Unmarried young men assigned to the Civilian Conservation Corps labored to reconstruct sites such as Mission La Purísima. They researched the historic layout of the structures and worked to rebuild the mission accurately—for educational purposes. At the same time, the debates intensified over the different treatments of the missions: conservation of mission ruins by simply mitigating further decay, preservation, or restoration/reconstruction of buildings at the sites. Although reconstruction at Mission La Purísima closely reflected evidence from the historical record, restoration and reconstructions at other missions, including San Carlos and San Juan Capistrano, was more heavily aimed at preserving the architectural style of the missions thereby falling in line with the established romanticized narratives of the idyllic Spanish past in California. However, architects excluded some components of the original structures that interfered with the look sought by designers. By the 1960s, all of the twenty-one mission sites had experienced some restoration and were no longer in complete ruin.[38]

### Outside Museum and Mission Walls: Land and "Wilderness"

Romantic interpretations of mission history inherently ignored the struggle of Native people to navigate the new Spanish institutions and indigenous perceptions of the changes under way. These forces worked to recolonize California for Euro-Americans—who replaced Mexican, Spanish, and Native heritages in the region with narratives that reflected Euro-American cultural ethos. This helped them appropriate mission sites to fit a Euro-American colonial narrative as they re-settled California. Although Euro-Americans in Southern California worked to preserve California mission ruins as symbols of a European antiquity, they ignored and attempted to erase indigenous ties to the land. In part, Euro-Americans administered this erasure more easily because Native Californians did not have brick-and-mortar ruins to prove their long-held relationship with the land. The differences between Native and Euro-American concepts of land use is important in understanding the divergent views of place, preservation, and a shared social history between the two groups in California and views in the popular culture.

Euro-Americans moving West viewed the land as "wild," "untamed," and unoccupied because they failed to recognize the ways Native peoples inter-acted with the land. Many significant sites for indigenous people consisted of natural earth formations tied to important cultural stories. Oral traditions told through generations informed Native people about the power of loca-tions—allowing only those with a certain level of spiritual power or tribal knowledge to visit some sites without facing risk of harm. In fact, Native people often restrict access and knowledge of these natural places to preserve and honor them.[39] Many Euro-Americans in the late nineteenth and early twentieth centuries mistakenly believed that Native Californians did not understand land management and had undeveloped cultures because they did not see visible changes to the "wild" land. Indeed, because they failed to understand Native cultures Euro-Americans neglected to recognize the importance and meaning found in Native landscapes.

"Where does nature end and culture begin?" This question, posed by historian Bonnie Stepenoff, exposes the conflict that exists when people perceive the natural landscape as inherently disconnected from built structures appropriate for preservation, such as the California missions.[40] Beginning with some of the first European explorations in the Americas, foreigners documented Native people and components of their cultures, just as they mapped the landscape and catalogued the flora and fauna of "unexplored" areas.[41] Some explorers concluded that Native Californians were so primitive and close to nature that they were nearly animals. Rawls detailed some of these first encounters documented by Europeans. For example, Capt. George Vancouver observed that the Indians at Mission San Fernando were "in the most abject state of uncivilization. . . . [T]hey are certainly a race of the most miserable beings, possessing the faculty of human reason, I ever saw."[42] As each wave of new-comers arrived in California, they did not envision Native peoples, or their cultures, as enduring into the future. As a result, scholars and anthropologists in the early twentieth century increasingly documented "vanishing" Native cultures, focusing especially on languages and, as described earlier in this chapter, their remains and the material objects indigenous people produced.

Euro-American writers portrayed Native peoples in popular culture using two distinct stereotypes. The "Noble Indian" or "Noble Savage" conveyed images of peaceful, egalitarian, nature-loving, innocent, and simple peoples.[43] Conversely, Americans vilified other groups of indigenous peoples as "Ignoble Savages"—wild, bloodthirsty, and violent marauders that jumped at any opportunity to slaughter whites and each other. Throughout the nineteenth century, western travelers wrote sensationalized narratives of Native people brutally attacking pioneer parties—killing any men, women, and children who crossed their paths. Travelers sent these tales back East to friends and family members who proliferated these stories without ever setting foot west of the Mississippi River.[44]

It was in the best interests of settlers and Euro-American businessmen to not recognize Native claims or ties to the land. Native peoples resisted Euro-American domination, but by the mid to late nineteenth century newcomers were far outnumbering and outgunning Native Californians.[45] To preserve their lives and important sites in the face of discrimination, many Native communities turned inward to protect themselves. They did not draw attention to their significant sites and did not encourage visitors to learn about their history. Land hungry newcomers welcomed the notion that lands in California and other areas of the West were "unoccupied" as they moved into the regions. Bernard W. Sheehan has argued that the "grand myth" of the unoccupied American West did not truly exist. What Euro-Americans perceived as wilderness in many places was actually a "*widowed* land" left destitute when thousands of indigenous people lost their lives in the wake of "Columbian discovery."[46] They reconstructed the historical landscape at the Spanish California missions as if no earlier history in the region ever existed.

Euro-Americans viewed "California, the beautiful and abundant land," as a place that "required an enterprising population to develop it."[47] Possessing little knowledge of Native land use traditions, Euro-Americans saw themselves as the tamers of this wilderness because people under the Spanish and Mexican flags supposedly failed to complete the task.[48] Yet for thousands of years Native Californians created meaning in natural spaces. They intrinsically altered the landscape by interacting with their environment, but they frequently did not physically change the appearance of the world around them to create this meaning. Thus only people privy to knowledge of specific places discern the cultural importance of the landscape.[49]

Euro-Americans throughout the twentieth century, and many today, fail to recognize the important ties Native people have with their ancestral homelands. This ignorance can be traced to the late nineteenth and into the twentieth century when Americans sought to preserve parts of the "pristine" wilderness and protect it from human development. In the face of industrial urbanization, Euro-Americans sought to preserve the past not only through mission buildings but also through the all-encompassing wilderness that symbolized the fading frontier mythology.[50] According to historian Mark

David Spence, Native people existed as a part of the "wild" in the minds of many Euro-Americans in the late nineteenth century. But preservationists increasingly viewed Native peoples' interactions with and mediation of the land as nuisances to maintaining their image of pristine wilderness. Spence pointed out that Euro-Americans frequently forced Native peoples out of particular areas to preserve the landscape. The U.S. government also removed Native peoples from desirable land in the late nineteenth and early twentieth centuries. According to William Cronon, this carefully constructed ideal of wilderness "had always been especially cruel when seen from the perspective of Indians who had once called that land home. Now they were forced to move elsewhere, with the result that tourists could safely enjoy the illusion that they were seeing their nation in its pristine, original state...."[51] All of this created the false impression that these environments existed uninhabited, waiting to be discovered and settled by Euro-Americans. Most poignantly, Spence noted that land preservation in the U.S. has "contributed to a sort of widespread cultural myopia that allows late-twentieth-century Americans to ignore the fact that national parks enshrine recently dispossessed land-scapes." In preserved areas where "humans are visitors who do not remain," the federal government forced Native people out of their homelands and created a false history of a wild and unoccupied landscape that attracted tourists to the region.[52] This perpetuated the vanishing Indian stereotype and helped marginalize the voices of Native peoples during the construction of the mission myth in popular culture.

In many places, Euro-Americans made the land a sacred "wilderness" by removing Native peoples, whose core mythologies and creation stories solidly grounded their history in the local landscape. As Cronon articulated, "The removal of Indians to create an 'uninhabited wilderness'—uninhabited as never before in the human history of the place—reminds us just how invented, just how constructed, the American wilderness really is."[53] To Euro-Americans, Native peoples did not exist in the constructed cultural narrative of California. In fact, to create their image of the wilderness, Euro-Americans *removed* Native peoples from the land and disregarded their cultural ties to the sites—as done similarly through the preservation of California missions.

This removal of Native people from the land and from popular histories of early California has created several problems for Native communities who now must work to preserve and mitigate damage to culturally significant sites.[54] While Native people in the nineteenth and early twentieth centuries worked to protect sites from gravediggers and collectors, many sites also face destruction by vandalism. According to the records of photographer Charley (Clayton) Howe, working for the Archaeological Survey Association of Southern California, people vandalized many Southern California sites, including rock art in the Mojave Desert, in the mid-twentieth century. Vandals spray-painted some sites, while other visitors attempted to remove the art using chisels. People riddled other sites with bullet holes, and paint stains are evident where trespassers tried to take rubbings of the rock art.[55] As mentioned earlier, vandals also frequented California mission sites before their restoration to the chagrin of local boosters and preservationists. However, in recent years Native burial sites at many missions have been threatened by the work of mission officials themselves—causing great outcry in Native communities to protect these sacred grounds.

## Protecting Sacred Sites on Mission Grounds

Many people in the late twentieth century, even those who are stewards of historic locations, failed to protect Native interests at the same sites. Working to maximize the usable space at Mission San Diego and Mission San Juan Capistrano, stewards at the sites built over Native graves.[56] Plans to construct a multipurpose hall and parking lot at Mission San Diego originally took precedence over a Native graveyard. And Mission San Juan Capistrano hastily constructed an unpermitted "Rectory Garden" on top of a known mission cemetery.[57] In both cases, the construction caused outrage in the local community.

Officials at Mission San Diego failed to inform Native people of construction and misrepresented or blatantly hid information about the history of the proposed sites to continue construction.[58] Kumeyaay elders and prominent scholars of San Diego Indian history such as Florence Shipek understood that missionaries founded Mission San Diego on the Native village site of Nipaguay. They also knew that the missionaries buried many Native peoples nearby. For nearly two decades, officials at Mission San Diego distorted the results of archeological research at the site in order to continue using the land. Shipek contended that mission officials such as Monsignor I. Brent Egan ignored archeological and historical evidence, including maps that proved that a Native cemetery existed under the proposed construction site.[59] Before construction, Egan claimed that "contrary to some opinions, there is not an Indian cemetery underneath the site of the proposed building."[60]

Under pressure from several local and state agencies, mission officials decided to build the hall on a raised structure to minimize disruption of the site. Mission officials hired Archeologist Richard Carrico to conduct a dig where the twenty caisson concrete pillars that support the structure would be anchored into the ground. Carrico and his crew discovered several human remains soon after excavations began—in fact, they found remains in all but one of the caisson holes. Altogether, the archeological team found the remains of nearly seventy persons whose burials were consistent with Christian funerals conducted at the missions.[61] The crew carefully removed the remains and temporarily stored them at the San Diego Museum of Man. Local leaders condemned mission officials' decision to continue construction at a proven cemetery site. Finally, in the face of a widespread public outcry and the possibility of a lawsuit brought by legal representation for the Kumeyaay, mission officials agreed to stop construction.[62] Mission interpreters do not address this controversy or the location of the graveyard in their contemporary presentations at the mission. The site now rests behind a gated fence with a large cross in the center. As a result of the public controversy and threat of lawsuit, mission officials allowed local Native community members to hold a ceremony and rebury the unearthed remains at the defunct construction site.

While public pressure and Native involvement helped stop the continued desecration of the graveyard at Mission San Diego, in 2007 officials at Mission San Juan Capistrano secretly and hurriedly constructed gardens and an outdoor kitchen for a retreat area on a portion of the mission cemetery in an attempt to avoid similar roadblocks.[63] They reportedly did not apply for building permits, nor did they conduct archeological studies to determine the significance of the construction site. However, maps and photographs from the mid-nineteenth century confirmed that the planned site for the retreat included the mission cemetery. Workers at the mission had to dig trenches and disturb the ground to construct the garden and barbeque area. According to site records, construction to build the rectory and earlier gardens in the 1930s and 1950s unearthed human remains. This led researchers to believe that workers would have found similar remains during construction in 2007.[64]

Once local Acjachemen (Juaneño) community members discovered this unpermitted and unresearched construction, they petitioned the city of San Juan Capistrano to issue a stop work order to examine disturbances to the site. Because construction was nearly complete, monitors merely supervised the site to mitigate future disturbances. Mission officials claimed they did not know the location was part of the old graveyard, and yet Acjachemen leaders had knowledge of the site and were appalled at the desecration of the sacred ground. Vice chairwoman of one Acjachemen faction, Sonia Johnston, argued that the mission had acted irresponsibly. She questioned the intentions of mission officials in an interview with the *Orange County Register*, asking, "How can you have parties and barbecues on the cemetery? I'd never go on my ancestral burial grounds and party on it. I don't understand."[65] Unlike the San Diego controversy, mission officials at San Juan Capistrano failed to notify the local community and nearly completed their construction project before concerned citizens intervened.[66] As is evident at Missions San

Diego and San Juan Capistrano, and in the problems encountered by the Serrano in protecting their sacred lands, many non-Native people continue to marginalize Native history and disrespect significant indigenous sites for private purposes.

Stewards at contemporary mission sites still greatly control the popular representation of Native peoples in mission history, just as collectors, museums, and regional promoters in the early twentieth century heavily influenced the perception of indigenous people in popular culture. Unfortunately, into the twenty-first century officials at some mission sites continue to minimize, ignore, or silence Native connections to mission history—even as the graves of tens of thousands of Native Californians rest beneath mission walls. Because Native Californians conceived of land use differently than Euro-Americans and left few permanent brick-and-mortar markers, the dramatized Spanish historical footprint overwhelmingly overshadowed Native history in the state. Following in the example of museums at the time, promoters at the turn of the twentieth century preserved, conserved, and restored the California missions for the appropriation of Euro-American audiences without paying heed to the perspectives of Native Californians.

In the absence of public knowledge of Native sites, the Spanish missions have become the symbols of California's earliest history. The popularity of the mission myth further played into the silencing of Native Californian experiences. As alluded to in *The Missions: California's Heritage*, the missions supposedly developed as sites for Native people to learn "civilized" ways of life, suggesting that any other history before this point was primordial and irrelevant.[67] Promoters of these constructed narratives focused on the benevolent religious and cultural agendas of Spanish colonizers. Their representations often ignored the hostility between indigenous people and foreigners who transformed California from the late eighteenth to early twentieth centuries. Native people and Spanish colonizers often fell into conflict over cultural differences and acceptable behavior, and yet mission representations marginalize these struggles and display the mission era as an idyllic time.

Inherent in both contemporary educational texts on the missions and the arguments by newcomers to California in the early twentieth century is an understanding that Native peoples did not or could not use the land in an effective and productive manner, and therefore they did not deserve to own the land. According to some educational texts, "since the Indians did not wish to continue the missions [following secularization], the buildings and land were sold, the Indians not even waiting for money or, in some cases, receiving money for the sale."[68] At this point, Native people frequently exit the mission narrative and the focus shifts to what became of the mission buildings themselves.[69]

Unlike the history presented in these texts, Native people did not simply fade into the past as newcomers increasingly encroached on their lands. Rather, Native communities resisted, accommodated, and adapted to change. Groups devastated by disease merged together, resettled lands, and formed new bonds. While Euro-Americans created notions of the vanishing Indian in popular culture, Native peoples demonstrated their perseverance in the face of the destructive forces brought by these colonizing powers.[70] They worked at mission sites and adapted to new economies outside of the missions. Euro-Americans arriving in the early twentieth century frequently failed to recognize this adaptation and survival because they encountered Native communities ravaged by over a century of hardships. However, many Native peoples negotiated through these trying times to preserve their lives and cultures.[71]

## Notes

1. Dydia DeLyser, *Ramona Memories: Tourism and the Shaping of Southern California* (Minneapolis: University of Minnesota Press, 2005), 179.

2. Richard White, *"It's Your Misfortune and None of My Own": A New History of the American West* (Norman: University of Oklahoma Press, 1993), 102–117.

3. James J. Rawls, *Indians of California: The Changing Image* (Norman: University of Oklahoma Press, 1984), xiii–xiv, 205–215. Emphasis in quotation is author's own. Not all Americans moving to California wanted to "exterminate" the Native population. Many philanthropic/humanitarian groups such as the Sequoya League emerged in the early twentieth century to help improve conditions for indigenous people in California and throughout the United States (see Chapter 2). Although these organizations sought to improve the contemporary plight of Native peoples, especially those on reservations, they rarely viewed preserving Native cultures as a part of their crusade. More often, these Euro-Americans sought to improve the lives of Native peoples by giving them tools to help acculturate them into American ways of life.

4. Clifford E. Trafzer and Joel Hyer, eds., *"Exterminate Them!": Written Accounts of Murder, Rape, and Enslavement of Native Americans during the California Gold Rush* (East Lansing: Michigan State University Press, 1999), 14–30.

5. Rawls, *Indians of California*, 116–201. The violence perpetrated by many American emigrants lured by the lucrative dreams of striking it rich during the gold rush in the mid- to late 1800s almost made this a reality. To avoid these violent offenders, many Native people disassociated from their cultures in public and instead identified as Mexican to protect their families from violent Indian hunters. Rawls examines the exploitation of and extermination campaigns against Native Californians.

6. Peter Iverson and Wade Davies, *We Are Still Here: American Indians since 1890*, 2d ed. (Malden, MA: Wiley Blackwell, 2015).

7. Michael Kelleher, "Images of the Past: Historical Authenticity and Inauthenticity from Disney to Times Square," *CRM: The Journal of Heritage Stewardship* (summer 2004): 6–19.

8. Information about the California missions was collected by means of tours and site visits from 2009 to early 2015.

9. Karen Coody Cooper addresses sites that worked to remedy issues of representation in *Spirited Encounters: American Indians Protest Museum Policies and Practices* (Lanham, MD: AltaMira Press, 2008).

10. White, *"It's Your Misfortune and None of My Own,"* 102–117; Frederick E. Hoxie, *A Final Promise: The Campaign to Assimilate the Indians, 1880–1920* (Lincoln: University of Nebraska Press, 2001), 64–67.

11. Moira G. Simpson, *Making Representations: Museums in the Post-Colonial Era* (New York: Routledge, 2001), 35.

12. *Ishi: The Last Yahi*, directed by Jed Riffe and Pamela Roberts (New York: Shanachie Entertainment, 1992), DVD.

13. Simpson, *Making Representations*, 35–36. Current exhibitions at the California State Indian Museum buck this trend by using photographs and material objects to help visitors understand the historical uses of objects. They also include narratives from contemporary indigenous people to address the ways in which Native Californians continue to incorporate traditional practices in their modern lives.

14. David Hurst Thomas, *Skull Wars: Kennewick Man, Archaeology, and the Battle for Native American Identity* (New York: Basic Books, 2000), 53–63.

15. Martin Padget, "Travel, Exoticism, and the Writing of Region: Charles Fletcher Lummis and the 'Creation' of the Southwest," *Journal of the Southwest* 37 (autumn 1995): 421-449.

16. Sonya Atalay, "Indigenous Archeology as Decolonizing Practice," special issue, *America Indian Quarterly* 30 (2006): 281.

17. Simpson, *Making Representations*, 119–128.

18. Thomas Biolsi and Larry J. Zimmerman, eds., *Indians and Anthropologists: Vine Deloria Jr. and the Critique of Anthropology* (Tucson: University of Arizona Press, 1997); Vine Deloria Jr., "Indians, Archaeologists, and the Future," *American Antiquity* 57 (October 1992): 595–598. Not until Vine Deloria Jr. wrote *Custer Died for Your Sins: An Indian Manifesto* in 1969 did major conversations develop among anthropologists about the proper treatment of Native communities. The late 1960s also marked the beginning of increased Native activism in academia.

19. Murray L. Wax, "Educating the Anthro: The Influence of Vine Deloria, Jr.," in *Indians and Anthropologists: Vine Deloria Jr. and the Critique of Anthropology*, ed. Thomas Biolsi and Larry J. Zimmerman (Tucson: University of Arizona Press, 1997), 50–60.

20. James J. Rawls, "The California Mission as Symbol and Myth," *California History* 71 (fall 1992): 347–352; Rawls, *Indians of California*, 357.

21. Rawls, *Indians of California*, 112–113.

22. Phoebe S. Kropp, *California Vieja: Culture and Memory in a Modern American Place* (Berkeley: University of California Press, 2006), 47–52.

23. Mary Null Boulé, *The Missions: California's Heritage—Mission San Diego de Alcalá* (Vashon, WA: Marryant Publishing, 1992), 5.

24. Ibid.

25. George Wharton James, *In and Out of the Old Missions of California* (Boston: Little Brown, 1906), 383–386.

26. The Pasadena Loan Association also planned to trace genealogies back to "the *Conquistadores* themselves." Anonymous, "The Pasadena Loan Association," *Land of Sunshine* 2 (February 1895): 54; Edna E. Kimbro and Julia G. Costello, *The California Missions: History, Art, and Preservation* (Los Angeles: Getty Conservation Institute, 2009), 62.

27. "To conserve the missions and other historic landmarks of southern California" was the slogan of the Landmarks Club. It can be found in blurbs about the club in *Out West* magazine.

28. Kimbro and Costello, *California Missions,* 58–59.

29. Ibid., 58–65; Kropp, *California Vieja*, 52–54.

30. Charles F. Lummis, "The Landmarks Club," *Land of Sunshine* 4 (December 1895): 85.

31. Charles Lummis, "Our Historic Treasure," *Land of Sunshine* 4 (December 1895): 117–120.

32. Ibid.

33. Ibid., 120.

34. Neither Lummis nor any other contributor to the *Land of Sunshine/Out West* magazine mentions vandals attacking mission cemeteries, although in the *Mission Play* Señora Yorba instructs Native people to not bury with the deceased padre a jewel-encrusted golden chalice "for sacrilegious thieves to dig up."

35. Zephyrin Engelhardt, *The Franciscans in California* (Harbor Springs, MI: Holy Childhood Indian School, 1897), 252–255.

36. Kimbro and Costello, *California Missions*, 67–83.

37. For a detailed examination of the development of the mission bell guideposts by the El Camino Real Association, see Kropp, *California Vieja*, 60–71.

38. Kimbro and Costello, *California Missions*, 67–83.

39. Peter M. Knudtson, *Wintun Indians of California and their Neighbors* (Happy Camp, CA: Naturegraph Publishers, 1977), 61–67. In 1973 Flora Jones, a Wintu shaman, claimed that the spirits informed her that she must call on the Wintu people and other Native Americans from diverse tribes to join together to "wake up" their sacred places. Because the U.S. Forest Service controlled thousands of acres in Northern California that were home to Wintu sacred sites, including the slopes of Mount Shasta, Jones contacted the Forest Service and asked permission to use the traditional Wintu lands so she could conduct doctoring ceremonies in the appropriate traditional power sites, including the Shasta volcano. Most Native Californians in the region do not travel to the upper slopes of Mount Shasta because of the sacred nature of the mountain.

40. This question comes out of the theoretical struggle created by the Wilderness Act (1964). Bonnie Stepenoff, "Wild Lands and Wonders: Preserving Nature and Culture in National Parks," in *Cultural Landscapes: Balancing Nature and Heritage in Preservation Practice,* ed. Richard W. Longstreth (Minneapolis: University of Minnesota Press, 2008), 91.

41. Rawls, *Indians of California*, 25–80.

42. Ibid., 28. Epidemics had ravaged the Native peoples Vancouver encountered—a significant factor in their "miserable" appearance.

43. Bernard W. Sheehan, *Seeds of Extinction: Jeffersonian Philanthropy and the American Indian* (New York: Norton, 1973), 8–31. Euro-Americans commonly applied this stereotype to the Pueblo people in the Southwest. They were sedentary agriculturalists whose lifestyle complemented contemporary Jeffersonian ideals.

44. Shepard Krech III, *The Ecological Indian: Myth and History* (New York: Norton, 1999), 16–17. For more on the fear of "Indian Wars," see Peter Silver, *Our Savage Neighbors: How Indian War Transformed Early America* (New York: Norton, 2008),

39–72.

45. Rawls, *Indians of California*, 139-141.

46. Sheehan, *Seeds of Extinction*, 8-31.

47. Rawls, *Indians of California*, 50–55.

48. Ibid., 34, 50–55; George Harwood Phillips, *Chiefs and Challengers: Indian Resistance and Cooperation in Southern California*, 2d ed. (Norman: University of Oklahoma Press, 2014), 323–338. Some Americans even blamed the mission system for creating the "heavy and dull" character that they applied to many Native Californians. But they failed to take into account the impact of generations of strain and adaptation brought on by European and American contact.

49. Susan Suntree showed the connection between scientific and Native understandings of the land in her poetic monograph *Sacred Sites: The Secret History of Southern California* (Lincoln: University of Nebraska Press, 2010); Keith Basso also demonstrated this connectedness in *Wisdom Sits in Places: Landscape and Language among the Western Apache* (Albuquerque: University of New Mexico Press, 1996).

50. Mark David Spence, *Dispossessing the Wilderness: Indian Removal and the Making of the National Parks* (New York: Oxford University Press, 1999), 4.

51. William Cronon, "The Trouble with Wilderness; or, Getting Back to the Wrong Nature," in *Uncommon Ground: Rethinking the Human Place in Nature*, ed. William Cronon (New York: Norton, 1996), 79.

52. Spence, *Dispossessing the Wilderness*, 5.

53. Cronon, "The Trouble with Wilderness," 79.

54. One such example is the development of the Big Bear area in Southern California. As described in the introduction to this volume, Big Bear Lake is a very significant site for the Serrano. But because of its large and natural structure, this sacred space has been defiled as Americans have constructed buildings, roads, and facilities for the local water district throughout the area. Other important Serrano cultural sites in the San Bernardino Mountains now exist on private property and similarly face the threat of damage and destruction. For a more detailed discussion of this issue see Clifford E. Trafzer, *The People of San Manuel* (Patton, CA: San Manuel Band of Mission Indians, 2002), 16–20.

55. The Pfau Library at California State University, San Bernardino, houses the Charley (Clayton) Howe Collection that includes photographic evidence of the vandalism.

56. Furthermore, the city of Sonoma built streets and homes over the Indian graveyards that surrounded Mission San Francisco de Solano.

57. Jennifer L. Trotoux, "Mission San Juan Capistrano Rectory Garden Site Plan Review Assessment," San Juan Capistrano and San Francisco, April 16, 2008. To help protect gravesites, California also passed the California Native American Graves Protection and Repatriation Act in 2001.

58. Ibid.; Clifford E. Trafzer, "Serra's Legacy: The Desecration of American Indian Burials at Mission San Diego," *American Indian Culture and Research Journal* 16 (1992): 57–75.

59. Ibid., 59–60. Historians Norman Neuerburg and Zephyrin Engelhardt both

described Mission San Diego in detail. They located the Native cemetery at the proposed construction site, near the original site of the mission church before it was destroyed and rebuilt in a different location on the same grounds.

60. Trafzer, "Serra's Legacy," 58.

61. Ibid., 63–64. Similar to many other Southern California Native communities, the Kumeyaay traditionally cremated their dead. Therefore, finding several human burial remains signified that the site was a Christian cemetery related to the mission.

62. Kumeyaay legal counsel proposed launching a lawsuit that would question the church's legal right to the land if the church did not agree to stop all construction and agree to Kumeyaay demands. Trafzer addressed the legal battle and public outcry against the construction at Mission San Diego in "Serra's Legacy," 57–75.

63. The Rectory Garden served as a gathering place for guests for the celebration of the San Juan Capistrano Mission Basilica retablo. A cardinal from the Vatican visited the mission in commemoration in 2007.

64. Trotoux, "Mission San Juan Capistrano Rectory Garden Site Plan Review Assessment."

65. Vik Jolly, "Mission Garden Center of Dispute," *Orange County Register,* October 8, 2007. David Belardes, a leader of another Acjachemen faction, argued that the church intentionally acted "with malice" in failing to follow the proper channels in building the gardens. He contended that mission officials knew they would need Native monitors because the site was over a cemetery. Mission representatives scoffed at Belardes's claim. They argued that he was only trying to gain publicity in making such accusations. Matt Coker, "Native American Battle over a Mission San Juan Capistrano Garden Gets Ugly," *Orange County Register,* December 24, 2008.

66. Some indigenous communities have successfully mitigated damage to cemeteries and other important sites. For example, Ohlone leaders in the San Francisco Bay area successfully petitioned the city to reroute the construction of Highway 680, which would have run directly through a cemetery related to Mission San Jose.

67. Boulé, *Missions.*

68. Ibid., 9.

69. George Harwood Phillips, *The Enduring Struggle: Indians in California History* (Sparks, NV: Materials for Today's Learning, 1990), 21.

70. Sheehan, *Seeds of Extinction*, 22–60.

71. Phillips, *Enduring Struggle*, 1–3.

# 4

# *Marginalizing Native Histories: Labor, Land, and Changes to Native Economies*

Viewing these buildings, imposing in their ruins and the vast amount of labor necessary, entailed in garden and field work, the caring for the great herds of cattle, the management of the extensive irrigation systems; the mind marvels over the results accomplished and a feeling of reverence for the robed and sandaled [*sic*] men of the brotherhood of St. Francis . . . surely impels one to hope that the men of this age will spare from the abundance God has showered upon them enough to restore and repair these priceless monuments of the past.
—F. A. Mann, "La Purísima Concepción Missions [*sic*] at Lompoc, California: A Historical Memorial" (1912)

Preservation and reconstruction projects, beautification efforts, and modernization of the surrounding landscapes have removed many contemporary missions from their historical contexts. Misrepresentations of the dramatically reconstructed Spanish ruins also help to divorce popular understandings of the mission myth from the more accurate historical accounts of Native interactions with these institutions. Mission San Gabriel Arcángel, one of the most productive missions along El Camino Real, is a prime example of the divide between Native accounts, scholarly understandings, and public presentations found at contemporary mission sites. Exhibitions at two of the more popular missions among contemporary tourists, San Juan Capistrano and Santa Barbara, similarly reflect the sanitized narrative many visitors encounter in these modern spaces. The Spanish colonizers brought disruptive changes to Native economies that rippled throughout California and what is now the American Southwest into the twentieth century.[1] Many scholars have documented that Native Californians became the central labor force supporting Spanish colonization.[2] Although scholars have examined the interplay of labor with power, control, and conversion, many contemporary presentations at California missions do not stress the role of Native labor as the most important component of mission life that sustained Spanish settlement in Alta California.[3]

Shifts in the California economy and Native labor strategies have been some of the most long-lasting legacies of the mission system. As noted, the arrival of the Spanish marked the beginning of significant changes in the lives and economies of Native Californians. The Spanish crown sought to make its overseas colonies more productive to reduce the cost of colonization.[4] Not just a secular act, the Spanish priests viewed labor as a "morally enriching disciplinary activity that hastened [Native] conversion from savagery to civilization."[5] Therefore, priests instituted regimented labor, believing that punishment for idleness or failure to perform was a means of achieving the eventual salvation of Native souls.[6]

As a result of Spanish colonization and the collapse of traditional economies and trade networks, many Native communities along the coast shifted from a trade and shell money–based economy to a system dependent on labor exchange. Over time, Native Californians became low-wage laborers for the new migrant groups that settled the region—first the Spanish colonists, then the Mexican rancheros, and finally the Euro-American settlers. Although missionization had a lasting negative impact on Native economies, contemporary mission representations continue to promote a romanticized depiction of the past that overlooks the memories and histories of Native Californians whose lives were transformed within the mission system. A closer look at Mission San Gabriel, the Gabrielino-Tongva, and the history presented by interpreters at San Gabriel's contemporary mission museum reveals the divide between popular representations of mission history and Native and scholarly understandings of the past.

## Museum Displays at Mission San Gabriel Arcángel

The physical descriptions of the landscape that surrounded Mission San Gabriel during the late eighteenth and early nineteenth centuries vary significantly from the landscapes people see today. Two hundred years ago, Mission San Gabriel was surrounded by leagues of supposedly unoccupied land available for grazing. Today, San Gabriel's Mission District is in the center of a bustling town, dominated by office buildings, homes, and busy streets. The city of San Gabriel defines itself through its mission heritage, "where the Los Angeles region began 200 years ago, at the San Gabriel Mission."[7] The restored Mission Playhouse, located only a few blocks from Mission San Gabriel, played host to the legendary *Mission Play* that defined the romantic mission era for over a million patrons in the twentieth century (see Chapter 2).

The museum at Mission San Gabriel, crowded with display cases of photos and objects, exhibits material that is not contextualized within a historical period. It does not include interpretation provided in organized labels. Upon entering the museum through the far-left room, patrons find information about Native Californian history. Pictures of Ishi, "America's last savage," hang on a wall behind the door. Interpreters do not describe Ishi's relationship to the mission, most likely because none exists. Also in this room is a display case of tiles, old keys, baskets, ceramics, spurs, and hardware made by neophytes. These material objects are well suited for use as interpretive devices in a discussion of Native labor at the mission, but the museum presents no more than a superficial discussion of the objects and their creators. Rather than describe a typical workday for neophytes, the mission museum displays tokens that reflect the romanticized past constructed during the early twentieth century by the likes of Charles Fletcher Lummis and John Steven McGroarty. These items also include Jackson's novel *Ramona* and early *Ramona* tourism memorabilia.[8]

The first room in the museum is the only space that includes the Native past to any detailed extent. However, the minimal description of the local indigenous population robs visitors of an opportunity to understand the rich history of the Gabrielino-Tongva that began centuries before the arrival of the Spanish.[9] The museum, which falls under church leadership, does, though, positively reflect the religious history of the former Spanish site. For example, one room of the museum houses an early nineteenth-century French organ, and is also cluttered with the artwork, vestments, and ceremonial clothing of the priests, as well as an early steam space heater. The walls of the museum's central room are covered in photos with little to no description of their relevance to the mission or California history in general. Furthermore, a case displays photos of the famous people who have visited the mission, including Charlie Chaplin, Mary Pickford, Lucille Ball, Desi Arnaz, Gen. George S. Patton, and Sen. Robert Kennedy.

Other rooms in the museum contain similarly eclectic collections of objects and photographs. For example, one room contains a bedroom set dating from 1623. However, the bed itself originated in the eighteenth or early nineteenth century. A clock on the wall dates from the 1880s, and a wall label reports that the timepiece stopped during the Whittier Narrows earthquake (magnitude 6.0) in 1987. Mission San Gabriel sustained significant damage during this earthquake. The walls had to be braced and reinforced to prevent further damage. However, the objects displayed by interpreters in the San

Gabriel mission museum appear to be more a collection of curiosities than materials related to the history of the mission and the people who labored on its grounds. By displaying visually pleasing photos and artifacts with minimal interpretation, officials at the mission sanitize its history and ignore the impact of the mission system on the Gabrielino-Tongva. Understanding the history of the Native peoples who populated the greater Los Angeles area for centuries before Spanish colonization is an essential component of a more inclusive history for Mission San Gabriel. Information about the Gabrielino-Tongva and other neighboring Native communities can be easily found in sources published by scholars and Native people from the early twentieth century to the present.

## The Gabrielino-Tongva and the Founding of Mission San Gabriel

The history of Mission San Gabriel began in late 1770 when the viceroy of New Spain, Carlos Francisco de Croix, ordered the establishment of Mission San Gabriel de Arcángel as well as five other missions north of present-day San Diego.[10] The Gabrielino-Tongva and Spanish built Mission San Gabriel near the Native village of Shivaanga.[11] Mission San Diego and the nearby military garrison provided guards and supplies for the founding of the mission. Contemporary interpreters at Mission San Gabriel focus their historical discussion on the establishment of the mission itself, ignoring the concurrent history of the Gabrielino-Tongva people and the residents of Shivaanga.

According to the history of Mission San Gabriel, upon arrival the Spanish met significant resistance from indigenous people in the area. Following in the dramatic tradition of mission lore, interpreters at Mission San Gabriel tell visitors that the local people gave up their weapons after the missionaries unveiled a painting of the Virgin Mary, Our Lady of Sorrows. This account is one of the most prolific stories about Mission San Gabriel, found in nearly every publication and discussion of the site. In more detail, it depicts the first encounter between the Gabrielino-Tongva and Spanish missionaries. Father Pedro Benito Cambón noted in a letter to his superior, Father Rafael Verger, that the missionaries faced opposition by the local Gabrielino-Tongva in their first efforts to establish the mission. Cambón recounted that the Spanish caravan "kept moving along in spite of the determined opposition of the *Indios,* who, in full war-paint and brandishing their bows and arrows . . . tried to prevent them from crossing the river." After members of the Spanish caravan barricaded themselves behind some bales and boxes, the missionaries unfolded a canvas painting of Our Lady of Sorrows. The Gabrielino-Tongva reportedly marveled at the sight of it "as if transfixed in wonderment."

**California Missions**

San Francisco Solano
July 4, 1823

San Rafael Arcangel
December 14, 1817

San Francisco de Asís
(Mission Dolores)
June 26, 1776

Santa Clara
de Asís
January 12, 1777

Santa Cruz
August 28, 1791

San Juan Bautista
June 24, 1797

Nuestra Señora
de la Soledad
October 9, 1791

San Antonio
de Padua
July 14, 1771

San Miguel Arcángel
July 25, 1797

San Luis Obispo
de Tolosa
September 1, 1772

La Purísima
Concepción
December 8, 1787

Santa Barbara
December 4,
1786

San Fernando Rey
de España
September 8, 1797

Santa
Inés
September 17, 1804

San Gabriel Arcángel
September 8, 1771

San Juan Capistrano
November 1, 1776

San Luis Rey
de Francia
June 13, 1798

San Diego de
Alcalá
July 16, 1769

Redding

Sacramento

Fresno

Los Angeles

Palm Springs

San Diego

South Lake Tahoe

0   50   100
Miles

Book Cover: Cars parked in front of Mission San Juan Capistrano with Serra statue in view, ca. early 1900s. (photCL 496 (210), Connie Rothstein Collection of California Missions, The Mission Play, and Southern California, The Huntington Library, San Marino, California.)

Etching of Mission San Diego de Alcalá, ca. 1883. (By Henry Chapman Ford, RB 37631, The Huntington Library, San Marino, California.)

Etching of Mission San Luis Rey de Francia, ca. 1883. (By Henry Chapman Ford, RB 37631, The Huntington Library, San Marino, California.)

Etching of Mission San Juan Capistrano, ca. 1883. (By Henry Chapman Ford, RB 37631, The Huntington Library, San Marino, California.)

Etching of Mission San Gabriel Archángel, ca. 1883. (By Henry Chapman Ford, RB 37631, The Huntington Library, San Marino, California.)

Etching of Mission La Purisima Concepción de María Santísima, ca. 1883. (By Henry Chapman Ford, RB 37631, The Huntington Library, San Marino, California)

Portrait of Helen Hunt Jackson, ca. late 1880s. (photCL Pierce 08629, C.C. Pierce Collection of Photographs, The Huntington Library, San Marino, California.)

Charles F. Lummis sitting at his desk, writing, 1902. (photPF 3909, The Huntington Library, San Marino, California.)

"Romances of the Mission Bells" pamphlet produced by the California Petroleum Company (CalPet), ca. early 1920s. (General Ephemera: Californiana, Indians and Missions, The Huntington Library, San Marino, California.)

Postcard produced for tourists that promoted "Ramona's Marriage Place." (photCL 56 (3522), Grace Nicholson Photograph Collection, The Huntington Library, San Marino, California.)

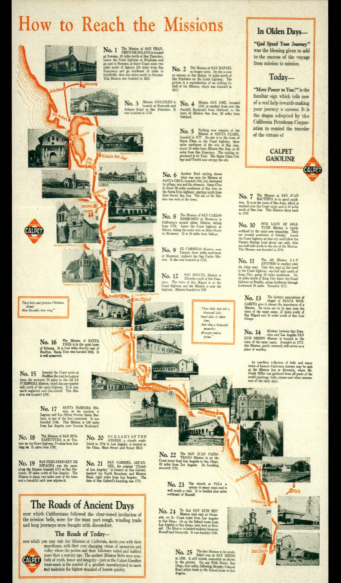

"How to Reach the Missions," Map guiding visitors to the California missions produced by the California Petroleum Company (CalPet), ca. early 1920s. (General Ephemera: Californiana, Indians and Missions The Huntington Library, San Marino, California.)

El Camino Real souvenir for the Mission bells, pamphlet, 1906.(General Ephemera: Californiana, Indians and Missions, The Huntington Library, San Marino, California.)

Indian Basket makers,
on Reservation
Warner Hot Sp
San

Postcard of Indian basket makers, on Reservation, Warner Hot Springs, San Diego. (photCL 56 (975), Grace Nicholson Photograph Collection, The

"The Mission Steps" - Mai Richie Reed with traveling companions on steps at Mission San Gabriel, photo from diary, 1908. (mssHM 64599, The Huntington Library, San Marino, California.)

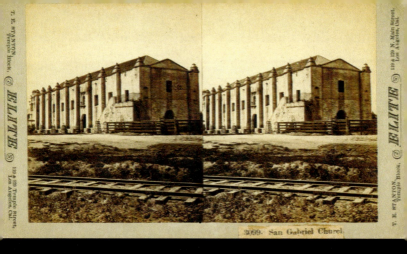

Mission San Gabriel, detail, pre-1885. (photCL 496 (875), Connie Rothstein Collection of California Missions, The Mission Play, and Southern California, The Huntington Library, San Marino, California.)

San Gabriel Mission Cemetery where several thousand Indians are buried, ca. 1900. (photCL Pierce 02699, C.C. Pierce Collection of Photographs, The Huntington Library, San Marino, California.)

Mission San Luis Rey seen through archway, ca. early 1900s. (photCL 496 240), Connie Rothstein Collection of California Missions, The Mission Play and Southern California, The Huntington Library, San Marino, California

A staged scene at Mission San Juan Capistrano, ca. early 1900s. (photCL 496 (203), Connie Rothstein Collection of California Missions, The Mission Play, and Southern California, The Huntington Library, San Marino, California.)

Mission San Juan Capistrano with visitor in a car posed in front, ca. early 1900s. (photCL 496 (186), Connie Rothstein Collection of California Missions, The Mission Play, and Southern California, The Huntington Library, San Marino, California)

SAN JUAN CAPISTRANO MISSION,—1776.

Postcard of Mission San Juan Capistrano in "Album of views of the missions of California," 1914. (photCL 496 (box 25), Connie Rothstein Collection of California Missions, The Mission Play, and Southern California, The Huntington Library, San Marino, California.)

VISITORS AT SAN GABRIEL MISSION.

Postcard image of visitors in front of Mission San Gabriel in Album o_ views of the missions of California," 1914. (photCL 496 (box 25), Connie Rothstein Collection of California Missions, The Mission Play, and Southern California, The Huntington Library, San Marino, California.)

Postcard image of the theatre garden at the Mission Playhouse, San Gabriel, California, ca. early 1900s. (Author's personal collection.)

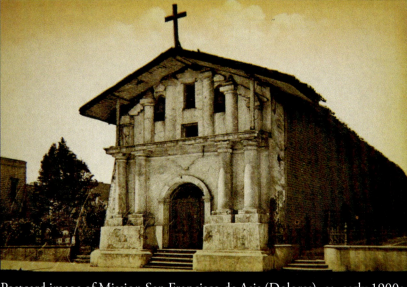
Postcard image of Mission San Francisco de Asis (Dolores), ca. early 1900s. (Author's personal collection.)

MISSION SAN FRANCISCO DE SOLANO. At Sonoma. Founded July 4, 1823, by Padre Altimira. The last of the great chain of California Missions, the like of which is not to be found elsewhere in the world. The picture shows the mission as it was many years ago. At present it is even more altered and fast decaying—a part of it being used as a wine vault. Its great bells could be heard many miles away, but now they, like its property, are scattered and gone. Its pretty gardens are obliterated and bloom no more.

Supplement San Francisco Sunday Chronicle, November 29, 1902.

Sketch of Mission San Francisco de Solano published as a supplement for the San Francisco Sunday Chronicle, November 29, 1903. (photCL 496 (box 25), Connie Rothstein Collection of California Missions, The Mission Play and Southern California, The Huntington Library, San Marino, California.

According to Cambón, the Gabrielino-Tongva dropped their weapons, and two headmen placed their necklaces at the feet of the portrait—a symbol of their peaceful intentions and instant adoration of the Virgin Mary.[12]

Following this display of submission, Native peoples helped the soldiers and priests prepare the mission site for construction. They also went out and returned with more people from neighboring villages, referred to as *rancherias* by the Spanish, bringing with them offerings for Our Lady of Sorrows. The company celebrated the first Mass at the mission after erecting a shelter and a large cross, marking the establishment of Mission San Gabriel on September 8, 1771.[13] This hopeful account sets the stage for mission interpreters to tell an optimistic version of history wherein Native people sought conversion from the very beginning. And it allows mission officials to discount the historical controversy over coercive conversion practices, harsh labor regimens, fugitivism (fleeing the mission), and instances of rebellion that do not correspond to the "joyful" history presented in mission mythology.

At Mission San Gabriel, just as at the other twenty-one mission sites, the Spanish put local indigenous people to work constructing buildings. During the first two years, missionaries at San Gabriel baptized seventy-three adults and children. They built the living quarters for the missionaries and soldiers, a defense stockade, corrals for cattle and horses, and a granary. Neophytes also planted wheat, corn, beans, and vegetables in nearby fields. The increase in food supplies allowed the mission to support more converts, and by December 1774 the missionaries had baptized an additional 148 people and conducted nineteen marriages. The growing number of neophytes at Mission San Gabriel between 1771 and 1774 provided a labor force capable of tending large herds of cattle, horses, sheep, and mules. The livestock population and grain production at Mission San Gabriel increased substantially every year after its founding.[14]

Indeed, Native peoples almost immediately contributed to the mission economies and constructed buildings at every mission from the ground up. They formed the adobe bricks from mud and water. They also fell trees, carried them miles to the mission sites, and shaped them into the planks and beams needed to frame the walls and roofs of the missions. Although the original site of Mission San Gabriel sustained the Spanish and Native populations for a time, flooding forced the padres to move the settlement a league north in 1775, to a location closer to El Camino Real. This move helped San Gabriel to become a trading center and resting point for travelers in Spanish and Mexican California. At this new site, indigenous people again worked to build more permanent structures from adobe and wood. Between 1775 and 1783, Native laborers constructed a majority of Mission San Gabriel's quadrangle, including a chapel, quarters for the missionaries, storage facilities, sheds and corrals, a kitchen, a two-room hospital, separate dormitories for girls and boys, a tannery, and soldier barracks. Construction continued at the mission into 1827, during which time the neophytes built many more structures, including the large stone and masonry church—remnants of which still stand on the mission grounds alongside a reproduced façade. They also built several granaries, dozens of homes for neophyte families, mills, hen houses, and facilities for a blacksmith.[15]

Production generally increased at San Gabriel throughout the mission period, especially after the padres moved the mission deeper inland into the Los Angeles basin. For example, the mission reported harvesting 960 bushels of wheat and 1,605 bushels of corn in 1780—both non-native foods that the Gabrielino-Tongva learned to cultivate after the Spanish arrived in Alta California.[16] George Phillips noted that "the Indians' vast knowledge of harvesting and processing wild foods probably allowed for a relatively easy transition to the planting and tending of domestic ones."[17] The mission benefited from an irrigation system constructed by the Gabrielino-Tongva and the missionaries after 1778. This aqueduct system supplied water for the kitchen, tannery, and the irrigated fields surrounding the mission complex.[18] The completed irrigation system contributed to the successful wheat harvests of over 4,500 bushels a year. Workers at Mission San Gabriel produced a record-setting 16,500 bushels of wheat in 1821. Native laborers also increased corn production over the years, reaching a high of 12,000 bushels in 1817. Many contemporary mission sites highlight the "sophisticated" aqueduct systems that the Spanish introduced to California—images that hark back to the aqueducts constructed by Roman architects during antiquity. At the same time, they neglect to address the extensive labor required to build the aqueducts and the number of workers needed to procure such bountiful harvests year-round.

Statistically, Mission San Gabriel was a success. However, the onset of Spanish colonization in Alta California marked the beginning of a downward spiral for many Native communities. Hispanicization of indigenous people under the threat of physical punishment compelled many missionized Native peoples to curb outward expressions of their cultures and conform to Hispanic styles of eating, dressing, praying, and living—during the day at the very least.[19] As just described, representations of the past at Mission San Gabriel generally ignore almost all aspects of indigenous history. According to Phillips, "when mentioned at all, Indians have been assigned an insignificant role" in the histories of missions, ranchos, and pueblos.[20] The Spanish entered into the Gabrielino-Tongva's sophisticated and established society with ethnocentric notions of indigenous peoples as primitive savages without culture or religion.[21]

In fact, the Spanish described many of the Native people they encountered as inherently indolent and undisciplined. In response, the priests established localized congregations so that the padres could remove indigenous people from their cultures and ways of life in order to control and "civilize" them more effectively.[22] However, Native people did not respond well to this coercion. Many secretly retained components of their traditional lifeways, while others fled the missions or actively resisted the Spanish. The Gabrielino-Tongva had long-established cultural and religious traditions that did not fade away with Spanish colonization. Instead, as Phillips noted, they incorporated their knowledge of the land and work ethic into life after the Spanish invasion.[23]

Contemporary interpreters at Mission San Gabriel note "it is difficult to picture early California more than 200 years ago when the wild, uninhabited miles of our Western land knew only the occasional footsteps of the Gabrielino-Tongva Indian tribes."[24] Contrary to this description, however, people populated nearly every region of California, from the Modoc plateau in northwestern California to the Kumeyaay lands in today's southern San Diego County. For thousands of years, Native peoples developed complex societies that transformed the cultural heritage of the region and enshrined the landscape with intrinsic meaning. The Tongva, or Gabrielino, are the indigenous people who historically occupied large portions of present-day Los Angeles and Orange Counties in California.[25] Tongva is a more recent name for this group, but the Spanish referred to them as the Gabrielino to distinguish the Native people who surrounded the San Gabriel Mission.[26] The Gabrielino-Tongva identified closely with their individual villages, but understood that they shared language and customs with other villages as a larger Gabrielino-Tongva culture as well. Gabrielino-Tongva territory spanned more than 2,500 square miles and included the region between Topanga Canyon, Mount Wilson, east to San Bernardino, and southeast to Aliso Creek. To the northwest, the Gabrielino-Tongva shared a border with the Chumash. Gabrielino-Tongva territory bordered Serrano and Cahuilla land to the east, and they also shared borders with the Acjachemen and Luiseño to the south.[27]

Despite the presumption made by some mission officials that California was an "untamed" land before Spanish settlement, scholarly analyses and Gabrielino-Tongva descriptions of their precontact religious, political, and socioeconomic structures reveal that Native people manipulated their surroundings to create a lifestyle in which they could thrive.[28] By overlooking important aspects of Gabrielino-Tongva society before sustained Spanish colonization,

Mission San Gabriel places the Gabrielino-Tongva into the periphery of its historical discussion. Representations that fail to acknowledge the complexity and longevity of Native communities *long before* Spanish colonization also help to elevate the romanticized mission myth. They falsely contend that the Spanish landmarks signify the beginning of history in California, when in fact rich Native histories far predate the "discovery" of America. In short, the Spanish entered a highly developed Native world.

The Gabrielino-Tongva hunted and harvested the landscape. They benefited from surplus production, but they also developed a complex economic influence in the region because of their advantageous location between the Chumash, Serrano, Cahuilla, Luiseño, Acjachemen, and the California coast. Although this structure seems fairly straightforward, anthropologists and Native peoples have documented complex aspects of Gabrielino-Tongva culture and societal organizations.[29] Strict rules of reciprocity and exchange gatherings greatly assisted in the development of a local economy among the many Gabrielino-Tongva communities and neighboring indigenous groups.[30] They shared culture and language, and they intermarried with people from other villages and Native nations. Native communities in Southern California frequently interacted with other local indigenous groups who did and did not speak their language. This thorough mixing allowed for semiporous boundaries between territories and helped create different indigenous communities with similar cultural values. For example, archeological artifacts and records left by Spanish priests reveal that the Gabrielino-Tongva shared similarities with the Chumash and the Acjachemen, including belief in the Chinigchinich religion.[31]

For the Gabrielino-Tongva, the leader of each local community was a *tomyaar*. The tomyaar, or headman, acted as the administrator of political, fiscal, legal, and religious affairs. The tomyaar also regulated communal food distribution and the exchange of shell-bead money between lineages and other communities. Tomyaars received their power and authority through their familial lineage. It also provided them with innate access to supernatural sources of power. Although many tomyaars were male, female tomyaars occasionally emerged in the historical records.[32]

Gabrielino-Tongvas and other neighboring Native communities viewed shell-bead exchange and redistribution as an important tie to bring their communities together. Neglecting to adhere to tribal laws of food or shell-bead reciprocity could result in conflict and warfare.[33] Shamans also held powerful roles in Gabrielino-Tongva society. They used their spiritual power and skill to protect and control society.[34] Some shamans and tomyaars retained important and active roles in Gabrielino-Tongva life within Mission

San Gabriel. Many times, these tribal figures, who concealed the extent of their spiritual powers from the Spanish priests, became the elected leaders of indigenous people within the mission. Mission officials relied on these Native leaders, or *alcaldes*, to help organize and facilitate day-to-day activities at the missions. Alcaldes frequently followed through with orders given by missionaries, such as enforcing punishments, but these leaders also protected Native interests within the Spanish institutions, and some continued to be powerful leaders after secularization.[35] Popular presentations based on romanticized mission myths do not acknowledge the presence of Native leaders at the mission.

Embracing the mission myth, contemporary interpreters ask patrons at Mission San Gabriel to "forget [their] cares and troubles as [they] relive the early days of the Western World."[36] The brief portraits of pre-Spanish Native existences painted by many mission officials reflect the romanticized stereotypes of Native peoples found in mission lore. According to this mythology, Native people lived serene and carefree lives before Spanish colonization, where "nature reigned supreme over man."[37] These kinds of generalizations allowed mission officials to establish the Spanish as a greatly positive influence in the lives of Native Californians. According to this flawed description, the Spanish introduced indigenous groups to "civility," teaching Native peoples to conquer their surroundings and cultivate the land. By contrast, Native-centered narratives of California history before Spanish colonization confirm that Native peoples, including the Gabrielino-Tongva, successfully managed their lands and had complex societies and cultures.

Occupying, like other tribes, some of the most topographically diverse and naturally rich lands in North America, the Gabrielino-Tongva developed settlement patterns that helped them utilize all of the plant, animal, and ocean resources available to them throughout the seasons.[38] Men typically hunted and fished, while women collected seeds, nuts, plants, and roots, and manufactured material goods, including baskets, cooking utensils, clothing, and adornments.[39] However, during harvests, when it was important to collect food quickly, all members of Gabrielino-Tongva communities participated in food-gathering efforts. For example, acorns were an important food for many Native Californians, but were only available for harvest seasonally. Both men and women collected the acorns that women brought back to village sites and processed into a meal.[40] Gabrielino-Tongva people arranged their settlement patterns to accommodate important harvests because other foods, especially seafood and wild game, were usually available throughout the year. Furthermore, they participated in trade with surrounding Native communities to supplement their stores in times of shortage and for gain in times of prosperity.[41] The Gabrielino-Tongva moved less frequently than other peoples because of their close proximity to the ocean and other natural resources. During Spanish colonization, the padres frequently established mission sites near larger villages to build trade relationships with local leaders and gain the trust of potential converts. However, the Native people did not welcome intrusion within their territory and frequently resisted Spanish settlement.

The Gabrielino-Tongva territory included important economic trading centers such as Nájquqar on Santa Catalina Island.[42] The mainland epicenter of Gabrielino society sat in the center of a large trade network that connected many Southern Californian Native groups. Gabrielino-Tongva territory was in a region that was so naturally rich that they relied minimally on trade for sustenance. However, they still traded with other indigenous peoples for goods not found in their territory.[43] For example, they traded soapstone and shell beads with the Cahuilla for fur, hides, and salt. They also traded sea otter pelts, fish, and shell beads to the Serrano for deerskin and seeds. Meanwhile, the Mohave from the Colorado River region traveled hundreds of miles to trade "luxury" goods such as deer or antelope skin shirts, red ochre, bighorn pelts, and blankets to the Gabrielino-Tongva for shells and soapstone from Catalina Island.[44] Trade provided outlets for specialized craftsmen, such as plank canoe builders who produced goods for profit. Also, trade among the Gabrielino-Tongva, Chumash, Cahuilla, and others helped create the shell-bead as a standardized medium of exchange.[45]

## Mission Life: Thrust in a Spanish System

The sophisticated socioeconomic system developed in Southern California was a testament to the generally rich and sophisticated lives of Native peoples long before Spanish intervention. Mission officials and foreign explorers who deemed indigenous peoples "simple" and "ignorant" failed to understand Native history and culture prior to Spanish contact. Native people were not "lazy" or "indolent" as described by many foreign explorers, Spanish priests, and soldiers. Rather, they developed complex socioeconomic systems that required strenuous work, but also allowed time for leisure, games, singing, dancing, and other cultural and religious activities.[46] Because Native peoples did not have a routine work day and had time for leisure, their lifestyles did not mesh with European standards of "civility."[47] Thus the cultural barriers between Native peoples and Spaniards bred conflict. The Spanish viewed idleness as a gateway to sin, and the padres forced a restrictive, stringent labor routine on Native peoples at many of the missions.

Thrust into a new and foreign mission landscape, Native people employed a combination of newly learned and older, more familiar methods to navigate their roles as laborers in the Spanish missions. Indigenous peoples at many missions refused to completely abandon their traditional subsistence strategies and other economic activities.[48] They held onto traditional practices, but also adapted to the occupations required by Spanish institutions to survive in a quickly changing world. For example, Native women within the missions continued to make baskets, but also learned to weave wool into clothing and rugs.

Before and after Spanish colonization, music, song, and dance were important components of Native Californian cultures.[49] Spanish priests also valued music and song, and they quickly established choirs and orchestras after founding a mission.[50] Although priests often considered Native dances to be "lascivious," they treasured talented musicians and angelic voices.[51] Priests placed a high value on musical instruction and trained talented young men to sing in the Spanish style. They allowed gifted performers and members of the all-male choirs to focus on music rather than participate in labor-intensive chores. According to historian of Spanish California James A. Sandos, in the social order of mission life members of the choir were among the elite. Priests considered music an important tool, leading to total conversion of indigenous peoples. The padres believed they could reach neophytes on a deeper level through the music of the Mass than through baptism alone. In fact, scholars point out that priests frequently provided indigenous peoples with very little spiritual instruction before baptism. Rather, they imparted "abbreviated catechism," which sometimes was as short as a day. These abbreviated catechisms helped populate the mission with enough "converts" to build and sustain the mission complex, but often did not convert the hearts of Native peoples.[52] Religious instruction, then, appears to have been a secondary concern for the Spaniards, who initially viewed many adult neophytes as laborers to fulfill their need to sustain the fledgling missions.

Along with choir members, the hierarchical organization of mission communities placed the most value on skilled artisans such as blacksmiths, carpenters, weavers, masons, and artists.[53] Representations of labor at contemporary missions focus nearly exclusively on this group, which produced many of the visible tools and objects displayed at the missions today.[54] For example, current displays at the museum at Mission Santa Barbara emphasize the work of neophyte artisans, painters, weavers, sculptures, blacksmiths, and potters rather than the laborious tasks undertaken by field hands and builders. By highlighting mission-trained artisans, exhibits at Mission Santa Barbara and reenactments on "Mission Days" at many other sites continue to reflect romanticized attributes of the mission system. They also continue to promote the romanticized myth of Spanish California by depicting the missions as training grounds for Native artisans while brushing over the stringent work routines instituted by the padres. As Edward and Mary Alexander question in *Museums in Motion*, "even if the equipment, process, and costumes [used in museums and reenactments] are thoroughly researched, is the . . . craft overly romanticized? What of the tedium of such work? Are the . . . demonstrators too neat and clean?"[55] Moreover, do they critically analyze the work of artisans as expressions of both Catholic and Native cultures? For example, Juan Antonio, the artist of *Via Crucis* (Stations of the Cross) now hanging at Mission San Gabriel, arguably expressed both a love for Jesus Christ and a distain for his crucifiers, whom Antonio depicted as Spaniards instead of Romans.[56] This complex series of paintings illustrates one way in which mission representatives could, but ultimately fail to, complicate the narrative of Native experiences at the missions. Many Native peoples today reject popular narratives that paint the missions as idyllic centers of religion. Rather, they contend that the Spanish kept indigenous people at the missions as captive laborers or even as slaves.[57]

Scholars debate the degree of force used by missionaries and soldiers to keep neophytes at the missions and disagree over whether Native peoples were slaves to the Spanish (also see Chapter 6). For example, Steven W. Hackel noted that neophytes worked at the missions not as slaves or indentured servants, but as a "semicaptive labor force" compelled to stay based on a need for food and community.[58] Similarly, Sandos claimed that scholars who relate the neophyte condition under the mission system to slavery in the American South are "unfair." Sandos supports a "peonage" model of labor in Spanish California in which Native laborers bound themselves to the mission and missionaries through baptism.[59] He argues that baptism symbolized a neophyte's commitment to the rules and regulations of mission life—including a strict labor routine and regulated movement away from the grounds of the mission.[60] Alternatively, testimonials in *The Missions of California: A Legacy of Genocide* provided by Native peoples in the late twentieth century depict a history of forced conversion and slavery in which missionaries and soldiers abused and killed many indigenous people.[61] Other oral histories provided by Native people throughout the twentieth century argue that Native peoples were slaves of the missions. For example, Tony Pinto, longtime tribal chairman of the Ewiiaapaayp Band of Kumeyaay Indians, recalled that "all of our elders knew what happened to those who were forced to go to the missions.... The Indians were slaves. They did all the work, and after a day's work, the priests lock them up. . . . They beat them and killed them if they were sick, or couldn't work, or didn't agree to certain work."[62] Overall, the missions were complex sites, and experiences varied for indigenous peoples, depending on the management of a mission and the "particular economic program introduced."[63]

Many components of Spanish colonization and the mission system such as labor, punishment, death, and disease left lasting imprints on Native Californian communities into the late twentieth century, and in many places stories passed down generationally reflect many of the negative aspects of mission life because, as expressed by Julia Bogany (Gabrielino-Tongva) "we learn the bad before the good."[64] And yet despite this well-known legacy in many Native Californian communities, popular representations of the missions continue to reflect glorified and romanticized perspectives.

Exhibition spaces at private Church-owned mission museums tend to focus heavily on the religious and Spanish cultural heritage of the missions. Phillips explained that "such an approach is understandable [to historians] because it is easier to write about those who produced the historical documents than about those mentioned intermittently in them."[65] Yet Native elders and culture bearers such as Bogany provide oral histories to supplement this often one-sided narrative. Bogany has worked for years to convince leadership at Mission San Gabriel to revise their presentation and include a stronger Gabrielino-Tongva perspective, but to no avail. "I understand that this is a time of History," she says, "but it's time to tell [the] *true* History [about the missions]." She questions the use of forced labor, violence, and physical restraint used against Native people at the missions, noting that "there was no sign offering jobs. Why did people have to be chained or locked in if they were not slaves—why shackle women if they were cooking?"[66]

Most contemporary mission sites do not address this negative history. Instead, they focus on religious and Spanish objects that reflect the lives of the priests and soldiers at the sites. For example, an exhibit in the "kitchen and dining room" at Mission San Juan Capistrano includes an outline of a priest's daily life. It fails to address the work Native peoples performed under strict supervision at the mission. The display explains that, besides their religious obligations, priests filled the roles of accountants and architects, and the padres "built the sun dried adobe brick, they planted fields and orchards, they drove livestock up from Mexico. They created the Missions of California."[67] Native laborers are completely absent in this assessment of mission history.

Pamphlets sold at the missions, many to fourth-grade students who produce school projects about the sites, conclude that "considering the period of history, the mission neophytes did less labor and lived better than the average worker or peasant in Europe."[68] According to Father Raymond Kammerer's idyllic description of mission life, priests punctuated three hours of work with a hearty meal of *pozole* and neophytes enjoyed "many feast days."[69] Kammerer did not explain that Native peoples labored to produce enough food to feed themselves and the increasingly unproductive Spanish settler and soldier populations. At the same time, they also built the Spanish California infrastructure *and* tended to the growing livestock population that skyrocketed into the hundreds of thousands. Bogany has a different perspective after assessing life for the Gabrielino-Tongva people at the beginning of Spanish contact: "We were here [at the missions] even though we were not hungry, in need of anything to survive, and yes . . . we might have learned new trades [but] we didn't at this time have need for [trade skills]."[70]

Within the missions, Native peoples worked under a stringent labor program harvesting newly introduced plants such as wheat, corn, barley, and grapes rather than their traditional food collected from fishing, hunting, and gathering from the locally managed land. Other neophytes managed vast herds of cattle, sheep, and horses. Spanish priests assigned Native women work in kitchens to make foods that appealed to the Spanish palate, including gruel made of cornmeal, known as *atole,* as well as tortillas, stews such as pozole and *puchero,* and dough breads, including *tarrejas.* These labor routines partially resembled the gendered divisions of labor familiar to indigenous peoples in California, but Native men frequently balked at agricultural work in the fields because women traditionally gathered plants.[71]

Although some Native peoples adapted to Spanish expectations and new gender roles, they also struggled to adjust to different social structures at the missions. At some missions, Native people constructed traditional semi-permanent tule-grass structures to house families in the areas surrounding the mission complex. They also built separate permanent adobe quarters for priests, soldiers, and young or unmarried Native women, known as *monjeríos.* Native women maintained the domestic sphere, adhering to the strict gender-based division of labor ingrained in Spanish society in the late eighteenth and nineteenth centuries. Conversely, indigenous men did much of the heavy labor-intensive work such as building and repairing the Spanish infrastructure at the missions, presidios, and towns (*pueblos*).[72] Unbaptized Native people, known as gentiles, worked in the pueblos and on the relatively few ranchos during the Spanish period, but they did not join in the social fabric of Spanish communities.[73]

Once Native peoples became members of the mission community, they began an extremely structured life as child-like wards of the missionaries. Each day, they rose before sunrise. At daybreak, the priests said Mass followed by recitation of Christian doctrine and hymnal singing. While the padres generally understood components of some Native languages, they preferred to instruct the neophytes in Castilian as an important part of the Hispanicization process. After these standardized Catholic rituals, converts ate breakfast and subsequently received their daily work assignments. Work

119

included tending the fields and livestock, preparing and cooking food, and assisting in the production of mission-made goods. The neophytes received lunch at noon and returned to work until sunset when they again recited doctrine and sang.[74]

Neophytes worked and lived under strict supervision at many missions. Missionaries used a Spanish overseer, known as a *mayordomo*, and alcaldes to monitor work and enforce daily routines under the threat of the whip.[75] Priests also doled out sentences in shackles and stocks to punish converts for skirting their chores, working too slowly, or being "lazy." According to Native testimonials published by contemporary scholars, the missionaries sometimes even forced offenders to work in the fields wearing weighted wooden stocks around their ankles as punishment.[76] Most mission sites do not acknowledge the punishments used by missionaries and soldiers to enforce the strict Spanish labor systems.[77] And yet images of the punishment devices are not far from sight. The two mission sites operated by the state of California address components of labor punishment—Mission San Francisco de Solano sells a coloring book that includes an image of a Native woman weaving in ankle stocks, and an exhibit at Mission La Purísima includes a physical reproduction of the heavy wooden stocks once worn by neophytes as a punishment. However, at many of the other contemporary mission sites, representations of the past still focus heavily on object-based displays that romanticize the Spanish past in the state and minimize Native experiences.

## Complicating Labor at Contemporary Mission Sites

An outward air of romance permeates Mission Santa Barbara, and yet representatives at the site do acknowledge that "the missions were built *for the Indians*, and, to a great extent, *by them*."[78] Nevertheless, publications produced for visitors to Mission Santa Barbara minimize labor regimens and paint work under the Spanish as more appealing than the stringent routines that modern scholars have documented. According to Franciscan historian Maynard Geiger, the Chumash of Santa Barbara traditionally "had quite a bit of leisure," but neophytes needed organized routines to adapt to Spanish culture. Geiger reported that these labor routines did not significantly disturb the lives of the Chumash—"few labor unions today have reached the working hour schedule and fringe benefits or the social security of the California Indians either at Santa Bárbara or elsewhere."[79] According to Geiger's idyllic representation of mission life, Native people worked only a handful of hours each day, and they enjoyed plenty of leisure for games and other recreational activities.[80]

120

Geiger's description of light workloads and leisurely time at the mission, originally written in 1960, reflects the glorified Spanish narrative popular in the United States in the early twentieth century. Much like other mission apologists, Geiger argued that indigenous peoples "lived under a benevolent and paternalistic regime, [they were] taught Christianity, and if [they] did not have the freedom enjoyed in pre-mission times, [they] received other social and economic gains in the form of social security."[81] Using statistical data recorded by missionaries and the journals and letters of Spanish officials during the mission era, historians today maintain that labor regimens at the missions were far less ideal for Native peoples than those described by Geiger. As Hackel illustrated, labor at the mission took a toll on neophytes, especially when combined with the threat of physical punishment. Fear of punishment became ingrained in their psyche and physically affected indigenous peoples, along with malnutrition and the epidemics found in neophyte communities (see Chapter 6).[82] Sherburne F. Cook also found that the psychological effects of coercive labor routines greatly affected neophyte morale because Native Californians were not accustomed to the intense workdays enforced by the Spanish.[83] However, Phillips claims that both mission "defenders" and mission "denigrators" have distorted mission life and "inadvertently overlooked what may be one of [the mission system's] more positive aspects—the development of a large and often efficient labor force."[84]

According to Cook, the highly structured daily labor regimens were not a part of Native life before Spanish colonization, and Native peoples continually struggled with the drastic change to their daily patterns of life. Cook argued that indigenous people disliked the tedious and orderly labor traditions that were a central part of mission life, noting that "the whole basis of the aboriginal system was the idea of intermittent effort, rather than steady, consistent exertion."[85] Native people operated on seasonal schedules based on locally available foods. They worked hard to harvest food when it was ripe and rested after the work was done. They also resented providing food and labor for the Spanish soldiers who did little work themselves. Unlike contemporary scholars such as Hackel, Sandos, Phillips, Robert H. Jackson, and Edward D. Castillo, who demonstrated that Native people quickly adapted to Spanish tools and labor systems, Cook claimed that Native Californians inherently could not adapt to the "necessities of the European and American economic system."[86] Reflecting common discriminatory notions towards Native peoples in the early twentieth century, Cook argued that because of their "innate inferiority . . . the race was doomed to severe depletion, if not extinction, in free competition with the whites simply because it could not sufficiently, rapidly and successfully adapt itself to the labor system basic to white economy."[87] Phillips disagrees; he maintains that Native people adapted quickly to labor at the missions. Scholars today discredit Cook's contention and point to how Native peoples have revived their traditional cultures while also contributing to changing economies.

James Sandos observed that labor and religious instruction served dual purposes to Hispanicize and control Native populations. He argued that "the primary purpose of the Franciscans in the missions was to mold good Christians" but the secular needs to economically sustain colonization in Alta California often superseded the goals of the padres.[88] Representations of Native labor at Mission San Gabriel are similar to the narratives at Mission San Juan Capistrano and Mission Santa Barbara. Professionally printed signs placed at key sites throughout the grounds at San Gabriel note that Franciscan missionaries and the Gabrielino-Tongva constructed the mission together. In reality, Native laborers did much more work than the handful of priests that served the mission, in part because they significantly outnumbered the Spanish in Alta California. According to mission interpretations, they also made clay aqueduct pipes, produced food, ground wheat, and cured leather. These signs differ from older hand-painted placards also found throughout the mission that passively describe the laborious tasks carried out at the mission, such as soap and candle making, without identifying who was responsible for manufacturing the goods. Although some brazen tour guides may elaborate on the scope of neophyte labor—even referring to Native people as "slaves" at the missions—the posted labels at mission sites and imagery used in related publications minimize the roles of indigenous people as the builders of the missions.[89]

Other significant aspects of mission life ever-present in historical interpretations at contemporary mission sites are cattle ranching and agricultural production. Missing at Mission San Gabriel, however, is a clear portrayal of the toll the livestock tending and hard labor had on Native peoples and their communities. The Spanish brought cattle to Alta California as early as 1769—coinciding with the founding of Mission San Diego. The Los Angeles basin provided some of the best land in Alta California for cattle ranching, and the Spanish utilized it widely. The meat, hide, and tallow that Native people cultivated from cattle quickly became staples for Spanish settlers, who relied heavily on the products developed from these raw goods in their daily lives.[90] The Native vaqueros who tended the herds as skilled horsemen were in the highest strata of the mission labor pool.[91] The hides and tallow products, such a soap and candles, also lured foreign merchant ships to the California coast. These ships helped supplement Spanish supplies in the region when the self-sufficient mission system left them wanting a variety of different tools and other goods not produced in Alta California.[92]

The Spanish crown found self-sufficient systems ideal for its Alta California colonies. Within this system, the crown supplied minimal resources, while, ideally, the soldiers, settlers, missionaries, and neophytes would all benefit from the food and goods produced at the missions and in the pueblos. But, according to many accounts by Native peoples and Spanish officials, indigenous people suffered great exploitation under this system. Besides the physical abuses Spanish soldiers and missionaries inflicted on Native laborers, neophyte populations had to absorb the shortfalls during poor harvest years, while missionaries and soldiers consistently received the same amount of food (a fact not included in the narratives of California missions).[93] Priests sometimes permitted Native peoples to leave the missions for a short time to harvest wild foods, hunt, and visit briefly with relatives, but they sent soldiers to bring back those who did not return to the mission after their leave period expired.[94]

Early on in the mission era, the Spanish established a reliance on Native labor instead of working themselves, both within missions and beyond their walls. In return, the Spanish compensated Native laborers with clothing, goods, and food. Missionaries allowed neophytes to work for settlers and soldiers—that is, they "rented" Native people to help construct buildings and harvest fields in exchange for a fee. Increasingly, the soldiers neglected to pay for this labor. Soldiers often received late or no payments from the government in New Spain, contributing to their inability to pay Native workers (or their disinterest in doing so).[95] As for the settlers, during the late eighteenth century many Spanish settlers petitioned the Alta California government for access to the large tracts of land surrounding the missions. The government granted some of these requests, whereas the missionaries demanded that the government deny others in the name of neophytes.[96]

Beginning in 1784, Gov. Pedro Fages granted large tracts of land in Southern California to four retired Spanish soldiers: Manuel Neito, Antonio Yorba, Jose Maria Verdugo, and Juan Jose Dominguez.[97] In the years that followed, the labor of both neophytes and non–mission Native peoples became central in the homes and fields of the emerging Californio class. The large ranches established by missions and settlers unleashed large numbers of cattle and horses in the Los Angeles basin, where the herds of grazing animals went unchecked and grew tremendously. They decimated the natural vegetation in the area and strained Gabrielino-Tongva access to traditional foods, forcing the local indigenous people to turn to towns for access to money and a stable food supply.[98]

Native peoples also worked as domestic servants and did much of the heavy physical labor in California. According to Hackel, the Spanish settlers and soldiers, who referred to themselves as *gente de razón*, (people of reason) insisted that Native peoples did the manual labor because they were inferior, *gente sin razón* (people without reason). This division of labor branded indigenous people as the working class—a distinction that lasted long after the Spanish flag came down in California. Native people filled the role of laborers to earn a subsistence wage in the wake of extreme cultural, economic, and environmental upheaval that made it difficult to continue traditional ways of life.[99]

In Alta California, Spanish settlers and soldiers also pressured the mission system for inexpensive food and goods. Presidios and settlements relied on the grains and meat produced at prosperous California missions such as Mission San Gabriel. Thus missions and Native laborers increasingly served secular needs. The products of Native laborers skilled in specific trades such as carpentry, blacksmithing, shoemaking, soap and candle production, tanning, and weaving contributed to even higher levels of trade between missionaries and soldiers and the foreign ships that frequented the California coast in the early nineteenth century.[100] Seeking the goods produced by Native laborers, foreign merchants engaged in the hide and tallow trade that helped erode Alta California's dependence on New Spain. These exchanges and heavy reliance on Native labor only increased under Mexican rule.

**Emancipation**

Many mission museums today point to secularization—the dissolution of the mission system by the Mexican government—as the cause of the widespread destruction of Native communities. According to this perspective, Native Californians faced abuses from incoming settlers once the Mexican government removed neophytes from the protection of the Spanish padres. Conversely, the historical records, including petitions for emancipation by Native Californians, demonstrate that many neophytes chose to leave the missions on their own accord once the governors of Alta California provided that liberty. Some indigenous peoples petitioned and received small land grants from the government, using their learned skills and years of labor at the missions as evidence of their ability to make the land productive.[101] Many others fled the missions, and following the emancipation decrees issued in the late 1820s, neophytes did not fear punishments for fugitivism. Many left the missions without recourse.[102] To significantly reduce the power of the church, the Mexican governors turned the missions into local churches, replaced missionaries with parish priests, and drastically cut funding for the missions in the 1830s.

Meanwhile, the missionaries did not adequately prepare Native peoples for this shift to life in secular society. According to Jackson and Castillo, "social disruption and psychological dislocation, results of the extreme paternalism practiced at the missions, left the Indians ill-prepared to deal with the new conditions that existed in California following the closing of the missions."[103] Secularization led to the almost immediate collapse of many mission sites. According to interpreters at Mission San Gabriel, "with secularization, with the missions destroyed, with the Indians dispersed to dusty reservations, one of the most idealistic adventures in colonization ever attempted came to a sad end."[104] As this disingenuous sign at Mission San Gabriel put it, the "idealistic adventure" of Spanish colonization abruptly concluded and Native peoples quickly moved into the social periphery.[105] This statement highlights both the simultaneous proliferation of the mission myth and a misunderstanding of basic Native history in the state. In fact, the U.S. government did not establish the first reservation in California until the early 1850s.

As emphasized frequently, interpreters at many contemporary mission sites, including San Gabriel, San Juan Capistrano, and Santa Barbara, promote the mission myth of a romantic Spanish past. By failing to include significant descriptions of Native cultures *before* Spanish settlement and sidestepping the realistic experiences of Native people at the missions, interpreters do not fully address how Spanish colonization affected Native economies and labor systems. Furthermore, mission sites fail to acknowledge the lasting effects that the Spanish missions had on Native communities.

In the midst of the contentious debates over the true nature of Spanish colonization, many contemporary missions continue to represent the history of the sites in a way that promotes a more positive view of California's Spanish past. However, the Native testimonials in Spanish mission records include labor regimens and harsh punishments as some of the many reasons underlying indigenous resistance to the mission system, which are described in the next chapter. The detailed accounts of resistance at the California missions counter benign narratives of Spanish colonization constructed by boosters in the late nineteenth and early twentieth centuries. Yet struggles to resist the Spanish left indelible marks on the region's history.

## Notes

1. Native people living along the California coast felt the greatest impact of Spanish colonization when the Spanish erected a majority of their missions, presidios, and pueblos within a league of the shoreline. Destructive changes to the Native landscape, including the introduction of intrusive plant and animal species, forced Native Californian communities to turn to the missions for support.

2. Sherburne F. Cook, *The Conflict between the California Indian and White Civilization* (1943; repr., Berkeley: University of California Press, 1976); James A. Sandos, *Converting California: Indians and Franciscans in the Missions* (New Haven, CT: Yale University Press, 2004); Steven W. Hackel, *Children of Coyote, Missionaries of Saint Francis: Indian-Spanish Relations in Colonial California, 1769–1850* (Chapel Hill: University of North Carolina Press, 2005), 272–320; Robert H. Jackson and Edward D. Castillo, *Indians, Franciscans, and Spanish Colonization: The Impact of the Mission System on the California Indians* (Albuquerque: University of New Mexico Press, 1995), 50–51, 91–110; George Harwood Phillips, *Chiefs and Challengers: Indian Resistance and Cooperation in Southern California*, 2d ed. (Norman: University of Oklahoma Press, 2014), 27–42; George Harwood Phillips, *Vineyards and Vaqueros: Indian Labor and the Economic Expansion of Southern California, 1771–1877* (Norman: University of Oklahoma Press, 2010), 69–79.

3. Mission La Purísima and San Francisco de Solano are two blatant exceptions to this statement.

4. Hackel, *Children of Coyote*, 273–274. More specifically, the Spanish crown instituted a mercantile system that sought to reduce significantly the costs of operating its colonies while maximizing profits from these overseas territories.

5. Ibid., 280.

6. Ibid., 280–282.

7. City of San Gabriel, *San Gabriel: Historical Walk* (San Gabriel: City Hall, n.d.). Although the city proudly proclaims its heritage in pamphlets and on its website, the actual "Mission District" includes Mission San Gabriel, the Mission Playhouse, and the Old Grapevine Room (referred to as the birthplace of Helen Hunt Jackson's novel *Ramona*).

8. *Ramona* itself represents an opportunity for a discussion of changes in Native labor as a result of the Spanish colonization. Set in the mid-nineteenth century, the main male character in the novel, Alessandro, works alongside other members of his local village as a traveling seasonal sheep-shearer on large ranchos owned by Californios. Native people began to pursue this type of seasonal work after mission secularization in the mid-1830s, using skills obtained from mission life. Mission life in California gave way to the sweeping livestock operations of the Mexican ranchos that relied heavily on Native Californians as their main source of inexpensive labor. From the 1830s to the end of the nineteenth century, the missions and presidios—symbols of the Spanish system that Mexico fought to escape—fell into disrepair and ruin.

9. William McCawley, *The First Angelinos: The Gabrielino Indians of Los Angeles*

126

(Banning, CA: Malki Museum Press, 1996). One of Mission San Gabriel's only lengthy notes on Gabrielino heritage is a framed copy of a single page from a scholarly publication about the Gabrielino-Tongva by William McCawley.

10. Zephyrin Engelhardt, *San Gabriel Mission and the Beginning of Los Angeles* (Chicago: Franciscan Herald Press, 1927), v–5.

11. Robert Heizer, ed., *The Indians of Los Angeles County: Hugo Reid's Letters of 1852* (Highland Park: Southwest Museum, 1968), 7, 107. Mission baptismal records and accounts given by Gabrielino-Tongva people refer to the nearby village where missionaries established Mission San Gabriel with variations of the same name. The name of the village appears in the mission baptismal records as Sibag-na, Sibapet, Sibanga, Sibap, and so on. Other people note that the name of the village was Tobiscanga or Toviscanga.

12. Thomas Workman Temple II, "Founding of San Gabriel Mission," in *The Pride of the Missions: A Documentary History of San Gabriel Mission*, ed. Francis J. Weber (Hong Kong: Libra Press Limited, 1979), 4–5.

13. Temple, "Founding of San Gabriel Mission," 4–5.

14. Jackson and Castillo, *Indians, Franciscans, and Spanish Colonization*, 117–118; Engelhardt, *San Gabriel Mission and the Beginning of Los Angeles*, 60. Grain production increased at the missions, and the number of livestock grew dramatically as well. For example, in 1780 Mission San Gabriel reported 450 head of cattle, 500 sheep, and 100 horses. Forty-five years later, the mission reported having 18,400 head of cattle, 14,000 sheep, and 2,400 horses. Because of these large resources, Mission San Gabriel was able to support its missionary and neophyte populations as well as the soldiers stationed locally. Furthermore, Mission San Gabriel generally produced enough surpluses to help supplement the food needed at other missions, such as Mission San Diego, located on less fertile ground.

15. Jackson and Castillo list the buildings constructed at the missions, including dates and descriptions, in *Indians, Franciscans, and Spanish Colonization*, 145–168.

16. Hackel, *Children of Coyote*, 441. The original name used by the Spanish for units of measurement was *fanegas*. All the data on grain production in Jackson and Castillo, *Indians, Franciscans, and Spanish Colonization*, is in *fanegas*. One *fanegas* is equivalent to 1.5 bushels.

17. Phillips, *Vineyards and Vaqueros*, 68.

18. The Gabrielino-Tongva and missionaries constructed an aqueduct system that brought water into Mission San Gabriel from Wilson Lake.

19. Phillips, *Vineyards and Vaqueros*, 32.

20. Ibid., 15.

21. For examples, see: Hubert Howe Bancroft, *History of California*, Vol. 1 in *The Works of Hubert Howe Bancroft*, Vol. 18 (San Francisco: The History Company, 1886), 72–73.

22. Hackel, *Children of Coyote*, 288–290; Phillips, *Vineyards and Vaqueros*, 32.

23. Phillips, *Vineyards and Vaqueros*, 16–17.

24. Val Ramon, *Mission San Gabriel Arcángel: Commemorative Edition* (Yucaipa,

CA: Photografx Worldwide, 2008), 4.

25. Native peoples occupied the Los Angeles County and Orange County region and much of the rest of California thousands of years before the Spanish missionaries set foot on the North American continent. Alfred L. Kroeber, *Handbook of the Indians of California* (Washington, DC: Government Printing Office, 1928), 620–621; Alfred L. Kroeber, "Shoshonean Dialects of California," *American Archeology and Ethnology* 4 (February 1907): 140–145; Bernice Eastman Johnston, *California's Gabrielino Indians* (Los Angeles: Southwest Museum, 1962). McCawley updated much of what Johnston wrote to appeal to a more scholarly audience.

26. McCawley, *First Angelinos*, 1–4.

27. Ibid., 89; Kroeber, *Handbook of the Indians of California*, 620–621.

28. McCawley, *First Angelinos*, 25. The Gabrielino-Tongva resided in many individual communities with populations that ranged from fifty to over two hundred people. A single village generally consisted of one or more ancestral bloodlines within individual family units.

29. Lowell J. Bean, *Mukat's People: The Cahuilla of Southern California* (Berkeley: University of California Press, 1972), 151–153.

30. Ibid., 85, 151–153.

31. Geronimo Boscana, *Chinigchinich: A Revised and Annotated Version of Alfred Robinson's Translation of Father Gerónimo Boscana's Historical Account of the Belief, Usages, Custom and Extravagancies of the Indians of This Mission of San Juan Capistrano Called the Acagchemem Tribe*, ed. Phil Townsend Hanna (1933; repr., Banning, CA: Malki Museum Press, 1978), 41–44; Kroeber, *Handbook of the Indians of California*, 622–627; McCawley, *First Angelinos*, 23.

32. McCawley, *First Angelinos*, 91–93; Heizer, *Indians of Los Angeles County*, 19–21.

33. Bean, *Mukat's People*, 69–70.

34. McCawley, *First Angelinos*, 99–103.

35. Steven W. Hackel, "The Staff of Leadership: Indian Authority in the Missions of Alta California," *William and Mary Quarterly* 54 (April 1997): 347–376; Phillips, *Chiefs and Challengers*, 45–47, 57.

36. Ramon, *Mission San Gabriel Arcángel*, 3.

37. Ibid. 4.

38. McCawley, *First Angelinos*, 25–26.

39. Phillips, *Vineyards and Vaqueros*, 51.

40. Helen McCarthy provided an in-depth analysis of the importance of acorns as a Native food source in "Managing Oaks and the Acorn Crop," in *Before the Wilderness: Environmental Management by Native Californians*, ed. Thomas C. Blackburn and Kat Anderson (Menlo Park, CA: Ballena Press, 1993), 213–228.

41. Heizer, *Indians of Los Angeles County*, 43–45; McCawley, *First Angelinos*, 111–117.

42. McCawley, *First Angelinos*, 76–82.

43. McCawley included a discussion of all of the resources available to the Gabrielino-Tongva within their territory in *First Angelinos*, 115–140.

44. Heizer, *Indians of Los Angeles County*, 43–44; Bean, *Mukat's People*, 123; McCawley,

*First Angelinos,* 111–112; Kroeber, *Handbook of the Indians of California,* 628–629. Island Gabrielino quarried soapstone and traded it with mainland Gabrielino and other indigenous people throughout the region who used the stone extensively to make cooking utensils, pots, pipes, and a variety of other goods.

45. Bean, *Mukat's People,* 151–159; McCawley, *First Angelinos,* 113–115. To regulate prices and keep demand steady, many Native communities in Southern California destroyed goods and beads during certain ceremonial activities, such as the Mourning Ceremony.

46. Boscana, *Chinigchinich,* 2–247. Religion was extremely important to many Gabrielino-Tongva people, who turned to their spiritual beliefs to define nearly every aspect of life, including economics, morality, politics, law, and life events. *Chinigchinich,* the religion of the Gabrielino-Tongva people at the point of Spanish contact, developed over time and reflected influences from the Chumash *'antap-yovaar* religion, traditions of the earlier Uto-Aztecan speakers in the region, and possibly Christianity. The Gabrielino in general took care to keep aspects of their religion private. Despite this, scholars do know some details about Gabrielino-Tongva religious beliefs, based on Geronimo Boscana's writings on the Juaneño.

47. Phillips, *Vineyards and Vaqueros,* 52.

48. Hackel, *Children of Coyote,* 280–281.

49. For example, communities in Southern California often used rattles from dried gourds while they sang, and some groups in northern and central California used flutes to accompany their song and dance.

50. Joseph Halpin, "Musical Activities and Ceremonies at Mission Santa Clara de Asís," *California Historical Quarterly* 50 (1971): 35–42; James A. Sandos, "Identity through Music: Choristers at Mission San Jose and San Juan Bautista," in *Alta California: Peoples in Motion, Identities in Formation, 1769–1850,* ed. Steven W. Hackel (Berkeley: University of California Press, published for the Huntington-USC Institute on California and the West, 2010), 111–128.

51. Halpin, "Musical Activities and Ceremonies at Mission Santa Clara de Asís," 35. Sandos examined Franciscan perspectives on dancing in *Converting California,* 167–168.

52. Sandos, *Converting California,* xvi–xv.

53. Ibid., 9–10.

54. Displays at several contemporary mission museums contain nails, horseshoes, adobe bricks, red roofing tiles, baskets, paintings, wine vats, and other materials that symbolize the dramatized labor by Native people at the "idyllic" California missions. This statement is based on observations of displays at the San Diego, San Gabriel, San Juan Capistrano, Santa Barbara, and San Juan Bautista missions from 2009 to 2015.

55. Edward Alexander and Mary Alexander, *Museums in Motion: An Introduction to the History and Function of Museums,* 2d ed. (Lanham, MD: AltaMira Press, 2007), 263.

56. Norman Neuerburg countered this perspective in "The Indian Via Crucis from Mission San Fernando: An Historical Exposition," special issue, *Southern California*

*Quarterly* 79 (fall 1997): 329–382; George Harwood Phillips, "Indian Paintings from Mission San Fernando: An Historical Interpretation," *Journal of California Anthropology* 3 (summer 1976): 96–100; George Harwood Phillips, "The Stations of the Cross: Revisited, Reconsidered, and Revised (Sort of)," *Boletín* 24 (2007):76–87; Lisbeth Haas, *Saints and Citizens: Indigenous Histories of Colonial Missions and Mexican California* (Berkeley: University of California Press, 2014), 108–115.

57. Tony Pinto, "All of Us Know about Slavery at the Missions," in *The Missions of California: A Legacy of Genocide*, ed. Rupert Costo and Jeannette Henry Costo (San Francisco: Indian Historian Press, 1987), 139.

58. Hackel, *Children of Coyote,* 281.

59. Sandos, *Converting California*, 107–108.

60. Ibid.

61. Costo and Costo, *Missions of California,* 136, 139, 141–142, 145–146, 154–155.

62. Pinto, "All of Us Know about Slavery at the Missions," 139.

63. Phillips, *Vineyards and Vaqueros,* 21. According to Phillips, "the missions concentrating on agriculture organized a different kind of workforce than did those emphasizing stock raising" (21).

64. Julia Bogany, personal communication with author, March 13, 2015.

65. Phillips, *Vineyards and Vaqueros,* 15.

66. Bogany, personal communication.

67. Raymond C. Kammerer, *Mission Life at San Juan Capistrano* (Cincinnati: KM Communications, 1991), 14.

68. Ibid., 47–48. Scholars agree that Hackel provided a more accurate account of mission life in *Children of Coyote,* 283–284.

69. Hackel, *Children of Coyote,* 283–284.

70. Bogany, personal communication.

71. Jackson and Castillo provide a detailed account of grain production and livestock at select missions in *Indians, Franciscans, and Spanish Colonization*, 113–131.

72. Ibid., 38–39.

73. Phillips, *Vineyards and Vaqueros,* 84–89.

74. Hackel, *Children of Coyote,* 283–284.

75. Spicer and Hackel separately address punishment and labor. Edward H. Spicer, *Cycles of Conquest: The Impact of Spain, Mexico, and the United States on the Indians of the Southwest, 1533–1960* (Tucson: University of Arizona Press, 1962), 294–295; Hackel, *Children of Coyote,* 280–309.

76. Jackson and Castillo, *Indians, Franciscans, and Spanish Colonization*, 83–84.

77. This image can be found in David Rickman, *California Missions Coloring Book* (New York: Dover Publications, 1992).

78. Maynard Geiger, *The Indians of Mission Santa Bárbara*, 2d ed. (Santa Barbara: Franciscan Friars, 2010), 2.

79. Geiger, *Indians of Mission Santa Bárbara*, 32.

80. Ibid., 36.

81. Ibid., 39; Doyce B. Nunis Jr. and Edward D. Castillo, "California Mission

Indians: Two Perspectives," *California History* 70 (1991): 206–215. Mission era "apologists" is a term Castillo used to classify scholars who frequently focused on the positive attributes of the Spanish missions and ignored or discounted negative components of the system.

82. Hackel, *Children of Coyote*, 282–283.

83. Cook, *Conflict between the California Indian and White Civilization*, 98–100; Phillips, *Vineyards and Vaqueros*, 18.

84. Phillips, *Vineyards and Vaqueros*, 18.

85. Cook, *Conflict between the California Indian and White Civilization*, 99.

86. Ibid., 100.

87. Ibid., 101.

88. Sandos, *Converting California*, 8–11.

89. Conversation with long-time Mission San Gabriel volunteer curator and docent. February, 2014.

90. Terry G. Jordan, *North American Cattle-Ranching Frontiers: Origins, Diffusion, and Differentiation* (Albuquerque: University of New Mexico Press, 1993), 7–35.

91. Phillips, *Vineyards and Vaqueros*, 144.

92. Jackson and Castillo, *Indians, Franciscans, and Spanish Colonization*, 126–127; Jordan, *North American Cattle-Ranching Frontiers*, 161–165.

93. Jackson and Castillo, *Indians, Franciscans, and Spanish Colonization*, 26–29. In times of shortfalls, missionaries still expected Native laborers to produce the same quantities, even though they had less nourishment.

94. Phillips, *Vineyards and Vaqueros*, 66.

95. Jackson and Castillo, *Indians, Franciscans, and Spanish Colonization*, 26–29.

96. Engelhardt, *San Gabriel Mission and the Beginning of Los Angeles*, 62–68.

97. J. J. Warner, Benjamin Hayes, and J. P. Widney, *An Historical Sketch of Los Angeles County: From the Spanish Occupancy, by the Founding of Mission San Gabriel Arcángel, September 8, 1771, to July 4, 1876* (Los Angeles: Mirror Printing, Ruling and Binding House, 1876), 8–10. Landscapes in Southern California still hold the names of some of these early Spanish land grants.

98. Ibid.

99. Hackel, *Children of Coyote*, 318–320.

100. Ibid., 272–277.

101. Haas, *Saints and Citizens*, 166–172.

102. Hackel, *Children of Coyote*, 369–381.

103. Jackson and Castillo, *Indians, Franciscans, and Spanish Colonization*, 53.

104. Excerpt from a sign in the museum at Mission San Gabriel.

105. Ibid.

# 5

# *Resistance at the California Missions*

That there was so little active hostility on the part of the savage tribes, that they looked so kindly as they did to the ways and restraints of the new life, is the strongest possible proof that the methods of the friars in dealing with them must have been both wise and humane.
—Helen Hunt Jackson, *Glimpses of California and the Missions* (ca. 1883)

It is something to be grateful for to Almighty God that one of the Fathers can give you an account of what happened. That certainly was not the intention of those wicked men. They meant to exterminate the entire white population and the Fathers in particular.
— Vicente Fuster, as quoted in, *Lands of Promise and Despair: Chronicles of Early California, 1535–1864* (1775)

The mission myth constructed and popularized in the twentieth century does not include discussions of indigenous peoples during Spanish colonization from *Native* perspectives. Interpretations at many contemporary California missions marginalize Native points of view and often neglect to present a clear understanding of the local indigenous peoples, as exemplified in the previous discussion of labor at the missions. It is nearly impossible to understand Native experiences within the mission system and their negotiation of these Spanish institutions without also having a basic understanding of the religious beliefs, customs, and tribal histories that shaped Native peoples' worldviews.[1] A case study of the Kumeyaay, who populated the region surrounding Mission San Diego, is an example of the skewed presentations of Spanish colonization promoted by contemporary California missions, especially when dealing with controversial topics including resistance, abuse, and fugitivism.[2] An analysis of the Kumeyaay and their interaction with the Spanish before and after settlement, focusing specifically on the motives behind key disputes in mission history such as the 1775 San Diego revolt, serves to illuminate the divide between Native knowledge, scholarly understanding, and romanticized portrayals of mission history still common in popular culture.

## The Kumeyaay: A Cultural Profile

Patrons who visit many of the California missions leave with a distorted understanding of the past, tinged by the biased history presented by promoters of "benevolent" Spanish colonization. Interpretations of history at Mission San Diego reflect the mission myth, as they focus on the site's history but oversimplify the local Kumeyaay people and their frequently contentious relationship with the Spanish. To insert a Native presence at the mission today, Kumeyaay people erected a life-size traditional dome-shaped house (an 'ewaa) in the mission's garden. While this structure brings a physical Native presence to the site, it lacks adequate interpretation and contextualization of Kumeyaay interactions with and responses to the Spanish during the mission era. Placards at the mission inform people that the Kumeyaay were hunters and gatherers who lived simple lives. Their lives were so simple, in fact, they had never seen cloth before, but instead used natural material such as grass, seashells, and stains to cover their bodies. They lived in crude huts constructed of brush and other nonpermanent materials. And because they did not have a sense of land ownership, the Kumeyaay lived as nomads, moving from place to place with the seasons.[3]

Although some of this information is accurate in its most basic sense, the lack of any further detail about these people and their continued existence contributes to the notion that Native people lived "primitively" with little social development. In reality, the Kumeyaay had long-established cultural histories with rich social and religious traditions. They resided in the greater San Diego region for centuries before European contact.[4] Some archeologists and anthropologists theorize that they originally emerged from a much larger society. This larger group occupied a vast territory that spanned north to the current-day Utah-Arizona border, east to Flagstaff, Arizona, and southwest to San Diego, Baja California, and portions of Sonora, Mexico.[5] Archeological evidence suggests that Kumeyaay ancestors constantly migrated to find more abundant food and better accommodations for their growing population, especially as climate and water sources shifted.[6] Between 1000 and 1500 C.E., these Yuman speakers migrated to the southwestern coastal regions of the described territory.[7] Scholars theorize that the complex organization and kinship structure of Kumeyaay culture developed and matured during this period.[8]

Kumeyaay conceptions of property allowed for mobility between territories. According to George Phillips, "the Kumeyaay exhibited a very flexible kinship system in that they often allowed individuals without any clear-cut societal identity to reside in their villages as long as they remained useful."[9] People from one village could hunt on the property of another but could not settle on it. This structure demonstrated a distinct concept of territorial possession.[10] It also suggests why the Kumeyaay initially cooperated with the Spanish but grew hostile once the foreigners built settlements and stopped trading goods with local people. Close kinship relationships over a vast territory permitted people within one family or village to take up residence with kinfolk in another village, no matter the distance.[11] This flexibility encouraged sharing between regions and assisted in trade relations important during years of drought. The geographic diversity in Kumeyaay territory also allowed for a more varied food supply throughout the changing seasons.[12] These relationships may have helped coastal Kumeyaay relocate to inland villages once the Spanish began to colonize the region.

The Kumeyaay maintained a flexible and semimobile society to accommodate a wide variety of hunting, gathering, and plant husbandry. The relatively short distances between the mountain, valley, and coastal regions within their territory also helped the Kumeyaay people to maintain a varied diet. Food redistribution was an important aspect of Kumeyaay society as well. The Kumeyaay managed their environment by planting seeds and utilizing controlled burns to stimulate plant growth for the future. The Kumeyaay also fished extensively and hunted as a major food source. Wild game became increasingly scarce as droughts reduced water supplies and Spanish livestock overgrazed the land in the late eighteenth century.[13] Native peoples responded to drought and the strain on the population in several ways. They dispersed all able-bodied members of the community to find food, adopted infanticide and abortion practices in extreme cases, and turned to the mission for assistance after Spanish colonization.[14]

According to anthropologist Florence Shipek, the Kumeyaay experienced a two-decade period of abundant rainfall before Spanish settlement began. An extended period of drought followed this time of plenty. The strain of Spanish settlement and drought severely damaged Native food supplies and restricted population growth.[15] Low food production in the San Diego area hindered the development of the mission. Meanwhile, both the Spanish and Kumeyaay relied on rainwater and a restricted food supply for sustenance in the late eighteenth century. Competition over scarce water and food supplies created tensions between the Kumeyaay and the intruding foreigners.[16] Interpretations at Mission San Diego do not engage many of these important details that highlight the ways Kumeyaay experiences in the years before colonization informed their interactions with the Spanish.

## The Seeds of Resistance

Interpreters leave in the shadows other important aspects of Native life at the mission as well. For example, displays at the historic site tell visitors that the missionaries relocated the mission to find a better water supply. While it is true that the missionaries originally founded the mission in a poorly irrigated location, presentations at the mission fail to mention that the missionaries had difficulties finding converts at the original mission site and moved the mission closer to larger Kumeyaay villages.[17] The padres also relocated the mission to put greater distance between neophytes and soldiers at the presidio who assaulted Native women. These attacks prompted anger toward the missionaries who failed to protect the women and lacked power to punish the soldiers. Soldiers who wanted to silence witnesses also threatened, beat, and punished Native peoples that witnessed these assaults.[18] The mission does not discuss any of this information, documentation of which can all be found in published letters by priests, in scholarly analyses, and contemporary Native testimonials. Rather, mission interpreters avoid addressing motives for resistance prompted by Spanish soldiers and missionaries that reflect negatively on missionization.

Just as Charles Fletcher Lummis strained to reconcile Native resistance to Spanish colonization in his booster writings, contemporary mission interpreters also struggle with themes of resistance and social control in their museum displays.[19] Inevitably, most mission sites respond much like Lummis by focusing on the heroism of the missionaries in the face of danger, blaming fringe groups of Native peoples for uprisings, or completely skirting resistance and obvious examples of indigenous discontent with the mission system. Romanticized mission mythology that heralds Spanish colonizers as benign intermediaries in the lives of Native peoples falters when contrasted with historical accounts of forced assimilation and Native resistance at the California missions.

At Mission San Diego, interpreters inform visitors that the Kumeyaay were peaceful and had a good relationship with the mission. These presentations do not acknowledge that the Kumeyaay were displeased with the Spanish when they first arrived in San Diego. The Spanish encountered Native resistance on several separate occasions, beginning with initial contact and continuing intermittently until mission secularization.[20] Even after secularization, many Native communities resisted foreigners. For example, they raided ranches for livestock to rebuild their economy and hinder the success of Mexican and Euro-American settlers in the region.

Native peoples employed policies of resistance, withdrawal, or cooperation when outsiders threatened their sovereignty, unity, or cultural integrity. Phillips argues that individual Native communities resisted foreigners for many reasons, but central to every response was "the preservation of political sovereignty, corporate unity, and cultural integrity."[21] Forms of resistance varied from total revolts in which local indigenous people assassinated missionaries, to nonviolent resistance wherein people fled the mission and moved inland, ideally outside the Spanish reach.[22] Contemporary mission narratives ignore potential motives for resistance such as mistreatment at the hands of the Spanish, sexual abuse, cultural conflicts, disease, punishment, and the unrelenting deaths that stalked Native communities after contact.

## The Myth of the Founding of Mission San Diego

The mission myth highlights joyful interactions between Europeans and Native peoples. However, early explorers documented contentious encounters between the Spaniards and indigenous peoples in some of their first writings from Alta California. For example, on September 28, 1542, Juan Rodriguez Cabrillo anchored in San Diego Bay, formally founding Alta California in the name of Spain. Many Native people fled the Spanish, but some met Cabrillo and his men on the beach. They informed Cabrillo, through gesturing, that other Spaniards had traveled inland and had attacked many Native peoples. These actions, most likely connected with expeditions led by Francisco Vázquez de Coronado, created an atmosphere of fear and distrust of the Spanish among indigenous communities. That night, local Kumeyaay people attacked and wounded three Spanish sailors who went ashore to fish.[23] Despite this foray, Cabrillo reported that his men did not respond with violence, although they did take two Native boys with them to use as translators as they continued north along the California coast.[24] The sailors traded food and beads with the indigenous people to show their "peaceful" intentions.[25] And yet these contentious interactions negatively tinged Kumeyaay responses to Spanish explorers for generations.

Naval voyages to Alta California died down between the early 1600s and 1760s in response to the Spanish discovery that the area lacked mineral riches. Native Californians saw Spaniards less often and usually only in emergencies when the sailors were ill or desperately needed provisions. Exploration began again in the late eighteenth century when the Spanish, responding to foreign interest in California, instituted a plan to settle their northern frontier. Under Father Junípero Serra, the Spanish established the first mission in Alta California at San Diego.[26]

Many contemporary mission narratives focus on Serra and his important

136

role as the founder of the Alta California mission system. Nearly all of the modern mission sites venerate Serra, declared a saint in September 2015, as the "Apostle of California."[27] They honor him with statues in which Serra stands alone or has a Native child under his arm. Although small in stature, Serra was a very determined man who worked feverishly to establish mission settlements throughout Alta California.[28] The padre raised the cross at the first San Diego mission on July 16, 1769, but he faced resistance from the Kumeyaay people. Serra labored to find Native converts, but language and cultural barriers between the missionaries and Kumeyaay made communication, let alone conversion, difficult.[29]

Curious people from local villages visited the temporary site frequently.[30] At first, many Native peoples cooperated with the Spanish. But as the newcomers established permanent camps and pressured indigenous communities for food without reciprocating in kind, local people began to resist.[31] And then on August 15, 1769, just one month after Serra raised the cross at the Spanish settlement, Kumeyaay men attacked the site. They stripped the clothes off the sick and took whatever else they wanted. According to Steven W. Hackel, in their raid the Kumeyaay sought to humiliate the weak Spanish encampment.[32] As stated by Serra, the Kumeyaay, seeing the number of sick and dying sailors, chose to attack suddenly when the mission only had four soldiers on guard. A skirmish began after soldiers returned to the site. Both Spaniards and indigenous people were injured during the skirmish, but Serra noted that "the one worst hurt was a young Spanish lad. . . . At first shot he darted into my hut, spouting so much blood at the mouth and from his temples, that I had hardly time to absolve him and help him to meet his end."[33] The padre recalled that the fighting stopped when the Native peoples realized how many of their own were injured. Serra did not believe the Spanish killed any indigenous people in this fight, which meant that the missionaries could still baptize them and bring them into the mission fold.[34] After violent encounters between indigenous peoples and the Spanish newcomers, Native peoples frequently kept their distance from Spanish settlements.[35]

Along with skirting instances of early Native resistance against the Spanish, mission interpreters do not discuss the problems missionaries encountered in their efforts to convert Kumeyaay people to Christianity; they concentrate instead on the positive intentions of the padres. For example, Serra faced several setbacks in his attempts to perform his first baptism in Alta California. Because the Spanish did not offer any improvements on the Kumeyaay economy, culture, and religion during the first years of colonization, the Kumeyaay rejected Spanish advances. After trying for months with no success, Serra eventually communicated sufficiently enough with the local Kumeyaay to express his desire to baptize a baby. Soon thereafter, a group of people came to the temporary mission, one cradling a baby, but the baby's nervous parents ran away with the child almost as soon as the padre tried to baptize the child.[36]

These actions contradicted Serra's earlier recorded encounters with Native peoples in Alta California while traveling on the expedition to San Diego. Serra recalled that "they [the Indians] came out to meet us both along the roads and at our camping places. They displayed the fullest confidence and assurance just as if we had been lifelong friends."[37] However, the contentious interactions between the two groups lead to increased tension and distance. Juan Crespí described other hostile exchanges with Native populations. He reported that twenty-nine indigenous people followed his expedition for three days, taunting the Spanish with gestures and eventually engaging them in a brief fight.[38] After traveling overland from San Francisco to San Diego, Crespí noted that "all this land [Alta California] is populated with a large number of Indians who are gentle, generous, and well-formed. The most savage natives that we have found are those of San Diego and a circle in the same neighborhood."[39] Fear of continued Native attacks plagued residents at the young San Diego mission. The Kumeyaay people were not happy that the Spanish had settled within their territory and expressed their unhappiness through raids in which Native peoples from local villages took clothing and valuables from the site.[40]

Examining these events from a Kumeyaay perspective reveals that they did not attack the Spanish without motivation. The Kumeyaay resided in an environmentally diverse area and relied on many different types of food found throughout the region. Luis Jayme, a priest at Mission San Diego, observed in a letter written on October 17, 1772, that rumors of Spanish soldiers who raped and mistreated Native women prompted many indigenous people to move further inland and forego their coastal food supply.[41] Thus Spanish actions encouraged Kumeyaay attacks and resistance to priestly efforts to baptize members of the community. In August 1774, the Spanish relocated Mission San Diego further inland near a large Kumeyaay village.

### The Kumeyaay Revolt

In conjunction with poor soil and inadequate irrigation sources at the original mission site, missionaries also moved their settlement further inland to put distance between neophytes and soldiers at the presidio. The padres allowed many neophytes to live outside of the mission complex while they struggled to reap successful harvests. Outside of the mission, neophytes collected food and lived with nonconverted communities.[42] Baptized Kumeyaay people maintained strong ties with their culture and heritage through these interactions. At the same time, the padres in charge of Mission San Diego, Luis Jayme and Vicente Fuster, increased their efforts to convert indigenous peoples in villages further inland. Many Native people who had already relocated to the interior likely did not appreciate Spanish encroachment further inland. Increased contact between the Spanish and indigenous peoples created hostilities that erupted in violence in November 1775.[43] The San Diego revolt led by the Kumeyaay people was one of the largest and most damaging attacks against a single mission in Spanish California history.

Today, students and visitors sitting in the restored Mission San Diego chapel learn that on November 5, 1775, a large group of Native people, ranging in numbers from 400 to 600, attacked the new fragile inland mission, which was made of brush, timber, and small portions of adobe.[44] After sacking the mission of valuables, the attackers burned it to the ground and killed Jayme in the midst of the fury. The purpose of recounting this story is not to describe Native discontent with the mission. Rather, it serves as a segue to a discussion of the "sacrifice" of Jayme, whom the mission champions as California's first martyr. Tour groups are told this story in the church so that the docents can show them Jayme's eternal flame, which burns in front of the alter in the Mission San Diego chapel. Mission booklets that describe the attack say that "perhaps a raid on the mission for the purposes of stealing clothing, ornaments, and articles, developed into an open attack. . . . The Indians broke open vestments cases and dispatched their women to the mountains with the plunder. They then began to set fire to the guardhouse, church, and living quarters."[45] Native people appear in these narratives as a wild horde of attackers seemingly without an organized purpose.

After a brief trip into the mission museum, patrons discover the underlying causes of the revolt according to mission interpreters. The label next to a depiction of the last moments of Jayme's life notes that the people who attacked the mission primarily came to take food, clothing, and valuables. But the assailants lost sight of their initial goal. In a furry, they sacked the mission and engaged in a total revolt, destroying the mission. They killed three Spanish men, including Jayme, who met his killers with the greeting "Love God, my children." Mission publications note that Jayme did not hide from the revolt as Fuster and some soldiers had done. Instead, Jayme approached his attackers, who took his clothes, beat him, and shot him with arrows several times. Many historical records indicate that neophytes found the body of the thirty-five-year-old missionary the next morning near the river—only recognizable by his "sacred hands."[46]

Many scholars active in the polemical debate over Spanish treatment of Native peoples during the mission era have varying interpretations of the ultimate reasons behind the attack in November 1775. Scholars Rose Marie Beebe and Robert M. Senkewicz write that Kumeyaay leaders rallied support for the attack based on their rejection of the culturally destructive practices of Spanish padres and soldiers at the mission and the presidio.[47] James Sandos and Richard Carrico more specifically argue that the revolt emerged from Native and Spanish competition over access to the scarce food supply, anger toward the Spanish soldiers who raped women, and Spanish encroachment on Native land.[48] On the other hand, supporters of the mission argue that the revolt began as a raid for food and valuables that evolved into violence.[49] Although the Native assailants did raid the mission complex for valuables, accounts of the attack by those present noted undoubtedly that the raiders came prepared for a violent revolt.

Scholars most commonly point to the Kumeyaay people's unhappiness with Spanish livestock destroying Native food sources as a direct cause of the revolt. Lazy soldiers failed to pen their livestock, and the animals indiscriminately ate native plants, including the grasses that were staples in the Kumeyaay diet. Carrico contends that Spanish soldiers allowed their cattle to graze on Native fields and grasslands, which drove the Kumeyaay people to take the livestock—an act that frequently resulted in punishment from Spanish officials. Carrico also argues that the Kumeyaay revolted because they feared being captured by the Spanish and forced to work at the missions.[50] Finally, Native people resented Spanish officials who neglected to adequately punish soldiers who raped women in Native villages. According to Sandos, the Kumeyaay viewed the proclaimed moral supremacy of the genté de razon as hypocritical. In the eyes of many indigenous people, Spanish soldiers continually behaved immorally and engaged in activities that countered the teachings of the padres. This led some Kumeyaay to believe that Christianity offered no improvement to their current belief structure. They called for removal of the Spanish from the region through revolt.[51]

Local Native leaders began planning the revolt months in advance. In the weeks leading up to it, the Kumeyaay people from nearby villages sought baptism in greater numbers than ever before. The overwhelming number of converts in a short time span forced the padres to allow large numbers of new neophytes to live outside of the mission where their Native cultures and religion continued to be main components of their daily lives. Nearly 100 people joined the mission in November alone. The new converts used the information they learned about the mission and its operations in planning many aspects of the attack, including the day and time.[52]

According to a variety of sources, the number of indigenous people reportedly participating in the revolt varies from between 600 and 1,000, as opposed to the lower figures reported by mission interpreters.[53] The attackers originally planned to use light from the full moon to assault the mission complex and the presidio simultaneously on the night of November 4, 1775. Although they successfully attacked the mission complex, no such attack occurred at the presidio.[54] The Kumeyaay waiting to assault the presidio abandoned their plan and joined the attack on the mission when they realized that the revolt at the mission had begun earlier than expected. They worried that the presidio soldiers had time to prepare for their impending assault. However, the soldiers remained unaware of the revolt until the next morning when survivors of the mission attack arrived at the presidio for protection.[55]

Fuster recounted the attack in a letter to Serra that highlights a clearly violent intent on the side of the indigenous attackers. The padre observes that "it is something to be grateful for to Almighty God that one of the Fathers can give you an account of what happened. That certainly was not the intention of those wicked men. They meant to exterminate the entire white population and the Fathers in particular."[56] Fuster details the violent scene in which Native people sacked the mission, burned the complex to the ground, and simultaneously attacked those living at the site and a near-by neophyte village. He also describes the large number of arrows shot at him and others at the mission to support his inference that Native peoples intended to stage a violent revolt.[57] The bloody and battered condition of Jayme's body also suggests that the attackers felt extreme anger toward the Spanish and the mission system. Fuster recalls that Jayme was "disfigured from head to foot, and I could see that his death had been cruel beyond description and to the fullest satisfaction of the barbarians." The attackers humiliated Jayme. They stripped his body "even to his undergarments around his middle. His chest and body were riddled through with countless jabs they had given him, and his face was one giant bruise from the clubbing and stoning it had suffered."[58] Clearly, Jayme was not an unintended casualty of this revolt. More explicitly, the Kumeyaay most likely saw him as a symbol of the system they sought to destroy.

In the end, the attackers killed three people: Jayme, a blacksmith, and a carpenter, and they injured numerous others, including Fuster. In the wake of the revolt, neophytes and missionaries in the region moved to the presidio for protection. Other missionaries and Spanish officials also relocated to the presidio, including expedition leader Fermín Francisco de Lasuén. The attack at Mission San Diego forced him to halt construction on nearby Mission San Juan Capistrano, which had begun only one week before the revolt.[59] The destruction of Mission San Diego and the abandonment of Mission San Juan Capistrano worried Serra, who advocated their quick reestablishment.[60]

Meanwhile, the troubling causes of the revolt and the details of the attack do not mesh well with mission mythology that praises Spanish colonizers. Descriptions of lazy, brutal, and immoral Spanish soldiers also resemble the Spanish "black legend" that promoters such as Lummis tried to dispel in the early twentieth century.

A formal investigation into the revolt conducted by officials, including Lieut. Francisco Ortega, resulted in two brothers, Francisco and Carlos, being charged with inciting the rebellion.[61] Francisco and Carlos were local Kumeyaay village leaders accused of thievery for taking fish and seeds from an unbaptized elderly women. According to Hackel, the two probably believed they were entitled to these goods. They interpreted attempts from the Spanish to exercise authority outside of the mission complex as a threat to their leadership. The brothers, along with five other neophytes, fled the mission and incited neophyte and gentile communities to join their resistance effort.[62] Phillips believes these two leaders "had come to the conclusion that Christianity was detrimental to Indian interests and sought to rid the region of its propagators." In doing so, they gained many allies among the Southern Kumeyaay.[63] Spanish abuses of Native peoples contributed to the large company that these two leaders were able to assemble against the mission.

In his report, Ortega recounted that people from over a dozen Christian and non-Christian villages participated in the revolt. The role of the neophytes living at the mission is unclear. Some sources believe the attackers used force to restrict neophyte involvement, while Lasuén and fellow expedition leader Juan Bautista de Anza postulated that the neophytes living at the mission took an active role in the revolt.[64] For example, Anza, in a January 1776 journal entry, speculates that Native peoples residing at the mission stole valuables from the church hours before the revolt started. He also contends that converts set fire to the mission before leaders sounded the war cry that officially began the attack.[65]

Spanish officials who analyzed the revolt found a range of other possible motives. Francisco Palóu attributed the attack to workings of the devil "because the missionaries, with their fervent zeal and apostolic labors, were steadily lessening his following, and little by little banishing heathenism from the neighborhood of the port of San Diego, [the devil] found a means to put a stop to these spiritual conquests." He argued that a malevolent Satan, "influenced a few of the new Christians not yet confirmed in the Faith to rebel, destroy the mission, and take the lives of the missionary fathers and soldiers who were guarding and defending him."[66] Interpreting what Palóu wrote, it is apparent that increased conversion efforts sparked a response against the Spanish assault on Kumeyaay religion and culture. In Palóu's statement though, mission officials attempt to place blame for the attack on outside forces. These efforts continue today in mission museums that stand as symbols of California's golden past and in the popular mission myth that paints Spanish colonization as a wholly positive influence in the region.

Many inconsistencies exist between Mission San Diego's interpretation of the revolt in November 1775 and eye witness accounts, records left by Spanish officials, and analyses of the event by contemporary scholars. Mission publications neglect to describe the Native attacks that preceded the revolt. They also fail to discuss the continued threats and rumors of other planned incursions in San Diego after 1775. More recently attributed causes of the revolt determined by Mission San Diego include the two Native leaders, noting that "Father Jayme and the other Franciscan Missionaries had great rapport with the Kumeyaay. . . . Unfortunately, two of the mission . . . Indians became dissatisfied with the regulations and conditions established by the Spanish authorities, and they incited hundreds of Indians in remote villages to riot."[67] To state that the discontent of merely two people caused hundreds to revolt is overly simplistic, minimizes wider discontent with Spanish colonization, and at least begs the question of what the kind of influence these two leaders wielded over so many "remote" communities to incite them to revolt. This source also notes that the padres rebuilt the mission in the same location, but to the specifications of a military fort because they worried about the possibilities of another attack.[68] Building a reinforced mission may seem excessive when, according to current public interpretations, Native people only attacked the mission once and the Spanish otherwise coexisted peacefully with indigenous peoples.

In reality, the Kumeyaay attacked the Spanish several times in San Diego after their arrival. Few padres described the local indigenous peoples as passive or submissive.[69] But these narratives do not fit into the utopian imagery promoters built around the Spanish era. To better situate Native people into this constructed past, contemporary signs at Mission San Diego tell visitors that "the padres encouraged the observance of many feast days and as a result, processions, fiestas, games, and celebrations were frequent." The quiet, serene atmosphere cultivated at current mission sites continues to encourage a vision of the Spanish missions that is incongruent with the harsh realities faced by Native people at these colonial institutions.

## Challenging Mission Representations of Resistance

Most striking in contemporary interpretations of the revolt is the claim that Mission San Diego was the only mission attacked by indigenous people. In fact, Native peoples attacked several missions throughout Alta California and the Southwest from the beginning of foreign colonization to the end of Spanish rule in the 1820s. And they continued to attack Mexican and Euro-American settlements for several more decades to resist their presence on Native lands. Scholars studied many revolts in California alone, specifically focusing on the attempted revolt at Mission San Gabriel in 1785 and the Chumash revolt in the Santa Barbara area in 1824. Furthermore, written documents by Spanish missionaries, soldiers, and officials described smaller attacks and resistance movements at nearly every mission in California from the late eighteenth to early nineteenth century.[70]

Interpreters at Mission San Gabriel and San Diego present similar misinformation and omissions about resistance efforts during the Spanish period. Presentations at San Gabriel provide little discussion about the attempted rebellion against the Spanish. The San Gabriel mission museum briefly mentions Toypurina, the "leader of the aborted Indian rebellion of 1785," whom Father Miguel Sanchez pardoned and baptized as Regina Josefa in 1787. They do not discuss or develop Toypurina's significant role in the Gabrielino community, past and present. Nor do interpreters in their popular presentations address the trials surrounding Toypurina's revolt. The mission also ignores important components of Native culture, including shamanism, despite its relevance to the revolt. Instead, popular depictions of Toypurina label her "a sorceress, medicine woman and witch."[71] Focusing on the realistic role of religion and shamanism in Gabrielino-Tongva society brings to light Toypurina's role as a powerful leader and female shaman.[72] Toypurina did not instigate calls for rebellion, but joined the movement later. Just as with the San Diego revolt, scholars have recently reexamined the historical documents surrounding planned resistance efforts against Mission San Gabriel to uncover contributing factors for Native displeasure with the mission, finding Spanish physical abuse and culturally destructive practices at the heart of their calls for rebellion.[73]

Throughout most of the twentieth century, many scholars and mission officials discounted Native perspectives and testimonials. They openly remarked that these sources were unreliable because many indigenous people depend on oral traditions rather than the written word to transmit history.[74] Historians who neglected to recognize Native perspectives also contributed to the types of misinterpretations found in presentations about Toypurina. But scholars in the late twentieth century increasingly reexamined Native sources to incorporate different perspectives into their analyses. These new perspectives shed light on the varied methods indigenous people used to resist Spanish colonial systems. Specifically, Hackel has reexamined Thomas Workman Temple's findings about the San Gabriel resistance movement. He notes that scholars have commonly cited Temple, but Temple misrepresented events and misread historical sources. Hackel reanalyzed sources, including trial testimonies, and found that Nicholás José actually instigated the rebellion because the Spanish refused to allow him to exercise his cultural practices.[75]

Native peoples employed several forms of resistance at many mission sites throughout the Spanish period. For example, indigenous people either attempted to poison or did poison priests at Mission San Carlos, San Miguel, and San Diego. Native people at Mission Santa Cruz also assassinated Father Andrés Quintana. Quintana's alleged cruelty and use of an iron-tipped whip pushed some neophytes to ambush and murder the man in 1812.[76] Indigenous people at Mission San Carlos in Monterey raided the mission and nearby settlements for horses and other goods into the Mexican era to supplement their food after the destruction of local resources by European livestock.[77] And the Chumash revolt of 1824 spread to several sites, including Missions Santa Inés, Santa Barbara, and La Purísima.[78]

In further examining forms of resistance and social control, mission scholars have distinguished between primary and secondary resistance and between active and passive resistance. Robert H. Jackson and Edward D. Castillo labeled traditional resistance led by shaman and village leaders during wartime as primary resistance, whereas secondary resistance included second-generation Native peoples born into the missions and neophytes living within the system for extended periods. However, because soldiers and priests continually brought new generations of Native peoples into the mission from the late eighteenth century to the early 1830s, Native peoples employed both forms of resistance throughout the mission era.[79] Common acts of resistance against the mission system included active uprisings and fugitivism. Native people also engaged in passive resistance such as noncompliance and performing work slowly. Fugitivism grew to be the most common form of active resistance—a tactic that also depleted mission labor forces. Hackel has examined fugitivism in detail as an important component of resistance and cultural expression in opposition to Spanish social controls. For example, Native testimony and death records have revealed that Native peoples fled the missions to escape unhealthy conditions after epidemics killed scores of people. Although missionaries generally blamed fugitivism on the bad influence of local unbaptized indigenous populations, Native testimonials show that people left missions in part to escape death and punishment.[80] Many contemporary mission sites do not address these common reasons for resistance.

Native people used resistance as a central forum to shape their own experiences with the California missions. To this end, scholars have demonstrated that Native people *outside* the missions also resisted the Spanish. Sherburne F. Cook examined Native interactions with the Spanish and found that Native people fled the missions and raided stock, and that interior groups developed defensive measures to protect themselves from violent Spanish intruders.[81] Phillips also analyzed indigenous communities living in the interior of California. He found that Native peoples raided stock to restrict Spanish settlements from spreading inland. They also used stock raiding as a means to profit from trade with the growing number of European and Euro-American migrants in California. These types of examinations incorporate Native perspectives and provide more complete analyses of indigenous responses to Spanish colonization.[82] They also include perspectives of Native communities in the interior, not just the coastal groups most frequently pulled into the missions.[83] Although many contemporary scholars work to find Native perspectives in historical documents, Rupert Costo and Jeannette Henry Costo, as well as Edward Castillo, pushed further to include Native voices. These historians paint "Indians as shapers of events, rather than as violent savages or helpless victims."[84] Interpretations that ignore or discount Native experiences frequently neglect to utilize the knowledge of contemporary Native culture bearers and the abundant work of scholars published in recent decades to build their narratives.

Contemporary interpreters at California missions face a difficult task in reconciling resistance to the Spanish missions with the idyllic utopia that regional promoters constructed around mission ruins. For that last century, many people have created a sense of collective identity around the mission sites—seeing them as the place where Christianity first found its way into California. The mythical past built around missions supports a romanticized depiction of California in all of its "grandeur and excitement." Recognition of Native resistance against the Spanish missions requires a revision of popular perceptions of this idealized past by acknowledging the complicated and negative impacts Spanish colonization had on indigenous peoples. It also pushes museum interpreters and site stewards to recognize the historic failures of the institutions they support.[85] Florence Shipek has observed that "it must be emphasized that any study of mission history and its relations to changes in Indian cultures and behaviors requires knowledge of the specific belief systems of each tribal group to be examined."[86] Still, many mission sites, as the direct inheritors of the booster efforts led by Lummis, John Steven McGroarty, George Wharton James, and *Ramona* enthusiasts, continue to promote positive interpretations of the Spanish past that minimize Native perspectives and overlook Spanish abuses. Along with "civilizing" institutions, foreigners introduced Native Californians to a range of new diseases that caused widespread destruction in Native communities. Resistance efforts against the Spanish often erupted when Native people became dissatisfied with the intentional or inadvertent changes brought by the Spanish. Violence, punishments, disease, and death emerged as some of the most vociferous complaints Native people levied against the missions. These complaints fueled resistance efforts that endured from the beginning of Spanish colonization to the end of the mission era and demonstrate the power Native people exercised to control their lives.

**Notes**

1. Steven W. Hackel, *Children of Coyote, Missionaries of Saint Francis: Indian-Spanish Relations in Colonial California, 1769–1850* (Chapel Hill: University of North Carolina Press, 2005), 1–26; Robert H. Jackson and Edward D. Castillo, *Indians, Franciscans, and Spanish Colonization: The Impact of the Mission System on the California Indians* (Albuquerque: University of New Mexico Press, 1995), 31–39; James A. Sandos, *Converting California: Indians and Franciscans in the Missions* (New Haven, CT: Yale University Press, 2004), 1–32; Lisbeth Haas, *Saints and Citizens: Indigenous Histories of Colonial Missions and Mexican California* (Berkeley: University of California Press, 2014), 13–82; Richard L. Carrico, "Sociopolitical Aspects of the 1775 Revolt at Mission San Diego de Alcala: An Ethnohistorical Approach," *Journal of San Diego History* 43 (summer 1997), http://www.sandiegohistory.org/journal/97summer/missionrevolt.htm; Florence Shipek, "California Indian Reactions to the Franciscans," *Americas* 41 (1985): 53–66; George Harwood Phillips, *Chiefs and Challengers: Indian Resistance and Cooperation in Southern California*, 2d ed. (Norman: University of Oklahoma Press, 2014), 12–53.

2. Doyce B. Nunis Jr. and Edward D. Castillo, "California Mission Indians: Two Perspectives," *California History* 70 (1991): 206–215. For example, Edward D. Castillo responded to this bias in a reply to *California History* after Nunis criticized Castillo's use of Lorenzo Asisara's narrative about the assassination of Father Andres Quintana. According to Nunis, it was a "document flawed in the extreme." However, Castillo retorted that many historians before the late twentieth century discounted Native testimonials as inaccurate or unreliable, especially when Native accounts countered the romantic mission myth that mission "apologists" continually upheld. Castillo argued that apologetic scholars selectively read historical documents left by Europeans to present a cozier narrative of the Franciscans.

3. I. Brent Eagen, "A History of Mission Basilica San Diego de Alcala: The First Church of California Founded by the Venerable Junipero Serra, July 16, 1769," (San Diego: Mission Basilica San Diego de Alcala, n.d.).

4. Michael Connolly Miskwish, *Kumeyaay: A History Textbook* (El Cajon, CA: Sycuan Press, 2007), 16–21; Phillips, *Chiefs and Challengers*, 23–24. In the literature, the Kumeyaay are also referred to as Mission Indians, Diegueño, Kumiai, Tipai, or Ipai. Tipai and Ipai are geographical designations for southern and northern Kumeyaay. Furthermore, many early writers used various spellings for Kumeyaay as found in reports, letters, and ethnohistoric studies conducted by scholars such as T. T. Waterman. This study uses the term *Kumeyaay* as an overarching term for the Tipai-Ipai. The label "Diegueño" emerged from the mission period. The U.S. government also used this term during the reservation era when it gave the "Diegueño" reservation land. This caused many of the Kumeyaay to use this mission-derived name to gain federal recognition.

5. M. Steven Shackley, ed., *The Early Ethnography of the Kumeyaay* (Berkeley: Phoebe Hearst Museum of Anthropology, 2004), 16. These theories are based on ceramic

findings throughout this region.

6. Ibid., 21.

7. Roland B. Dixon and Alfred L. Kroeber, "The Native Languages of California," *American Anthropologist* 5 (1903): 1–26.

8. Shackley, *Early Ethnography of the Kumeyaay*, 22.

9. Phillips, *Chiefs and Challengers*, 24.

10. Miskwish, *Kumeyaay*, 25–26.

11. Shackley, *Early Ethnography of the Kumeyaay*, 29–35.

12. Miskwish, *Kumeyaay*, 31–35.

13. Leslie Spier, "Southern Diegueño Customs," in *The Early Ethnography of the Kumeyaay*, ed. M. Steven Shackley (Berkeley: Phoebe Hearst Museum of Anthropology, 2004), 334–340.

14. Florence C. Shipek, "A Native American Adaptation to Drought: The Kumeyaay as Seen in the San Diego Mission Records 1770-1798," *Ethnohistory* 28 (autumn 1981): 295-312.

15. Ibid., 296–297.

16. Ibid., 298–299.

17. Florence Shipek, "Kumeyaay Socio-Political Structure," *Journal of California and Great Basin Anthropology* 4 (1982): 293–303. The Ortega investigation noted that people from many villages surrounding Mission San Diego and from dozens of miles away participated in the attack. Leaders from these villages most likely learned about the attack through the intricate system of runners. Runner was a prized and sought-after position for Kumeyaay boys. These runners played a key role in keeping lines of communication open between villages throughout Kumeyaay territory, spreading vital news quickly.

18. Luis Jayme to Raphel Verger, San Diego, October 17, 1772, in *Letter of Luis Jayme, O.F.M. San Diego, October 17, 1772*, ed. and trans. Maynard Geiger (Los Angeles: Dawson's Book Shop, 1970). Hereafter referred to as Jayme to Verger, San Diego, October 17, 1772.

19. Sherry L. Smith, *Reimagining Indians: Native Americans through Anglo Eyes, 1880–1940* (New York: Oxford University Press, 2000), 129–131.

20. George Phillips examined Native forms of resistance in *Indians and Intruders in Central California, 1769–1849* (Norman: University of Oklahoma Press, 1993), 3–165.

21. Phillips, *Chiefs and Challengers*, 3.

22. Jackson and Castillo, *Indians, Franciscans, and Spanish Colonization*, 73–86.

23. Iris H. W. Engstrand, "Seekers of the 'Northern Mystery': European Exploration of California and the Pacific," in *Contested Eden: California before the Gold Rush*, ed. Ramon A. Gutierrez and Richard J. Orsi (Berkeley: University of California Press, 1998), 83–86; David J. Weber, *The Spanish Frontier in North America* (New Haven, CT: Yale University Press, 1992), 41–42.

24. Hackel, *Children of Coyote*, 33.

25. Zephyrin Engelhardt, *The Missions and Missionaries of California: San Diego*

*Mission* (San Francisco: James H. Barry Company, 1920), 7–9.

26. Engstrand, "Seekers of the 'Northern Mystery,'" 86–92; Hackel, *Children of Coyote*, 40–47; Hubert Howe Bancroft, *History of California*, Vol. 1 in *The Works of Hubert Howe Bancroft*, Vol. 18 (San Francisco: The History Company, 1886), 126–139.

27. Pope Francis's announcement in late January 2015 of his intention to canonize Serra reignited a firestorm of controversy about Serra and the larger impact of the mission system on Native Californians. Native people and scholars of California mission history came together to discuss Serra's canonization during the symposium "California Indians, Canonization of Junípero Serra, and Consequences of Colonialism" at the University of California, Riverside, on March 13, 2015.

28. Steven W. Hackel, *Junípero Serra: California's Founding Father* (New York: Hill and Wang, 2013), 139–236.

29. Sandos, *Converting California*, 39–42.

30. Ibid., 41–42.

31. Ibid.; Phillips, *Chiefs and Challengers*, 27–28.

32. Hackel, *Children of Coyote*, 44–46.

33. Junípero Serra to Juan Andres, San Diego, February 10, 1770, in *Writings of Junípero Serra*, Vol. 1, ed. Antonine Tibesar (Washington, DC: Academy of American Franciscan History, 1955), 149–155. Hereafter referred to as Serra to Andres, San Diego, February 10, 1770.

34. Ibid.; Sandos, *Converting California*, 42. Sandos noted that five Native people lost their lives during this skirmish.

35. George Harwood Phillips, *Vineyards and Vaqueros: Indian Labor and the Economic Expansion of Southern California, 1771–1877* (Norman: University of Oklahoma Press, 2010), 21–22.

36. Serra to Andres, San Diego, February 10, 1770. Sandos also describes these events in *Converting California*, 42–43.

37. Junípero Serra to Francisco Palóu, San Diego, July 3, 1769, in *Writings of Junípero Serra*, Vol. 1, ed. Antonine Tibesar (Washington, DC: Academy of American Franciscan History, 1955), 141–147.

38. Francisco Palóu, "Juan Crespí to Francisco Palóu, San Diego, June 9, 1769," in *Historical Memoirs of New California*, Vol. 4, ed. and trans. Herbert Eugene Bolton (New York: Russell and Russell, 1926), 253–265.

39. Juan Crespí to Francisco Palóu, San Diego, February 6, 1770, in *Historical Memoirs of New California*, Vol. 4, *Francisco Palóu*, ed. and trans. Herbert Eugene Bolton (New York: Russell and Russell, 1926), 269–285. Hereafter referred to as Crespí to Palóu, San Diego, February 6, 1770.

40. Junípero Serra to Francisco Palóu, San Diego, February 10, 1770, in *Writings of Junípero Serra*, Vol. 1, ed. Antonine Tibesar (Washington, DC: Academy of American Franciscan History, 1955), 157–161.

41. Jayme to Verger, San Diego, October 17, 1772. Similar information was also provided to the author during a discussion with educational interpreters at the Barona Cultural Center and Museum, Lakeside, California.

42. Shipek, "Native American Adaptation to Drought," 299; Sandos, *Converting California,* 55; Phillips, *Vineyards and Vaqueros,* 30–31.

43. Sandos, *Converting California,* 55–60.

44. Hackel, *Children of Coyote,* 57–59. Some docents attributed the San Diego attack to the Yuma Indians, the Quechan and Mohave, who did revolt against Spanish settlement. However, the attacks associated with this revolt occurred in Yuma in July 1781. Historians attribute this revolt to increased pressure by the missionaries and demands for food and land for pasture by Spanish settlers. This revolt caused the closure of the overland route of the Spanish between Alta California and Sonora and cut off land travel to Alta California from New Spain.

45. Eagen, "History of Mission San Diego."

46. Ibid.; Sandos, *Converting California,* 55–68. Sandos provides a thorough scholarly description of the revolt.

47. Rose Marie Beebe and Robert M. Senkewicz, "1775: Rebellion at San Diego, Vicente Fuster," *Lands of Promise and Despair: Chronicles of Early California, 1535–1864,* ed. Rose Marie Beebe and Robert M. Senkewicz (Santa Clara: Santa Clara University, in conjunction with Heyday Books, 2001), 186.

48. Sandos, *Converting California,* 55–68; Carrico, "Sociopolitical Aspects of the 1775 Revolt."

49. See information published and distributed by Mission San Diego de Alcalá such as Eagen, "History of Mission San Diego."

50. Carrico, "Sociopolitical Aspects of the 1775 Revolt." This information was further corroborated by contemporary Kumeyaay cultural educators, who said that stories surrounding these types of fears have been transmitted orally throughout the generations.

51. Sandos, *Converting California,* 55–57.

52. Maynard J. Geiger, *The Life and Times of Fray Junípero Serra, O.F.M.; or, The Man Who Never Turned Back, 1713–1784, A Biography,* Vol. 2 (Washington, DC: Academy of American Franciscan History, 1959), 58–59; Sandos, *Converting California,* 55–58; Carrico, "Sociopolitical Aspects of the 1775 Revolt."

53. Hackel, *Children of Coyote,* 259; Sandos, *Converting California,* 59. Sandos contended that six hundred people participated in the attack, and Hackel noted that up to 1,000 Native people participated in the revolt.

54. See the varying accounts given by people such as Fuster, Anza, and Lasuén as demonstrated in Bancroft, *History of California,* 1: 249–255.

55. Beebe and Senkewicz, "1775: Rebellion at San Diego, Vicente Fuster," 187–192.

56. Vicente Fuster, as quoted in Beebe and Senkewicz, "1775: Rebellion at San Diego, Vicente Fuster," 187.

57. Bancroft, *History of California,* 1: 249–251.

58. Beebe and Senkewicz, "1775: Rebellion at San Diego, Vicente Fuster," 191.

59. Fermín Francisco de Lasuén to Fray Juan Prestamero, January 28, 1776, San Diego, in *Writings of Fermín Francisco de Lasuén,* Vol. 1, ed. Finbar Kenneally (Washington, DC: Academy of American Franciscan History, 1965), 59–61.

60. Junípero Serra to Antonio Maria de Bucareli y Ursua, Monterey, December 15, 1775, in *Writings of Junípero Serra*, Vol. 2, ed. Antonine Tibesar (Washington, DC: Academy of American Franciscan History, 1956), 401–407.

61. Claudio Saunt argued that the interrogators tortured Francisco and Carlos to extract a testimony. Claudio Saunt, "'My Medicine Is Punishment': A Case of Torture in Early California, 1775–1776," *Ethnohistory* 57 (fall 2010): 679–708.

62. Hackel, *Children of Coyote,* 259–261; Geiger, *Life and Times of Fray Junípero Serra,* 2: 58–59.

63. Phillips, *Chiefs and Challengers,* 30–31.

64. Bancroft, *History of California,* 1: 249–251; Miskwish, *Kumeyaay,* 47–48.

65. Juan Bautista de Anza, Diary of Juan Bautista de Anza, Thursday, January 11, 1776, University of Oregon, Web de Anza, http://anza.uoregon.edu/anza76.html.

66. Francisco Palóu, *Historical Memoirs of New California,* Vol. 4, ed. and trans. Herbert Eugene Bolton (New York: Russell and Russell, 1926), 62–63.

67. Mission San Diego de Alcalá, "History," http://www.missionsandiego.org/visit/history.

68. Ibid.; Eagen, "History of Mission San Diego."

69. Crespi to Palóu, San Diego, February 6, 1770.

70. Edward D. Castillo, "Blood Came from Their Mouths: Tongva and Chumash Responses to the Pandemic of 1801," *American Indian Culture and Research Journal* 23 (1999): 47–61. For a discussion of the attempted revolt at Mission San Gabriel, see Thomas Workman Temple II, "Toypurina the Witch and The Indian Uprising at San Gabriel," reprinted in *Spanish Borderlands Sourcebook: Native American Perspectives on the Hispanic Colonization of Alta California,* ed. Edward D. Castillo (New York: Garland Publishing, 1992), 326–152; Steven W. Hackel, "Sources of Rebellion: Indian Testimony and the Mission San Gabriel Uprising of 1785," *Ethnohistory* 50 (2003): 643–669.

71. Francis J. Weber, "Toypurina the Temptress," in *The Pride of the Missions: A Documentary History of San Gabriel Mission,* ed. Francis J. Weber (Hong Kong: Libra Press Limited, 1978), 29–30.

72. For more on Toypurina's revolt, see Edward D. Castillo, "Gender Status Decline, Resistance, and Accommodation among Female Neophytes in the Missions of California: A San Gabriel Case Study," *American Indian Culture and Research Journal* 8 (1994): 67–93; Hackel, "Sources of Rebellion," 643–669; Antonia I. Castañeda, "Sexual Violence in the Politics and Policies of Conquest," in *Building With Our Hands: New Directions in Chicana Studies,* ed. Adela de la Torre and Beatríz M. Pesquera (Berkeley: University of California Press, 1993), 15–33.

73. Hackel, "Sources of Rebellion," 643–669.

74. For a debate between two scholars on precisely this point, see Nunis and Castillo, "California Mission Indians," 206–215.

75. Hackel, "Sources of Rebellion," 643–669.

76. Lorenzo Asisara, "The Assassination of Padre Andrés Quintana by the Indians of Mission Santa Cruz in 1812: The Narrative of Lorenzo Asisara," in *Spanish Bor-*

*derlands Sourcebook: Native American Perspectives on the Hispanic Colonization of Alta California*, ed. and trans. Edward D. Castillo (New York: Garland Publishing, 1992), 3–11. For more general information on resistance to California missions, see Sherburne F. Cook, *The Conflict between the California Indian and White Civilization* (1943; repr., Berkeley: University of California Press, 1976), 64–90; Randall Milliken, *A Time of Little Choice: The Disintegration of Tribal Culture in the San Francisco Bay Area, 1769–1810* (Menlo Park, CA: Ballena Press, 1995); James A. Sandos, "Between Crucifix and Lance: Indian-White Relations in California, 1769–1848," in *Contested Eden: California before the Gold Rush*, ed. Rámon A. Gutiérrez and Richard J. Orsi (Berkeley: University of California Press, 1998), 196–229; Sandos, *Converting California*, 154–173; Jackson and Castillo, *Indians, Franciscans, and Spanish Colonization*, 73–86; Hackel, *Children of Coyote*, 228–271.

77. Sylvia M. Broadbent, "Conflict at Monterey: Indian Horse Raiding, 1820–1850," reprinted in *Spanish Borderlands Sourcebook: Native American Perspectives on the Hispanic Colonization of Alta California*, ed. Edward D. Castillo (New York: Garland Publishing, 1992), 364–379.

78. Thomas Blackburn, "The Chumash Revolt of 1824: A Native Account," reprinted in *Spanish Borderlands Sourcebook: Native American Perspectives on the Hispanic Colonization of Alta California*, ed. Edward D. Castillo (New York: Garland Publishing, 1992), 59–68; Rose Marie Beebe and Robert M. Senkewicz, "The End of the 1824 Chumash Revolt in Alta California: Father Vicente Sarría's Account," *Americas* 53 (October 1996): 273–283; James A. Sandos, "*Levantamiento*! The 1824 Chumash Uprising Reconsidered," *Southern California Quarterly* 67 (1985): 109–133.

79. Jackson and Castillo, *Indians, Franciscans, and Spanish Colonization*, 73.

80. Hackel, *Children of Coyote*, 92.

81. Cook, *Conflict between the California Indian and White Civilization*, 227–229.

82. Kenneally, *Writings of Fermín Francisco de Lasuén*; Tibesar, *Writings of Junípero Serra*; Crespí, *Description of Distant Roads*; Palóu, *Historical Memoirs of New California*. For archives of translations of Anza's diaries, see University of Oregon, "Web de Anza," http://anza.uoregon.edu. Much of the information about raids, attacks, and revolts can be found in easily accessible locations for current scholars. Scholars have translated and published many of the letters of Serra and Lasuén, along with the exploration journals of Crespí and Anza. Researchers can easily locate these resources online and in the libraries of universities throughout California.

83. Phillips has done extensive work on this subject; see Phillips, *Chiefs and Challengers*, 3–9; Phillips, *Indians and Intruders*, 14–64.

84. David J. Weber, "The Spanish Borderlands of North America: A Historiography," special issue, *OAH Magazine of History* 14 (summer 2000): 7.

85. Thomas S. Bremer, "Tourists and Religion at Temple Square and Mission San Juan Capistrano," special issue, *Journal of American Folklore* 113 (autumn 2000): 422–435.

86. Florence Shipek, "California Indian Reactions to the Franciscans," *Americas* 41 (1985): 53–66.

# 6

# *Death, Disease, and Punishment at the California Missions*

That there were occasionally individual cases of harsh treatment is possible. The most loving and indulgent parents are now and again ill-tempered, fretful, or nervous. The fathers were men subject to all the limitations of other men. Granting these limitations and making due allowance for human imperfection, the rule of the fathers must still be admired for its wisdom and commended for its immediate results.
— George Wharton James, *In and Out of the Old Missions of California* (1906)

The vast decline in the population of Native Californian communities after sustained Spanish and Euro-American contact left a legacy that helped silence Native people in popular history. From the early nineteenth century to the beginning of the twentieth century, settlers to the region frequently pushed Native peoples into the social periphery. Many thousands of Native people lost their lives to disease, malnutrition, and starvation, and the ruthless violence that newcomers unleashed on Native communities also affected survivors in many ways. The colonization process undertaken by the Spanish attempted to strip Native peoples of their customs and languages and replace them with Spanish culture, labor strategies, and religion. This cultural indoctrination may have helped some Native peoples assimilate more smoothly into life as "Mexican" citizens after secularization and during the early American era; however, the Spanish introduced large-scale systems of destruction to Native communities generations before the wagon trains crossed the continent and Euro-Americans settled in California.[1]

Scholars writing in the late nineteenth and early twentieth centuries such as Hubert Howe Bancroft, Herbert Eugene Bolton, and Sherburne F. Cook highlighted the devastation that death and disease brought to Native populations in Spanish California. They argued that Franciscan missionaries treated Native peoples poorly; yet they relied solely on non-Native sources for information. The Spanish instituted stringent labor regimens and took rations before indigenous populations in years of shortages. Spanish livestock roamed the California landscape freely, devouring Native food sources and causing malnutrition and starvation in many communities. Moreover, as a result of Spanish settlement, Native peoples faced contact with extremely deadly European diseases. Native Californians turned to the missions as potential havens from malnutrition, starvation, and disease. The mission communities did offer them food, but continued to expose indigenous peoples to a wide variety of maladies.[2] Reflecting the same prejudices toward Native peoples as many Euro-Americans in the early twentieth century, Cook contended that Europeans could not expect "semi-savages" to maintain modern standards of cleanliness. Discounting Native sources as unreliable, he claimed that sexual "promiscuity" and preferences for the "wild" contributed to the demographic collapse of Native Californian populations.[3] With their cultures under threat, and in response to persistent struggles with violence, malnutrition, and disease, Native peoples frequently stopped cooperating with the Spanish and instead employed resistance tactics to defend their communities against continued destruction.[4]

## Interpretations of Death and Disease during the Mission Era

Historians of Spanish California note that death and punishment are some of the strongest memories kept and passed on by Native Californians.[5] Candid docents at contemporary California mission sites observe that some Native peoples still refuse to visit the historic sites because they view the missions as negative places where many of their ancestors suffered and died. But this is not the only perspective. Others visit the missions for healing and to rebury Native remains found at other sites.[6] Some indigenous people visit the mission graveyards and memorials to reflect on the loss of life that these places symbolize. The impacts of death and disease are ubiquitous at contemporary California missions, and yet they frequently remain unexamined and ignored in mission museums.

As noted in previous chapters, many mission museum presentations give little space to discussions of the negative impacts of Spanish colonization such as disease, death, and punishment—factors that frequently encouraged resistance movements among both neophytes and non-missionized Native peoples. Resistance, stringent labor routines, health, and well-being were all interrelated facets of Native life at the California missions. Priests at many of the missions constantly expressed their concern about the high levels of disease and death that haunted mission grounds. They further conveyed their frustration about the violence inflicted on Native peoples by the Spanish soldiers. The padres understood the connection between these negative impacts of Spanish colonization and increased hostility among Native peoples.[7] Yet Franciscan scholars throughout the twentieth century such as Zephyrin Engelhardt and Francis F. Guest presented a one-sided perspective of mission history. They countered the negative portrayal of the missions with focused examinations of the institutional history of these sites and the lives of padres in Alta California.[8] Guest, who replied to Cook's scathing examination of the demographic collapse of Native Californians following Spanish colonization, argued that scholars must understand the cultural perspectives of the Spanish priests before condemning their actions in California. Specifically, Guest defended the continued spread of the mission system even though the missionaries recognized and bemoaned the significantly high death rate among neophytes. To justify these mortality rates, Guest argued that premature aging and death at an early age were common in the eighteenth century. Guest contended that priests from small rural towns in Spain experienced food shortages, frequent epidemics, and inadequate health care that made them accustomed "to rubbing elbows with death" from childhood.[9] Yet Native peoples in California did not have the sanitation issues or constant threat of epidemics common in Spain that fueled this familiarity with death. On the contrary, Native populations throughout much of California thrived before Spanish contact.[10]

Guest claims that to solve the problem of epidemics at the missions the priests commissioned mission residents to build hospitals. But a lack of doctors knowledgeable of these European ailments and inadequate medical supplies hindered the development of more advanced health care in the region. He insisted that Native people did not die because the padres neglected their duty to protect them; the missionaries cared for Native people to the best of their abilities. The padres were not "callous and indifferent," but the restraints of the mission system itself lent to the death and disease that marred the period. According to this perspective, disease was too rampant and the missions had too few resources to combat the maladies that infected so many neophytes.[11] This may have been true, but the Spanish were ultimately responsible for introducing several devastating diseases to the Native Californian peoples.

Contemporary scholars including Robert H. Jackson, James A. Sandos, and Edward D. Castillo have examined the many nonepidemic causes of death among missionized Native people such as limited medical attention, malnutrition, poor sanitation, and cramped living quarters for women and small children, as well as the high death rate among neophytes from epidemics and disease. According to Jackson and Castillo, labor and high stress levels affected the bodies of missionized Native peoples. This stress contributed to weakened immune systems and lethargy.[12] Sandos also studied lethargy among neophyte populations, but found the probable cause to be related to a high incidence of syphilis.[13] Meanwhile, within these academic debates that focus on demographic collapse, sanitation, and disease, the emotional impact of death often becomes secondary. But as Gregg Castro (Salinan/ Ohlone) has pointed out, the role of Native people today, "as the survivors of that academic event is to keep alive the emotional context of such heady debates. These were Real People—Our People—with Real Lives and Real Pain, pain that is continued and fed by the denial of this real history."[14]

## Locating Painful Histories at Contemporary Mission Sites

Native Californians faced the threat of epidemics throughout their lives at the missions, and yet contemporary displays at mission sites say little about the effects of disease on indigenous populations. Scholars have documented the effects of illnesses on the Native people in widely available publications that mission interpreters can easily access. However, graveyards filled with headstones bearing the names of priests and prominent members of the local community greet patrons as they pass through the garden courtyards at several missions. At Mission San Gabriel, a towering crucifix in the center of the mission gardens marks the gravesite of over 6,000 unnamed Gabrielino-Tongva people. According to interpretive panels at the mission, the people who occupy this mass gravesite died from the "cholera and small pox epidemics of 1825." This memorial points to epidemics in the early Mexican era as the cause of large-scale death. It ignores the widespread devastation caused by venereal diseases, malnutrition, violence, and sexual exploitation that affected Native peoples during the mission era. It also attributes the deaths to common maladies that killed many Native Americans during colonial times, rather than the specific venereal diseases and intestinal ailments that contributed to a majority of deaths following Spanish colonization in Alta California.[15]

The gravesites of priests and prominent community members also frequently are found in markedly different spaces than the Native cemeteries at many of the missions. These separate sites underscore the duality of presentations in mission histories. Mission sites freely honor deceased priests, military and political leaders, and noteworthy residents in individually marked graves, but they fail to adequately address the historical importance of the thousands of Native people buried in mass gravesites nearby. Furthermore, publications sold at contemporary missions primarily focus on sensationalized or accidental deaths in Spanish California that lend themselves to entertaining ghost stories or tales about the haunted landscape.[16] Many missions today present sanitized narratives that neglect to impart a clear understanding of life for Native peoples during the Spanish period that included early death, disease, punishment, and violence.

## Malnutrition and Starvation

These contemporary mission sites highlight themes that correspond to church history and the productive contributions the Spanish made to California society. In doing so, they obscure the role of Native people in the missions. For example, displays at many of the most productive missions, including San Gabriel, San Luis Rey, and La Purísima describe the ranching and agriculture ventures of the missions. They tell visitors that livestock populations thrived in Spanish California. Laborers at missions produced enough leather, soap, and meat to support themselves as well as supply those at less prosperous missions.[17] Regrettably for Native Californians, grazing animals such as horses, cattle, and sheep brought by the Spanish multiplied into the tens of thousands, far beyond the control of the missions. These animals ate and trampled the plants and seeds that Native Californians relied on for food.[18]

While mission herds doubled and tripled in size, California experienced a drought that diminished local food supplies and exacerbated the shortage beyond what livestock had already eaten and crushed.[19] However, anthropologists argue that drought alone did not cause the high rates of death and malnutrition that pushed Native people into the missions. For example, archeological evidence reveals that Native groups, such as the Chumash in the Santa Barbara area, experienced cycles of drought and El Niños several times in their 11,000-year history in the region without suffering severe population decline. Furthermore, Spanish documents from the early mission period in California describe thriving Native communities that relied heavily on the local landscape for food.[20] Many scholars agree that the introduction and propagation of European livestock and grains in California destroyed Native food resources and caused widespread malnutrition and starvation. Contemporary exhibitions at Mission San Gabriel highlight the productive ranching, tanning, soap, and candle-making facilities manned by Native laborers at the mission, but they do not discuss the toll of hard labor on Native bodies or the effects of livestock on Native food supplies and health.

Historical records indicate that Native peoples commonly came to the missions for sustenance. Pedro Font, who accompanied the Anza expedition from Sonora to Monterey, noted in January 1776 that the missionaries did not force baptism on local Native peoples. Nevertheless, hungry people turned to the missions as a solution to their food shortages. Indigenous people stayed at the missions and followed the instructions of the priests to maintain access to a stable food supply. As starvation lead many indigenous peoples to relocate to the Spanish missions, many priests mistook Native reliance on the missions' food sources for devotion to the Catholic faith. Although experiences varied at each of the twenty-one eventual mission sites, scholars maintain that the missionaries frequently provided abbreviated catechisms for adults before baptism, lasting as little as a few hours or one day, in order to supply the missions with an ample labor force.[21] Hugo Reid, who lived at Mission San Gabriel in the 1840s, noted that neophytes and Spanish soldiers used persuasion and force to bring in new converts.[22] The padres informed the neophytes after baptism that if they left the mission without permission, soldiers would hunt them down and return them to the mission for punishment. Font observed that many times neophytes asked for permission to leave to gather food and visit relatives nearby, which missionaries allowed periodically.[23] Thus people who turned to the missions for food quickly found themselves bound to the sites through a ritual that many did not fully agree with nor understand.[24]

People from more distant villages moved to the missions as livestock grazed on lands farther away from the Spanish settlements. According to Font, "at times they come with a pagan relative who stays for the catechetical instruction, either drawn by the example of others or attracted by the *pozole*, which suits them better than the herbs and the food they gather in the hills. So these Indians are wont to be collected through the stomach."[25] Missionaries such as Font recognized that the availability of food drew Native peoples to the missions. To provide adequate sustenance for their neophyte populations, less productive missions and those with extremely large populations such as Mission San Luis Rey had more lax guidelines about Native peoples' movement in and out of the mission complex.[26] Even though Native Californians survived for thousands of years from the resources provided by the land, food produced by neophytes at the missions offered stability for hungry populations following great changes brought by the Spanish.[27]

## The Ravages of Disease

Scholars of Spanish California argue that Native people also moved to the missions to escape disease in their own communities. Many indigenous peoples in California saw their friends and family members die from starvation and the newly introduced European diseases that Native healers could not treat effectively.[28] They also realized that Spanish soldiers and priests did not die from the same diseases. Some Native peoples turned to the mission complexes in the hope of protecting themselves and their families from death, but the missions could not stop the spread of the pestilence, proving instead to be a breeding ground for the foreign diseases. Epidemics spread like wildfire in mission communities where Native peoples worked, ate, prayed, and slept in close proximity to one another. According to scholars, venereal diseases were the most heinous European maladies that infiltrated Native populations, introduced by the Spanish expeditions. These diseases caused indigenous peoples to die in large numbers and left survivors in decimated villages to turn to the missions for help.[29]

Missionaries José de Miguel and José María Zalvidea at Mission San Gabriel wrote that Spaniards traveling with the overland expedition led by Juan Bautista de Anza in 1777 first introduced venereal diseases to the Gabrielino-Tongva. Moreover, James Sandos has noted that people traveling with the Portolá expedition in 1769 also spread disease throughout Native communities. During these expeditions, indigenous peoples from Baja California, whom the Spanish previously infected, had sexual encounters with people in Alta California. Spanish soldiers also raped Native people and infected them with sexually transmitted diseases such as syphilis and gonorrhea.[30]

Priests lamented the mistreatment of Native women by the soldiers. And Native peoples in villages near Spanish settlements changed their lifestyles to protect women from sexual assaults. Through archeological evidence and historical documentation, scholars have found evidence that suggests that some indigenous women who previously worked collecting plants on the outskirts of villages rarely left the safety of their homes after Spanish colonization. Others reoriented their communities and dug ditches around village sites so Spanish soldiers could not quickly ride through on horseback.[31] Most scholars believe that a wide range of venereal diseases did not exist in California prior to Spanish contact; however, these diseases spread swiftly after the Spanish arrived in Baja and Alta California.[32]

Syphilis, the deadliest of the venereal diseases Native peoples encountered with Spanish contact, progressed in several stages in the human body. People unfamiliar with syphilis could easily overlook the first symptoms of the disease—a rarely painful sore that developed at the infection site known as a "chancre." The secondary stage began between two to six months later and lasted for up to two years. People with stage-two syphilis break out in a highly contagious rash, and mucous sores erupt around the mouth, throat, rectum, and genitals. During this stage, noninfected persons may easily contract syphilis by coming into contact with an infected person's body fluids (and Native people at the missions shared clothing and bedding). Men and women with stage-two syphilis experienced fever, headaches, joint and bone pain, and hair loss. Pregnant women with stage-one or stage-two syphilis had a high chance of passing the disease on to their newborn child if they did not miscarry or experience a stillbirth.[33]

Late-stage syphilis symptoms developed after a dormant period that ranged anywhere from a few weeks to fifteen years. Infected people at this stage frequently experienced blindness, debilitating arthritis, memory loss, dementia, aneurysms, and death. Children born to mothers with syphilis had a high chance of developing deformed skulls and showed signs of late-stage syphilis early in life. Many children born with congenital syphilis died within their first few years. Advanced stages of syphilis also caused scarring of the fallopian tubes in women that significantly lowered their fertility.[34]

Poor reproductive health triggered by disease also caused women to miscarry or deliver still-born babies. Some priests punished women who miscarried. They thought these women had possibly aborted their babies, a practice sometimes employed by Native women, especially when their pregnancies resulted from rape by Spanish soldiers. For example, George Phillips noted that after Father Zalvidea became aware of Native men and women using herbs and sweating to induce miscarriage in pregnancies conceived by Indian-Spanish sexual contact, the priest assumed that all miscarriages were intentional. Under Zalvidea, the humiliating punishment for stillbirths or miscarriages included shaving the woman's head and forcing her to hold a painted wooden baby in her arms near the alter every Sunday for church—in conjunction with physical punishments of floggings and three months in iron ankle cuffs.[35] Punishment and humiliation tied to pregnancy losses induced by disease probably further affected the psyche of female neophytes. The high rate of death of women and children contributed greatly to the destruction of Native populations. Native people moved to missions as places of possible refuge from death and disease, but found the missions to be hubs of both.[36]

Today, many mission museums do not discuss the impact of venereal diseases on Native populations. A discussion of Native deaths from deadly venereal diseases does not seem appropriate for an institution that welcomes thousands of fourth-grade schoolchildren each year. Nonetheless, to attribute the high number of deaths to two epidemics that occurred in the 1820s, in the case of Mission San Gabriel, does not accurately represent the consistent battle with death and disease that Native peoples faced at the missions from 1769 to the 1830s.

## Monjeríos and Spanish Attempts to Control Native Bodies

The romanticized mission myth portrays the padres as benevolent forces in the lives of Native Californians. In reality, Spanish priests attempted to regulate the most intimate aspects of life for Native peoples, in part to curb the spread of disease. For example, they regularly used *monjeríos*, or female dormitories, to closely monitor and separate young women from the rest of the mission population until marriage, typically in their mid to late teens. Guarding "the purity of their spiritual daughters," priests segregated unmarried girls for their "protection" from Native men and Spanish soldiers. Missionaries called for monjeríos to be among the first buildings erected at mission sites, along with missionary residences and chapels.[37] At night, the priests and their assistants locked girls as young as age 8 in the single-room dormitories.[38] The Spanish used these spaces, important components of the mission complex, as tools of surveillance and control.[39] These poorly ventilated rooms were instrumental in spreading disease among the girls locked in the cramped spaces.

The matron, or *llavera*, who watched over the monjerío also supervised unmarried young women during their daily work. Interpretations at contemporary mission sites gloss over the lived experiences of young Native women isolated in the monjeríos. They focus instead on the daily chores of women and girls such as weaving, basket making, and food preparation. English and Russian explorers to Alta California during the Spanish era described women doing similar chores, but they also provided condemning descriptions of the ways in which mission officials treated the young women. German navigator Otto von Kotzebue, who worked in service for the Russians in the 1820s, described the "poor girls" he viewed at several missions. Some of the girls wore shackles, and all were eager to take in fresh air during their quick walk between the monjerío and church. He wrote: "We were struck by the appearance of a large quadrangular building, which having no windows on the outside, and only one carefully secured door, resembled a prison for state-criminals. It proved to be the residence appropriated by the monks, the severe guardians of chastity, to the young unmarried Indian women, whom they keep under their particular superintendence, making their time useful to the community by spinning, weaving, and similar occupations."[40] Foreigners and Spanish priests in Alta California described the monjeríos as protective sites that shielded young women from the brutality and depredations of both indigenous men and Spanish soldiers.[41]

Restricting all unmarried females over age 8 to the dormitories gave missionaries the power to intimately control the lives of converted women from a young age. Monjeríos forcibly separated young women from their families. This separation allowed the missionaries to ingrain Spanish customs and Catholic teachings in the secluded women at an early age. It stripped indigenous parents of the ability to teach their children about their Native culture, language, traditions, and religious beliefs. As a result, some women who matured within the mission system and had children with neophyte men produced new generations of indigenous peoples disconnected with their Native heritage.[42]

Presently, few missions provide insight into the lives of neophyte women in monjeríos. For example, the single wall panel at Mission San Gabriel that discusses the monjerío in the museum actually stands as a tribute to Eulalia Pérez, the "keeper of the keys." The label notes that Pérez held the keys to the monjerío for fourteen years, took care of the unmarried girls, and supervised the production of food, soap, and clothing at the mission. A sign notifying patrons of the different rooms housed in the south side of the quadrangle briefly recognizes the space originally occupied by the monjerío or, as the mission refers to it, the "quarters for unmarried girls." Missions San Juan Capistrano and San Luis Rey similarly mask the negative impact of monjeríos on the lives of Native women. They also neglect to address the monitoring and surveillance roles of the dormitories in the mission complex. Some of this misrepresentation began in the early and mid-twentieth century when inaccurate reconstruction and restoration efforts by church officials or regional boosters omitted monjeríos from the reconstructed sites.[43]

Mission officials formally established monjeríos to protect the "virtue" of Native women from the Spanish-perceived social ills of premarital sex. For example, priests at Mission San Gabriel condemned Gabrielino-Tongva culture for its acceptance of premarital and extramarital sexual encounters. The strict boundaries the missionaries established around the lives of neophytes caused some Native peoples to turn to desperate measures to find a semblance of happiness. Priests also created social boundaries to restrict the sexual relations of converts, and they further regulated marriage through Catholic doctrine to control sexuality. Native communities had their own customs regarding sexuality and marriage. Specific beliefs on marriage, sex, and divorce differed among indigenous peoples, but many Native communities shared a similar general understanding of marriage as a cultural institution also related to the economic and political needs of the family or community. They placed taboos on incest and adultery, but not on premarital relations or divorce as did the Spanish.[44]

Viewing sex outside of marriage as sinful behavior, many padres showed little flexibility in punishing Native peoples who violated the very conservative belief structure of the Catholic Church.[45] To reinforce Catholic conceptions

163

of marriage and sexuality, priests in Alta California vigorously questioned couples about their sexual exploits during premarital investigations. Many mission sites display the confessionals used at the mission, yet they do not contextualize their use in regulating the lives of neophytes in California. The padres sometimes coerced neophytes into admitting sinful acts in the eyes of the church. They further inquired into the sexual lives of married neophytes on an annual basis to consistently reinforce Roman Catholic concepts of sin, penance, punishment, and forgiveness.[46] Scholars argue that priests often confused indigenous people by preaching against certain behaviors and yet forgiving others of the same sins.

Many Native peoples began to resent the Spanish who attempted to regulate the sexual relations of neophytes. Historical records indicate that indigenous people often resisted Spanish attempts to control their marriages and divorces. Conflicts between the two groups emerged especially when conservative Spanish practices clashed with Native cultural views of personal relationships. According to some historians, the Spanish documented instances in which priests, alcaldes, or soldiers punished Native people at the missions for their sexual exploits. Steven W. Hackel has provided examples of conflicts between priests and neophytes over punishments for premarital or extramarital affairs at Mission San Carlos, San Miguel, Santa Cruz, and San Juan Capistrano. The priests punished offending neophytes with penalties that included cutting their hair, floggings, confinement sentences at the presidio, and hard labor terms in shackles. In one of the most extreme examples, a man and woman, Aurelio and Tomasa, trapped in an unhappy marriage at Mission San Juan Capistrano, faced punishment on several occasions for embracing extramarital lovers. Aurelio eventually murdered Tomasa for being "a bad wife" after missionaries punished his mistress and forced Tomasa's lover to stop compensating Aurelio for his wife's company. Aurelio and Tomasa's circumstances were not unique. Mission records indicate that men and women trapped in unhappy marriages murdered or attempted to kill their spouses at several missions so that they could remarry without facing continual punishments for adultery.[47] Representations at modern mission sites do not delve deeply enough into the personal lives of neophytes to uncover these complicated narratives found in the historical record.

Spanish missionaries attempted to regulate marriage and sexuality to control "illicit" behavior, but also hoped to halt epidemics among neophyte populations. As described earlier, the priests tried to stop the spread of disease through forced chastity by compelling unmarried Native women, and sometimes men, to sleep at night in separate, locked rooms. At some missions the missionaries locked the single men in at night, but they did not station a guard at the male dormitory.[48] Priests especially tried to restrict sexual relationships between neophytes to help curb the spread of venereal diseases such as syphilis and gonorrhea, even though these diseases originated from Spanish soldiers.[49]

Nonetheless, young women within the mission system had relatively short life expectancies. They frequently died in childbirth, endangered further by endemic diseases. At Mission San Carlos, one-third of all married women who reached child-bearing age (15 years old) died before their nineteenth birthday. Young men and women died more often in their early adulthood from diseases transmitted by intimate contact with other neophytes. The high mortality rate among Native people of child-bearing age also affected the infant death rate. Pregnant women infected with either syphilis or gonorrhea lost one out of three pregnancies. Babies commonly inherited diseases from their mothers. They also frequently lacked proper nourishment—their mothers may have died in childbirth or suffered from malnourishment themselves. Indigenous women also commonly lost a quarter of pregnancies to miscarriages and stillbirths. These tragedies probably weighed heavily on the minds and hearts of Native women and men as they saw their children die and communities deteriorate.[50] Hackel noted that "for the Franciscans, without Indians alive, working, and undergoing a process of civilization, the conquest had lost its object and could even be deemed a failure."[51] Most mission sites do not describe the impacts of disease and fail to acknowledge that 60,000 of the 81,000 Native people baptized during the mission era, beginning in 1769, had died by the time of mission secularization in 1834.[52]

### Violence, Punishment, and Other Abuses

Historic mission sites rarely refer to the violence, punishment, and other abuses the Spanish inflicted on Native people during the mission era. And Franciscan scholars in the twentieth century worked to counter many of the negative narratives that historians unearthed on the punishments, abuse, and violence perpetrated by the Spanish. For example, priests commonly used whips in their daily lives, but, according to Franciscan scholars, the padres viewed the discipline as a form of penance that helped a person become closer to Christ. Conversely, contemporary accounts provided by Native people argue that the Spanish punished and abused indigenous peoples. They contend that the missionaries used physical threats as a powerful form of coercion to force Native peoples into the Spanish Catholic fold. Writing in the late twentieth century, Lorena Dixon and Hazel Maldonado recalled that the missionaries did not understand Native lifeways "so [the missionaries] had to browbeat their religion into us. Whipping was common. . . . So the missions [sic] . . . was the worst thing that could happen to our people."[53]

Many Native people expressed similar sentiments condemning the way the Spanish treated their ancestors during the mission period. In the unusual instances in which present-day museum exhibitions address abuses, mission representatives blame the Spanish soldiers for exacting harsh punishments on indigenous peoples. The padres remain kind, compassionate, and devoted figures in mission presentations, just as in Helen Hunt Jackson's novel *Ramona* and John Steven McGroarty's *Mission Play*.[54]

Officials in Spanish California punished indigenous people for a variety of wrongdoings as a central tool in maintaining social control. Crimes ranged from grave misdeeds such as murder and livestock theft to far less serious offenses, including a worker's failure to complete daily chores, a young woman not returning to her dormitory in a timely manner, or a neophyte excessively mourning the death of a relative. Mission and civil officials prescribed punishments depending on the severity of the crime. The punishments included whippings, attachment of shackles, hard labor, or confinement sentences at the presidio. Many Native Californians viewed Spanish teachings and their actions as contradictory. The padres punished Native peoples for rather trivial offenses, while soldiers ravaged the countryside, attacked Native women, stole from them, and killed indigenous peoples but faced less severe punishments.[55] Meanwhile, Native peoples rarely used physical punishments or imprisonment to discipline their children or other community members before Spanish colonization. Rather, the community understood that offenders were in the debt of those they had wronged and must compensate victims for their crimes. For Spanish Franciscan priests, discipline was as central to their faith as "their rosary, or even their missal or breviary."[56] Father President Fermín Francisco de Lasuén, Serra's successor, defended missionaries who physically punished Native peoples to his inquiring superiors. He argued that "here are aborigines whom we are teaching to be men, people of vicious and ferocious habits who know no law but force, no superior but their own free will, and no reason but their own caprice."[57] Lasuén assumed that force played a central role in Native Californian cultures. But in reality, as noted, many Native peoples in California used physical punishment very infrequently before Spanish contact.[58]

According to Lasuén and Guest, twenty-one to twenty-five lashes were moderate sentences for any infraction requiring discipline. Students in Spain frequently received worse punishments for lighter offenses than Native people in California, they pointed out.[59] Whereas whippings averaged about twenty per charge, lashing sentences could range into the hundreds for severer crimes. For example, the men accused of murdering Father Andrés Quintana at Mission Santa Cruz in 1812 received two hundred lashes each, as well as prison terms at the presidio.[60] Physical punishment strained the relationship Native people had with the missions.[61]

Guest claimed that scholars cannot condemn the padres for the high mortality rate, overwhelming disease contagion, and use of corporal punishment in Alta California. He responded to what he called the "newsreel" history—reports of early California that emphasized sensational accounts of abuse and contended that these things were common in eighteenth-century Spanish society, not just colonial California. However, he did not acknowledge that corporal punishments, rampant epidemics, and wide-scale death were uncommon facets of Native life *before* Spanish colonization. Guest questioned why Native people "submit[ted] to these whippings so patiently," and he concluded that neophytes saw the whippings as an extension of the religious fervor of the padres, who practiced self-discipline almost daily.[62]

Scholars have argued more recently that Native people did not submit to punishments as acceptingly as Guest suggested. Neophytes often fled the mission to escape humiliating punishments and refused to work under threatening conditions as the mission system progressed.[63] Moreover, changing ideologies in Spanish Catholicism under reformist Bourbon policies in the late eighteenth century increasingly questioned the need for corporal punishment. They banned parish priests from using the whip for discipline. However, missionaries did not adopt these changes and found themselves defending their use of corporal punishment to the governors of Alta California.[64]

The tension between civil officials and missionaries in Alta California regarding the punishment of Native people was only one part of a power struggle between the two colonial authorities. The government questioned the priests' excessive use of the whip on neophytes, but secular officials still believed that errant indigenous peoples should face physical punishments—at the hands of the military. The Spanish believed that Native peoples must fall in line with Spanish colonial society, become productive members of the Hispanic community, or face punishment for their perceived misdeeds.[65] Native people responded by fleeing the missions, attacking priests, or staging revolts to demonstrate their displeasure.[66]

Guest argued that "American scholars, inclined to view [the whipping of the Indians] at the missions from the standpoint of either secular or Christian humanism, understand it less perfectly" than Latin American or Spanish scholars who are more familiar with "the discipline."[67] Guest insisted that scholars use cultural and historical perspectives when examining punishment, disease, and death in the missions. What he failed to recognize was that Native perspectives are as relevant as Euro-American views to framing historical interpretations. Native perspectives also provide a much-needed counternarrative to the traditionally religious-centered story commonly found in popular interpretations of mission history.

Since Guest's inquiry, a new generation of scholars have claimed that Native people found themselves drawn to the missions out of necessity—to escape the malnutrition, starvation, disease, violence, and death that stalked their communities following Spanish colonization. In this light, Native people endured strict discipline as a more appealing fate than almost certain death. Neophytes also reacted forcefully when necessary. They fled the missions and others responded with violence against the Spanish when they felt neglected or abused in the mission system. Even though Native peoples did not sit by passively and allow the Spanish to exert control over them, many contemporary mission sites continue to place Native people in passive roles while they interpret the past from the perspectives of the Spanish missionaries and colonizers.

## Notes

1. James J. Rawls, *Indians of California: The Changing Image* (Norman: University of Oklahoma Press, 1984), 116–201.

2. Robert H. Jackson and Edward D. Castillo, *Indians, Franciscans, and Spanish Colonization: The Impact of the Mission System on the California Indians* (Albuquerque: University of New Mexico Press, 1995), 41–58.

3. Sherburne F. Cook, *The Conflict between the California Indian and White Civilization* (1943; repr., Berkeley: University of California Press, 1976), 32, 71.

4. Cook, *The Conflict between the California Indian and White Civilization*, 227–229.

5. Jackson and Castillo, *Indians, Franciscans, and Spanish Colonization*, 73–87; George Harwood Phillips, *Vineyards and Vaqueros: Indian Labor and the Economic Expansion of Southern California, 1771–1877* (Norman: University of Oklahoma Press, 2010), 142.

6. For more on the varying views of missions by the Gabrielino-Tongva people, see Claudia Jurmain and William McCawley, *O, My Ancestor: Recognition and Renewal for the Gabrielino-Tongva People of the Los Angeles Area* (Berkeley: Heyday Books, 2009).

7. Francisco Palóu, *Historical Memoirs of New California*, Vol. 4, ed. and trans. Herbert Eugene Bolton (New York: Russell and Russell, 1926); Antonine Tibesar, ed., *Writings of Junípero Serra*, 2 vols. (Washington, DC: Academy of American Franciscan History, 1955–1956); Luis Jayme, *Letter of Luis Jayme, O.F.M. San Diego, October 17, 1772*, ed. and trans. Maynard Geiger (Los Angeles: Dawson's Book Shop, 1970).

8. Francis F. Guest, "An Examination of the Thesis of S. F. Cook on the Forced Conversion of Indians in the California Missions," *Southern California Quarterly* 61 (1979): 1–77. Guest directly responded to Cook's arguments, especially his contention that the mission complex was a breeding ground for disease and that missionaries forcibly converted Native peoples to Christianity.

9. Francis F. Guest, "Cultural Perspectives on California Mission Life," *Southern California Quarterly* 65 (1983): 4.

10. M. Kat Anderson, Michael G. Barbour and Valerie Whitworth, "A World of Balance and Plenty: Land, Plants, Animals, and Humans in a Pre-European California," special issue, *California History* 76 (summer-fall 1997): 12–47.

11. Guest, "Cultural Perspectives on California Mission Life," 4–6.

12. Jackson and Castillo, *Indians, Franciscans, and Spanish Colonization*, 51–52.

13. James A. Sandos, *Converting California: Indians and Franciscans in the Missions* (New Haven, CT: Yale University Press, 2004), 111–127.

14. Gregg Castro, "Mission Accomplice (But NOT Accomplished)," in *News from Native California* 28 (winter 2014): 62.

15. Steven W. Hackel, *Children of Coyote, Missionaries of Saint Francis: Indian-Spanish Relations in Colonial California, 1769–1850* (Chapel Hill: University of North Carolina Press, 2005), 114.

16. For example, many mission gift shops sell Richard Senate's *Ghosts of the California Missions and El Camino Real* (Santa Barbara, CA: Shoreline Press, 2011).

17. Terry G. Jordan, *North American Cattle-Ranching Frontiers: Origins, Diffusion, and Differentiation* (Albuquerque: University of New Mexico Press, 1993), 161–165.

18. Hackel, *Children of Coyote,* 65–123.

19. Ibid., 79–81.

20. Deana Dartt-Newton and Jon M. Erlandson, "Little Choice for the Chumash: Colonialism, Cattle, and Coercion in the California Missions," special issue, *American Indian Quarterly* 30 (2006): 416–430.

21. Sandos, *Converting California,* 128–134.

22. Phillips, *Vineyards and Vaqueros,* 65–66.

23. Zephyrin Engelhardt, *San Gabriel Mission and the Beginning of Los Angeles* (Chicago: Franciscan Herald Press, 1927), 33–34.

24. Phillips, *Vineyards and Vaqueros,* 65–66.

25. Engelhardt, *San Gabriel Mission and the Beginning of Los Angeles,* 33–34.

26. Phillips, *Vineyards and Vaqueros,* 65.

27. Kat Anderson, *Tending the Wild: Native American Knowledge and the Management of California's Natural Resources* (Berkeley: University of California Press, 2005), 76; Hackel, *Children of Coyote,* 65–72. While Hackel focuses on the Rumsen of Mission San Carlos near Monterey, the general aspects of his study can apply to many of the experiences of Native peoples throughout California.

28. James A. Sandos, "Between Crucifix and Lance: Indian-White Relations in California, 1769–1848," in *Contested Eden: California before the Gold Rush,* ed. Rámon A. Gutiérrez and Richard J. Orsi (Berkeley: University of California Press, 1998), 205.

29. Cook, *Conflict between the California Indian and White Civilization,* 227–229; Sandos, *Converting California,* 111–127; Hackel, *Children of Coyote,* 65–72.

30. Sandos, *Converting California,* 111–127.

31. Barbara L. Voss, "Colonial Sex: Archeology, Structured Space, and Sexuality in Alta California's Spanish-colonial Missions," in *Archaeologies of Sexuality,* ed. Robert A. Schmidt and Barbara L. Voss (New York: Routledge, 2000), 41.

32. Sandos, *Converting California,* 111–127.

33. Ibid., 114–115.

34. Ibid.

35. Phillips, *Vineyards and Vaqueros,* 142.

36. Sandos, *Converting California,* 111–127.

37. Jackson and Castillo, *Indians, Franciscans, and Spanish Colonization,* 48–49.

38. *Monjerío* translates as nunnery. Engelhardt, *San Gabriel Mission and the Beginning of Los Angeles,* 36–38.

39. Chelsea K. Vaughn, "Locating Absence: The Forgotten Presence of Monjeríos in the Alta California Missions," *Southern California Quarterly* 93 (2011): 141–174. The monjeríos also helped the priests and the matron in charge of the girls regulate the punishments meted out to young women.

40. Otto von Kotzebue, *A New Voyage Round the World, in the Years 1823, 24, 25, and 26,* Vol. 2 (London: Henry Colburn and Richard Bentley, 1830), 95.

41. Vaughn, "Locating Absence," 147–155.

42. Robert Heizer, ed., *The Indians of Los Angeles County: Hugo Reid's Letters of 1852* (Highland Park, CA: Southwest Museum, 1968), 87; Jackson and Castillo, *Indians, Franciscans, and Spanish Colonization*, 81–83.

43. Vaughn, "Locating Absence," 156–164.

44. Hackel, *Children of Coyote*, 182–185.

45. Ibid., 189–191. This belief structure was outlined in the codes from the Council of Trent (1545–1563). These codes sought to regulate the type of marriage deemed appropriate in the eyes of the church. For example, they banned marriage between close relatives. The codes made marriage a sacrament between two Catholics in the church based on an investigation carried out by a priest before the nuptials. A priest would also announce a couple's intent to wed for three consecutive days to ensure there were no communal objections to the marriage based on the regulations set forth in the codes.

46. Ibid., 199–202.

47. Ibid., 197–213.

48. José del Carmen Lugo, "Industrious Indians," trans. Nellie Van de Grift Sanchez, in *The Pride of the Missions: A Documentary History of San Gabriel Mission*, ed. Francis J. Weber (Hong Kong: Libra Press Limited, 1979), 136–139.

49. Heizer, *Indians of Los Angeles County*, 32–33. Gonorrhea and especially syphilis were spread directly through sexual intercourse, contact with open wounds, and the Native medicinal practices of blood-letting, and indirectly through contact with contaminated clothing and sheets.

50. Hackel, *Children of Coyote*, 96–115.

51. Ibid., 122.

52. Lisbeth Haas, *Saints and Citizens: Indigenous Histories of Colonial Missions and Mexican California* (Berkeley: University of California Press, 2014), 5.

53. Lorena Dixon and Hazel Maldonado, "Some Were Fooled," in *The Missions of California: A Legacy of Genocide*, ed. Rupert Costo and Jeannette Henry Costo (San Francisco: Indian Historian Press, 1987), 148–149.

54. Hackel, *Children of Coyote*, 321–331. The missionaries often tried to protect Native people from Spanish soldiers and settlers. They wrote to colonial civil authorities and requested that officials reassign or punish offending soldiers. However, some priests also abused Native people. For example, neophytes from Mission Santa Clara accused Father Tomás de la Peña of beating them. They argued that he was so brutal and "hotheaded" that he beat two men and a young boy to death. De la Peña was not the standard, but, at the least, many priests ordered punishments for neophytes.

55. Ibid., 321–366; Robert R. Archibald, "Indian Labor at the California Missions: Slavery or Salvation," *Journal of San Diego History* 24 (spring 1978): 172–182.

56. Guest, "Cultural Perspectives on California Mission Life," 15.

57. Lasuén, as quoted in Sandos, *Converting California*, 89.

58. Hackel, *Children of Coyote*, 322–330.

59. Sandos, *Converting California*, 89.

60. Guest, "Cultural Perspectives on California Mission Life," 14–17.

61. Jackson and Castillo, *Indians, Franciscans, and Spanish Colonization*, 52–53.
62. Guest, "Cultural Perspectives on California Mission Life," 14–17. Guest said that self-flagellation and whippings played a crucial role in the religious exercises of many Catholics in the eighteenth century. Some religious people during this time viewed voluntary self-flagellation as a form of penance and an expression of faith. According to Guest, "religious practice at the time was dominated by devotion to the passion of Christ and by the spirit of penance that issued from it" (p. 14). Bodily pain personified this religious devotion.
63. Jackson and Castillo, *Indians, Franciscans, and Spanish Colonization*, 78–85.
64. Hackel, *Children of Coyote,* 322–331.
65. Ibid., 329–330.
66. Jackson and Castillo, *Indians, Franciscans, and Spanish Colonization*, 78–85.
67. Guest, "Cultural Perspectives on California Mission Life," 20.

# 7

# *Native Voices and Experiences at California Missions*

> There are still living, wandering about, half-blind, half starved, in
> the neighborhood of the mission sites, old Indians who recollect the
> mission times in the height of their glory. Their faces kindle with a
> sad flicker of recollected happiness, as they tell of the days when they
> had all they wanted to eat, and the *padres* were so good and kind:
> "Bueno tiempo ! Bueno tiempo !" they say, with a hopeless sigh and
> shake of the head.
> —Helen Hunt Jackson, *Glimpses of California and the Missions* (1907)

Francis F. Guest argued that people must view the Spanish mission system
in its cultural perspective.[1] The Spanish established the California missions
as a component of their goal to claim Alta California for Spain. They used
methods that other societies at the time viewed as arcane, including excessive
punishment and humiliation tactics, hard labor regimens, religious indoctrination, and attempts to eradicate Native cultures. However, champions
of the mission myth in the late nineteenth and early twentieth centuries
sanitized narratives of Spanish colonization. Museum exhibitions at many
California missions today have immortalized this romanticized version of the
past, creating alternative narratives that remove the story of early California
from its cultural perspective. The perpetuation of romanticized mission mythology continues to relegate Native experiences during the mission era to
the periphery. Yet stewards of mission history at a few of these historic sites
buck the mission myth and provide more realistic interpretations of the past
that highlight Native experiences and provide alternative ways to understand
the impact of Spanish colonization on Native peoples in California.

Mission sites operated by the California Department of Parks and Recreation
work to override the unrealistic depictions of mission history common in
popular venues. Interpretations at these venues feature Native perspectives
more prominently. The typical religious narrative prominent at many mis-

sions becomes one of the many stories told in their exhibition spaces. The history presented at some of these missions also pulls back the curtains on the Spanish "white legend" popularized by Charles Fletcher Lummis, John Steven McGroarty, and *Ramona* enthusiasts. These sites interpret the mission system for what it was and some acknowledge that early twentieth-century preservation and reconstruction efforts helped to promote the romanticized mission myth. They provide Native voices that are missing in other mission representations and work to improve understandings of Native experiences with the Spanish for future generations. Moreover, a recently re-created version of the *Mission Play* and a *Toypurina* (2014) production that graced the stage of the Mission Playhouse communicate a more visible Native presence in the telling of mission history.

The contemporary Spanish missions that dot the landscape in California are centers of historical interpretation. Visitors to California, residents of the state, and schoolchildren often turn to these sites to learn about the early history of the region. Unbeknownst to many visitors, the history presented at many contemporary California mission sites reflects an incomplete, skewed, and biased perspective of the past created in the early twentieth century. This manufactured history focused on a romantic and idyllic representation of the mission era. Narratives centered on the benevolent work of Spanish priests and promotional efforts to preserve the mission ruins. However, the histories presented at Mission La Purísima Concepción and San Francisco de Solano, as well as the church-owned San Francisco de Asís (also known as Mission Dolores), reflect alternative interpretations of mission history that include Native experiences informed by Native voices and recent scholarship.[2] Recently as well, civic groups have worked to revise public presentations of mission history to impart a more accurate narrative to audiences. These public sites and private venues promote mission history by incorporating more accurate historical interpretations and Native perspectives in representations of the past.

## Revising the Myth at the San Gabriel Mission Playhouse

In recent years, the San Gabriel Mission Playhouse, once a center for romanticized mission tourism, has presented new perspectives that revise some of the old booster narratives. Civic groups in Los Angeles reinvented McGroarty's work to reflect contemporary understandings of the mission era to highlight Native experiences and their contemporary perspectives. The *Mission Play* once again graced the stage of the Mission Playhouse in early April 2013 in celebration of the city's centennial. Foregoing the romanticism that epitomized the original incarnation of the production, the newly "reimagined" *Mission Play* examines the impact of the California missions from multiple perspectives to reflect the diversity of San Gabriel today. The reimagined play begins in modern-day San Gabriel with a group of teenage hip-hop dancers gathering outside of Mission San Gabriel. Four of the teens are visited by the apparition of a man named Ubaldo, who takes them back in time to witness the history of California firsthand. The reenvisioned performance seeks to be educational and entertaining, reframing the dramatic original presentation with more honest and inclusive perspectives.[3]

Like many young students learning California history, the teens in the reconceived *Mission Play* are familiar with basic components of Spanish California history, but they are surprised to see the complex interactions among Native peoples, Spanish soldiers, and the padres. The young people witness Spanish soldiers and priests straining to survive in San Diego, Native peoples grappling with changes brought by the Spanish, and Junípero Serra's struggle to find converts. In the first act, the play addresses abbreviated catechisms and points out faults in the baptismal practices used by Spanish priests interested in finding converts as quickly as possible. It demonstrates that the priests desperately wanted to baptize a child to prove that the mission system would be viable in Alta California. Throughout the play, one of the teen observers continually criticizes Spanish colonization. She acknowledges the destruction done to Native communities and describes the historical implications of what she witnesses. She criticizes the Spanish for the disease, death, and the legacy of "genocide"—a term used in the play—they brought to Native Californians.

The retooled production removes much of the idyllic delusions of early California promoted by McGroarty, even while maintaining his general storyline and communicating Spanish colonization through the lens of a love story. The second and third acts illustrate the personal impact of Spanish colonization as it follows Serra's adopted ward, Anita, a half-Native and half-Spanish girl, and a young indigenous man named Pablo. Pulling from documented experiences found in historical records, the commandante of the Alta California presidios, Capt. Fernando de Rivera y Moncada, asks Anita to be his "personal servant," but Serra rebuffs the captain. Serra recognizes that Moncada had perverse intentions for the young woman. To protect Anita from further exploitation, Serra marries the young woman to her true love, Pablo, at Mission San Carlos Borroméo.[4] To avoid falling into a trap of romanticizing the era in the modern reproduction of the *Mission Play*, the padres present at the marriage ceremony acknowledge that the newlyweds will have a hard life and will likely not be accepted in either the Native or Spanish community.[5]

Highlighting the contemporary cultural diversity in San Gabriel, a procession

175

of misplaced Chinese dancers performs at Anita and Pablo's marriage cere-mony before the Spanish flamenco dancers. Spanish flamenco dancers were a popular yet unrealistic component of the original *Mission Play* that became part of the mission myth. To illustrate the multiple historical perspectives, the revised play includes several songs and dances by Gabrielino-Tongva performers, along with the Spanish flamenco and Chinese routines. Drunken Spanish soldiers invade the church and shoot Pablo after a brief confrontation following the marriage celebrations. The revised version of the *Mission Play* paints the Spanish soldiers as the main perpetrators of violence and disruption in the region. The missionaries remain benevolent forces, even if their actions had unintended negative consequences for indigenous communities. This is a common thread found in many presentations that critically examine the impact of Spanish colonization. Interpreters tread carefully to not place fault on the missionaries and the church. As a result, Spanish soldiers bear the brunt of the burden for spreading disease and abusing indigenous peoples.

McGroarty's original version of the *Mission Play* and interpreters at contem-porary California mission sites all point to secularization under Mexican rule as the downfall of the mission system. The end of the mission system is a turning point, and often an end point, in representations of early California history. Demonstrated in the third act of the reinvented *Mission Play*, the missions fall into ruins during this period. Ubaldo, the first baby brought to Serra for baptism in Alta California, remains the sole caretaker for Mission San Juan Capistrano. Ubaldo contemplates his life as a part of the mission system and the future of the crumbling site. Rather than use Señora Yorba to romanticize preservation of the Spanish landscape, as in the original *Mission Play*, the ghost of Ubaldo tells the modern-day teen observers that people must reconcile the past with the present—not to forget but to move forward. Significantly, Ubaldo then attempts to reconcile his anger with the abandonment of the missions with concerns about the incoming American settlers. The final curtain falls with a single Gabrielino-Tongva man standing under a spotlight, center stage, slowly beating a drum, as if to say "we are still here." Affirming and reiterating Native cultural continuity is a central theme in mission histories that aim for accuracy and improved representations.

Father Bruce Wellems, former parish pastor of Mission San Gabriel, has observed that "as Catholics, the work of reconciliation is what we embrace." According to Wellems, reconciling "the struggle of cultures" between the Catholic Spanish and Native Californians is an important component of the new *Mission Play*.[6] This is further reflected in *Toypurina* (2014), a play that illustrates the Gabrielino-Tongva struggle with the Spanish, seen through the experiences of Toypurina and the attempted revolt against Mission San Gabriel in 1785.[7] In moving forward and away from the romanticized portrayals of Spanish colonial history presented at many California missions, a number of interpreters at some mission sites work to present a different and more inclusive narrative to their audiences.

## Spanish History at State-Controlled Mission Sites

Promoting a new understanding of mission history will require many venues to reexamine and rephrase the traditional narratives told to the public as done in the *Mission Play*. For example, the California Department of Parks and Recreation controls the only building left at Mission Santa Cruz, the housing built for neophyte families at the mission. The exhibitions at Mission Santa Cruz focus on the experiences of the Ohlone and Yokut— the indigenous peoples associated with the mission. The mission presents a video of the Ohlone entitled "We are Still Here," that provides visitors with the Ohlone perspective on life *after* the mission period, emphasizing the cultural complexity and richness of Native communities. The film recounts that "to gain a foothold for Spain in [the] new world, the Spanish made the Indians work as laborers to build the missions. The padres used the missions to culturally change, civilize, and convert the California Indians into Christians." The narration further explains that "[Native people] built the mission buildings, they raised fields of grain, tended cattle and sheep and labored in workshops to sustain hundreds of Indians and the few Spaniards living at the mission." The film emphasizes the significant stress and change that the Spanish brought, including diseases that killed thousands of indigenous people. It pointedly notes that "the way [Native Californians] had lived for thousands of years would never be the same again." Similarly, Mission La Purísima Concepción and San Francisco de Solano focus much less on church history and veneration of the padres and more on the realities of mission life gleaned from Native voices, historic records, and current scholarship. They recognize that Native peoples overwhelmingly outnumbered Spanish padres, soldiers, and settlers in Alta California. Presentations at both of these missions sufficiently work to tell the story of early California from the perspective of Native Californians at the sites.

### Recognizing Spanish Failures at Mission La Purísima

Mission La Purísima boasts the most complete narrative and professional displays of any of the twenty-one California missions.[8] Indeed, it could serve as a model for other popular representations of California during the Spanish era because it articulates the "struggle of cultures" that accompanied Spanish settlement from a Native, specifically Chumash, perspective.[9]

Interpreters at the mission tactfully challenge the romanticized narratives upheld at many of the other California missions.[10] Instead of contextualizing the mission period through the lens of religion, interpreters at Mission La Purísima communicate the interactions between Native peoples and the Spanish through a sociocultural analysis of the period. Interpretive labels in the mission museum state that Mission La Purísima was, ultimately, a failure.

The visitor's center and exhibition hall, opened in 2009, promotes an understanding of mission history that places Native peoples at the center of its discussion. As the most populous residents of the missions by far, indigenous people and their experiences with the mission are front and center for visitors to explore. The history presented at Mission La Purísima begins with a discussion of the Chumash before contact and ends with mission restoration in the twentieth century. A team of museum professionals, park service leaders, local scholars, and knowledgeable volunteer docents known as the "Prelado de los Tesoros," worked to create an acceptable narrative that they shared with Chumash peoples.[11] This team of professionals, in conjunction with members of the Chumash community, examined every component of the exhibition to ensure they presented this history with truthfulness and compassion for the experiences of indigenous peoples. Representations of history at La Purísima have increasingly aimed for accuracy since reconstruction efforts began in the 1930s with the Civilian Conservation Corps.

Similar to many of the other California missions, La Purísima fell into ruins after mission secularization in the 1830s. A variety of Euro-American occupants used the buildings to shelter sheep and cattle, to accommodate a blacksmith shop, and even to house a saloon. Treasure hunters and collectors in the early twentieth century rummaged through the mission for relics. These vandals removed many of the iconic red roof tiles and flooring from the crippled site.[12] Stewards of the mission took down the remaining deteriorating roof tiles to prevent injury to site visitors. However, they unintentionally exposed the adobe walls to the natural elements, and the bricks deteriorated into mud over several decades. Just as Lummis and other mission conservators feared, vandals, negligence, and the passing of time caused significant damage to Mission La Purísima. Thus little of the original mission structure was standing by the early twentieth century. As one observer—an advocate of mission mythology— noted, by 1912 many missions, including La Purísima were "melancholy ruins, whose crumbling walls and remains of reservoirs . . . testify to the skill and the intelligent direction of the thousands of Indian converts who once congregated in these now lonely deserted ruined shrines and prospered under the rule of the gentle Franciscan brotherhood as never before or since."[13]

Lummis had an opportunity to preserve the crumbling mission through his work with the Landmarks Clubs. Union Oil Company offered the Landmarks Club the deed to the La Purísima ruins, provided that the civic organization raised enough funds to protect the site.[14] However, under the financial stress brought on by World War I, the Landmarks Club failed to meet its required financial commitment of $1,500 to maintain holding deed to the structure. Soon thereafter, under ever-greater financial strain, the Landmarks Club folded completely.[15] Union Oil eventually turned the property over to the state of California. After another generation of neglect, the National Park Service assigned members of the Civilian Conservation Corps to restore Mission La Purísima in 1933 as a part of the national effort to provide relief work during the Great Depression. The group of young men assigned to this task conducted research and used historical documentation to accurately reconstruct the mission.

Rather than serve as a museum itself—the practice at the other California missions—each of the rooms in the rebuilt mission reflects the actual use of the space in the 1820s, thereby giving visitors a more accurate understanding of the mission and its secular and religious goals. For example, the church does not contain pews for parishioners because Native peoples sat on mats placed on the floor during Mass. At many of the other contemporary mission sites, the churches contain ornate altars and are lined with modern pews. Mass is held at the mission church only once a year in celebration of the mission's founding day on December 8, 1787. For this occasion, the mission brings in folding chairs for attendees, allowing the lack of pews to serve as a learning experience for visitors. Because La Purísima is not officially affiliated with the local Catholic diocese, the church and interpretative spaces provide limited references to the religious components of Spanish colonization. They do not devote a majority of the exhibition space to venerating Serra, the Spanish priests that helped build the mission, or other religious relics as seen at San Gabriel, San Luis Rey, San Juan Capistrano, San Juan Bautista, and many other missions.

As noted, the exhibitions and displays at the interpretive center do not reflect the romanticized narrative told at many of the other California mission sites. The histories at many mission sites often glaze over monjeríos and the living arrangements for neophytes. At La Purísima, the walls of the monjerío, the dormitory for girls, are lined with plank bunks similar to the ones young Native women slept on during the mission period, and a group of dome huts near the mission demonstrates the living arrangements used by many neophytes. Aligning its discussion with leading scholars, the narrative told at Mission La Purísima introduces Spanish settlement in Alta California as a primarily colonial and economic undertaking. Religious conversion was a parallel goal of the system. Representations of religion do not overshadow the need for Native labor or the devastation brought by the Spanish to Native peoples. Interpreters at La Purísima emphasize that the Spanish crown intended the missions to be temporary institutions for use in claiming Alta California while they indoctrinated Native peoples in European culture and Catholicism—not the monolithic symbols of religion and the coming of "civilization" as suggested by other mission sites.

Like other mission sites, La Purísima's interpretive center includes a diorama of the mission during the Spanish period. However, Native laborers populate the set doing chores such as making adobe bricks, constructing buildings, carving wood, working the grist mill, tending gardens, and managing livestock, while others converse with the priest. Other than the priest, the only Spanish person in the scene is the mayordomo who oversees the laborers. Visitors are not misguided by lush gardens, ornate statues, or cityscapes that encroach into the mission landscape. The mission grounds at La Purísima remain on several hundred acres of undeveloped land. Visitors walk over un-landscaped dirt pathways dotted with holes dug by ground squirrels and gophers. In many ways, visitors at Mission La Purísima can experience a mission landscape that seems nearly unchanged.

The presentation at La Purísima lays out evidence in topical and chronological order, focusing on the tangible experiences of Native people during the Spanish era. Throughout the displays, interpreters foretell the inescapable failure of the mission instead of dramatizing a romantic foregone time. For example, under the heading "From Humble Beginnings to a Bustling Community," interpreters explain that the perceived success at the mission by 1804, measured by baptisms and agricultural production, actually masked the growing unhappiness among the Native community. In the nearly life-size exhibits, Native peoples rarely have smiles on their faces but rather show concern when interacting with the Spanish. The text for one exhibit explains that "corporal punishment and the regimented lifestyle fueled discontent among the neophytes. As more Chumash die from disease, the work from those remaining grows more difficult, and discontent increases."

To present a more Native-centered narrative, site interpreters at Mission La Purísima focus on labor. Backdrops display indigenous peoples working at the mission ranch with acres of farmland in the background. In the foreground of the display, visitors can see and touch cattle hides, blankets, reproduced farming tools, and iron implements made by the blacksmith—interactive components that appeal to the fourth-grade schoolchildren who frequent the mission. Mission La Purísima hosts several events during the year, including Mission Life Days. Visitors can see demonstrations and participate in tortilla and bread baking, candle and soap making, as well as weaving, carpentry, blacksmithing, and pottery production. Using live animals at the site, interpreters host a Sheep Shearing Day in late April, during which patrons learn about the labor-intensive process of wool cleaning and pro-duction—both activities carried out by women at the mission. Docents use the wool to weave blankets similar to the ones neophytes received annually during the Spanish era. Site interpreters also highlight the roles of children at the mission during Children's Mission Life Day. Although it is difficult to fully re-create mission life, interpreters inform visitors that Chumash children worked to support the mission economy by assisting in food production, wool cleaning, and a variety of other tasks.

Mission La Purísima also hosts several Village Days that combine reenact-ments of life at the neophyte village near the mission walls. Visitors can play Chumash games, learn basic basketry, grind acorn into meal, help build tule houses, and make dolls out of tule. Several times a year, the mission holds living history reenactment days, known as Purísima's People Days. During these times, interpreters "transform" the mission back to 1822, where it is again populated by "Native" men, women, and children working at the mission. Spanish officials, including Father Payeras and the mayordomo who directed the ranching and agriculture at the mission, also make appearanc-es. The reenactors highlight the daily chores neophytes performed but do not replicate the surveillance and control the Spanish exercised over them. Similarly, the interpretive center addresses the high rate of death and disease throughout the mission system, and yet living history days present a more attractive past that appeals to visitors as educational and fun experiences.

Nonetheless, professionals at Mission La Purísima have responded to shifts in social history that shine light on more diverse and complicated narratives in their museum interpretations. In their examination of authenticity in museums, Spencer R. Crew and James E. Sims observed that museums fre-quently create exhibitions based on their collections, which are made up of materials that collectors at one point deemed valuable and worthy of saving. At California missions, these objects overwhelmingly reflect the religious and colonial structure of mission life while far fewer objects echo the experiences of Native Californians because "the objects of ordinary individuals . . . did not have the same historical significance in the eyes of curators or other scholars" when museum collections were developed.[16] Many exhibitions at mission museums are "object-driven," and these objects "control the focus of the exhibition; they shape the themes and concepts presented to the public, and are the ideas of the curator [that] are transmitted to visitors. So, if the objects are not available to support a particular theme or to raise an issue, that theme or issue is not stressed in the presentation."[17] To counterbalance the lack of objects that reflect Native experiences at the mission, interpreters at La Purísima display selected objects and use visual pictorial displays to communicate the history of the site. This approach reflects a more authentic historical experience according to Crew and Sims's framework because La Purísima has broken from the "concept of object driven exhibitions and produce[d] presentations controlled by historical themes rather than by available objects."[18] Although Mission La Purísima does incorporate objects into its displays, the objects supplement its narrative of the past instead of standing as lone representations of history.

## Building Connections to the Past at Mission San Francisco de Solano

Presentations provided by docents at Mission San Francisco de Solano in Sonoma also contain more inclusive discussions of the past. Site interpreters report that students are very interested in learning what happened to indigenous peoples after the mission era. According to these mission interpreters, students are not frightened or traumatized from learning about the negative components of the mission system, including death and disease. Presented sensitively and correctly, students may learn a great deal about the perils of mission life and the complicated relationship between Native people and the Spanish.[19] Docents at Mission Solano tackle these difficult tasks in their tours.

Mission San Francisco Solano was the last of the twenty-one California missions established by the Franciscans in 1823. It is owned and operated by the state of California. Because the mission is not an active Catholic parish church like a majority of the California missions today, the historical narrative told at Mission Solano focuses more heavily on the experiences of Native peoples rather than the few Spanish priests and soldiers who occupied the mission sites. Yet the Sonoma mission is one of the smaller mission sites, with downtown Sonoma pushing against the mission walls on all sides. It is only partially reconstructed, and the building at the site currently is an inaccurate representation of the original mission, with a less than ideal layout for museum displays. Site interpreters are quick to point out that the displays at Mission Solano are outdated and boring. To make up for the humble displays and inaccuracies in the layout of the reconstructed site, docents have worked to create a well-rounded and engaging narrative in tours geared toward the schoolchildren who visit the mission. Visitors who do not take these guided tours have a difficult time contextualizing the history presented at the mission, characterized by dated, dry displays that contain wordy labels and minimal artifacts.

In an effort to address Native representation more directly, an interpretive planning firm hired by the State Parks conducted research and provided recommendations for a new interpretation master plan for Mission Solano. The firm recommended that leaders at Sonoma State Historic Park make Native experiences central to the themes presented at the mission. They suggested that the park consult local Native communities "to ensure Native American culture and history of the Mission is properly interpreted."[20] The firm also recommended recreating tule homes to form a neophyte village at the mission site to help visitors understand "the interwoven cultures of Native American neophytes and Hispanic colonizers."[21] While reinterpretation of the site's exhibition space has been slow, docents work to include Native perspectives in their discussions of mission history. To do this, some site interpreters provide each schoolchild with a lanyard inscribed with the Christian name of a Native child during tours.[22] As the children tour the mission, they learn about the varied reasons Native people originally came to the missions. Guides explain that many missions offered Native people a reliable source of food after Spanish livestock and plant species decimated traditional food sources. Native people also came to the missions because they were interested in goods the Spanish brought. Some indigenous peoples also recognized similarities between shamans and Spanish priests. They were curious about the spiritual power of the Spanish missionaries. Native people also valued song, dance, and music, and the missions offered access to new instruments and songs.

The history of the site, as at La Purísima, is "idea-driven." In these types of museums, "more importance is given to the research done by scholars," and voices found in primary sources—including contemporary Native testimonies.[23] Rather than mask the realities of life for Native peoples during the Spanish era, guides at Mission Solano explain to children that indigenous people often lived in villages outside the walls of the mission. The original mission quadrangle was not full of beautifully landscaped gardens, so Mission Solano does not have large lush foliage in its courtyard. Instead, the inner courtyard has a fountain and trees, but also a large cactus grove in the back that illustrates the type of natural "living" walls Native peoples used for food and to manage livestock herds. Once in the modest mission complex interior children learn that the Spanish used the hundreds of Coast and Lake Miwok, Pomo, Patwin, and Wappo peoples who once occupied Mission Solano as the main source of labor. Again, the discussion focus is on the experiences of Native Californians instead of the material objects of priests and Spanish colonizers found in many mission collections.

Docents weave a narrative around the lives of the Native children whose names the students wear around their necks. Mission guides place the students in the figurative shoes of their historical counterparts and explain the daily lives of Native Californian children roughly their own age. They explain that children as young as 10 or 11 worked at the missions. They helped tan hides, harvest food, prepare and cook meals, assist with construction, and many other jobs. Students at Mission La Purísima also learn that children frequently followed in the footsteps of their parents; thus a baker, weaver, or field worker's child would often be relegated to the same work. At both Solano and La Purísima, children learn that the Spanish housed all the young girls in a single dormitory. Docents explain that the living conditions in the monjeríos were so bad, with only a tiny window for ventilation, thick walls, and a dirt floor, that many young women died. Rather than skirt the negative aspects of mission life, including malnutrition, disease, and death, some docents at Mission Solano tackle these topics head-on.

By the end of their mission tour, guides have exposed schoolchildren to a more realistic narrative that dispels the mission myth. Students learn that the missions were complicated places where Native peoples sometimes went to try to improve their lives. More frequently, however, indigenous people had to negotiate a foreign world filled with much pain and hardship. Using an image from early explorers, docents show how local Native people singed their hair short as a sign of mourning. Interpreters tell students that it was not unusual to see indigenous people with short hair because the high death rate meant that neophytes constantly were in mourning. A memorial of the dead buried at the mission reflects this sad reality for Native peoples living at Mission Solano. Through this idea-based narrative, students do not encounter authoritative objects from the mission era that stand as representations of the site's history. Instead they are asked to use their imaginations. Curators and tour guides purposely shape the experience so that, as Crew and Sims observed, "imaginative truth is experienced, for the aware audience collaborator, as present truth."[24]

Outside the west wall of Mission Solano rests a striking black stone memorial that honors the names of the nearly 830 people buried at the mission. A coalition of local scholars, including Edward D. Castillo, community members, and the church, helped to raise funds for this memorial, and Castillo researched mission records for the project. The mission cemeteries rest below a street adjacent to the west wall of the mission and a small housing complex bordering the eastern side of the site. At the memorial, tour guides encourage the students to look for the name they have been wearing around their neck. Some students find the name of their historical counterpart—such as Pasqual, Juan Diego, Thomasa, Evanisto, and Delfina—marked with an asterisk and realize that this child died at the mission, as did many adults during the brief tenure of Mission Solano's existence. Others find that their assigned person lived a much longer life beyond mission secularization.

## Curating Native-centric History at Mission Dolores

California mission sites controlled by the state and the church-owned Mission San Francisco de Asís make great efforts to reconcile the problems of the Spanish missions with the experiences of indigenous peoples. They publically recognize the astonishingly high death rate of Native peoples after Spanish colonization, but also demonstrate Native cultural continuity into the twenty-first century. Andrew Galvan, curator at Mission San Francisco de Asís, also known as Mission Dolores, is Ohlone/Miwok, and some of his ancestors were baptized at the mission. He works to create a museum atmosphere that focuses on Native people and their continued presence, noting that "I proudly remind people that the mission was built by and for Indians. I'm determined to tell that neglected history."[25] Church leadership at the mission supports Galvan and his message.

The contemporary museum at Mission Dolores is a tribute to the Ohlone who populated the San Francisco Bay area. It includes reproductions of baskets, buckskin clothing, tools, and other implements used by local indigenous peoples. Galvan worked to change the shared graveyard and traditionally idyllic garden space in the mission courtyard after he took over curatorship at the mission a decade ago. Under Galvan's guidance, the mission planted local plants and built a dome-shaped Ohlone house in the mission courtyard. Much like Mission Solano, the complete narrative is not necessarily displayed in signs and labels that accompany exhibited objects. Again, docents and interpreters at Mission Dolores provide accounts of the complexities of mission history through their tours. Visitors who take self-guided tours of the mission site receive far less information than those who benefit from a tour led by Galvan and his assistant curator, Vincent Medina (Ohlone). In recent years Galvan and Medina worked to present "the other side of the mission story, from the viewpoint of the Indians."[26]

Together, the two curators created a narrative that recounts accurate and controversial histories of Spanish California as documented by Native peoples and contemporary scholars. From the perspective of curatorial staff at the mission, the Spanish sought to extinguish Native cultures and religions but ultimately failed. The Spanish baptized indigenous peoples and "gave them new names. They enslaved them, and forced them to perform heavy labor." The Spanish punished converted Native Californians with beatings, "and worked to eradicate their culture and replace it with their own."[27] Galvan and Medina argue that the contemporary church is not like the Spanish missions established in California nearly 250 years ago. They observe that many Native people continually work to reconcile contemporary Catholic beliefs with the abuses their ancestors endured under the Spanish system.[28]

Galvan argues that "the missionaries were well intentioned but they weren't anthropologists. Father Serra was [a] very, very good person in a very, very bad system."[29]

Other indigenous people disagree with the positive assessments of Serra. Many Native Californians from around the state have voiced their opposition to the romanticized perspective of California mission history and strongly object the canonization of Serra who was declared a saint by Pope Francis on September 23, 2015. Others, writing in the late twentieth century, argue that people who romanticize the mission era and want to venerate Serra must ask themselves "whether or not the understanding of those priests of the eighteenth century would be one which we would wish to proclaim today."[30] Efforts to understand the California missions in their cultural perspective demonstrates a divide between practices at the missions, such as whippings, and behavior deemed acceptable by the Catholic Church in subsequent generations.[31] Yet Serra and other Spanish missionaries are venerated at several California missions today.[32]

### Attempts to Reconcile with Spanish California Mission History

Some local leaders in the Catholic Church have begun to acknowledge the abuses and cultural destruction the Spanish missions inflicted on Native Californians. Church leaders at a few sites have made public apologies to contemporary Native communities for the injustices imposed on their ancestors by the Spanish. For example, Bishop Francis Quinn apologized to the Coast Miwok during a special Mass in December 2008 that celebrated the 190th anniversary of the founding of Mission San Rafael in the northern San Francisco Bay area. Quinn acknowledged the mistakes of the Spanish priests who should have offered Native people Catholicism rather than force the religion and Spanish lifeways on them.[33] He observed that "the padres tried to impose a European Catholicism upon the natives. . . . The church this evening apologizes for trying to take Indian out of the Indian."[34] According to reports, this watershed apology was met with audible gasps by the many Native people in attendance.

Similarly, Bishop Richard Garcia held a special "Reconciliation Mass" at Mission San Juan Bautista on December 22, 2012. Garcia acknowledged and apologized for Spanish Catholic mistreatment of Native peoples, especially the Amah Mutsun whom he personally addressed at the Mass. Some contemporary church leaders work to reconcile present ministering efforts with past mistakes by working with local Native communities and apologizing for the misdeeds of Spanish Catholicism from the sixteenth to early nineteenth centuries. Amah Mutsun tribal chairperson Valentin Lopez has observed that "there is a history here [that] the Catholic Church has wanted to deny for many years, so this [apology] is really something of a breakthrough in reclaiming our history, and gaining recognition as the survivors of cultural genocide."[35] Moreover, in early July 2015 Pope Francis, speaking in Bolivia, publically recognized the atrocities committed against indigenous peoples during colonization and asked for forgiveness for the "grave sins . . . committed against the native people of America in the name of God."[36] Although these apologies help some Native communities reconcile with the Catholic Church, many public representations of the Spanish missions and the canonization of Junípero Serra continue to promote the mission myth—and thereby continue to ignore the complex interplay between Native peoples and the Spanish during this period.

At the same time, today some Native Californians embrace the church and have come to terms, in some ways, with the troubling history of Spanish missionization. As Janice Ramos observed, "As negative as the missions were in so many ways, they allowed my great-great-great-grandmother to survive. They gave her skills to survive in the world that was becoming. They gave her . . . the ability to speak the language. . . . That's what the mission gave her. . . . As negative as it was, it was still a meeting place where we were together. So this land had to be sacred to my family because it allowed her to be with her people."[37] For other Tongva-Gabrielino people, the Spanish missions and Catholicism provide a common identity with a documented heritage that serves almost as "another place of origin as far as [a] historical place where people are connected to, to some people a sacred space."[38] Conversely, Linda Gonzales has said, "I have a different background. . . . We always hated any acknowledgement of San Gabriel. . . . We have a revulsion. Usually if it's mentioned, or any of the missions, it would be with a sneer from my parents."[39]

Outside this divide, many understand the need for more accurate representation of Native histories in public spaces and classrooms, because "any time you talk about Indians—[in] the fourth grade in California you learn about Indians and the Mission Period."[40] Zevi Gutfreund observed that the still popular fourth grade project to construct models of the physical mission structures "has left generations of California children with the impression that the missions were idyllic sanctuaries for the Catholic padres and Indians who lived there."[41] These projects pay quiet homage to the promotional efforts of Lummis and other boosters who romanticized the Spanish missions over one century ago and continue to marginalize the frequently negative experiences of Native peoples in the missions.[42]

Traveling along the mission trail, from San Diego to Sonoma, tourists have an opportunity to experience California history at reconstructed mission sites. Yet the prevalent narratives at California missions today reflect a romanticized history popularized by writers and promoters at the turn of the twentieth century. Lummis, McGroarty, James, Jackson, and many others used the mission ruins to dramatize early California history, effectively constructing the mission myth. At that time, few popular writers or scholars included analyses of the rich histories and cultures of Native Californians in their descriptions of the region's past. As heirs of this tradition, many mission sites today neglect to fully address the ways in which Native peoples negotiated the changes brought by foreign colonization. These struggles included maintaining control of their ancestral homelands, protecting indigenous belief systems in the face of forced cultural assimilation, enduring the constant threat of disease and death, learning new regimented labor strategies, and suffering from harsh and humiliating punishments, malnutrition, and a high mortality rate. The counternarratives provided by contemporary Native communities in California and new generations of scholars, informed by indigenous sources, indicate that Native people did not passively submit to Spanish colonizers. They responded in a variety of ways and worked to find opportunities to preserve their lives and cultures.

**Notes**

1. Francis F. Guest, "Cultural Perspectives on California Mission Life," *Southern California Quarterly* 65 (1983): 1–65.
2. California State Parks, "We Are Still Here," California Department of Parks and Recreation, http://www.parks.ca.gov/?page_id=27198.
3. In its effort to celebrate San Gabriel's diversity today, including a large Chinese population, Chinese dancers enter center stage during celebrations in the second and third acts. However, this is unrealistic as large-scale Chinese migration to California did not begin until the early 1850s with the gold rush.
4. In the original production, Serra marries Anita to another neophyte to protect her from the commandante, thereby removing Anita's agency to choose her partner while glorifying the padres as the protectors of Native Californians. Chelsea K. Vaughn, "Locating Absence: The Forgotten Presence of Monjeríos in the Alta California Missions," *Southern California Quarterly* 93 (2011): 141–174.
5. Because Pablo was not a neophyte and Anita was half-Spanish and raised at the missions with Father Serra.
6. Jennifer Wing Atencio, "Reconciliation: 'The Mission Play,' Reimagined, in San Gabriel," *Tidings Online,* March 29, 2013, http://www.the-tidings.com/index.php/news/newslocal/ 3271-reconciliation-the-mission-play-reimagined-in-san-gabriel.
7. *Toypurina* was performed October 23–24, 2014 at the Mission Playhouse. This production was directed by Johnathan Salisbury (who also directed the reenvisioned *Mission Play*) and co-written by two members of the Gabrieleño-Tongva Band of Mission Indians, Matthew Lovio and Andrew Morales.
8. Information about Mission La Purísima was gleaned from visits to the site in the spring of 2013.
9. The interpretations at La Purísima are not without flaws. For example, they continue to sanitize their reenactments of mission history by presenting the simple chores conducted by Native people, including tortilla and bread making. They do not have reenactors do heavy manual labor as many Native people did during the Spanish and Mexican periods.
10. The visitor's center is a few hundred feet from the mission buildings at La Purísima. Visitors do not have to file through the exhibition hall and gift shop to see the mission. This is unlike the layout of many of the other California missions where visitors must pay for admission or provide a donation at the gift shop.
11. Prelado de los Tesoros translates to "Keepers of Treasure."
12. Joseph H Engbeck Jr., *La Purísima Mission: A Pictorial History* (Sacramento: Department of Parks and Recreation, State of California, 1987), 17.
13. F. A. Mann, "La Purísima Concepcion Missions [*sic*] at Lompoc, California: A Historical Memorial," 1912, pamphlet, Huntington Library, San Marino, California, 14–15.
14. Union Oil Company held title to Mission La Purísima and the surrounding land in the early twentieth century as a part of its oil land holdings in Santa Barbara

County. The company sold off much of its agricultural land in the Lompoc valley around 1904.

15. Edwin R. Bingham, *Charles F. Lummis: Editor of the Southwest* (San Marino, CA: Huntington Library Publications, 1955), 111.

16. Spencer R. Crew and James E. Sims, "Locating Authenticity: Fragments of a Dialogue," in *Exhibiting Cultures: The Poetics and Politics of Museum Display*, ed. Ivan Karp and Steven D. Levine (Washington, DC: Smithsonian Institution Press, 1991), 165.

17. Ibid.

18. Ibid., 167.

19. Information about Mission San Francisco Solano was gathered from visits to the site from 2013 to 2015.

20. California State Parks, "Sonoma State Historic Park: Draft Recommendations Section for the New Interpretation Master Plan," California Department of Parks and Recreation, June 6, 2011, http://www.parks.ca.gov/SonomaPlan.

21. Ibid.

22. One docent explained that the mission uses Native people's Christian names because local Native traditions reveal a preference for not using the indigenous names of people after their death.

23. Crew and Sims, "Locating Authenticity," 169.

24. Ibid., 173.

25. Edward Guthmann, "Mission Dolores Curator Andrew Galvan," *San Francisco Chronicle*, March 20, 2011, http://www.sfgate.com/entertainment/article/Mission-Dolores-curator-Andrew-Galvan-2388292.php.

26. Dana Perrigan, "Ohlone Descendant and Devout Catholic Tells Painful Truths about Mission Days," *Catholic San Francisco* September 7, 2012, http://catholic-sf.org/news_select.php?newsid=23&id=60242.

27. Ibid.

28. Perrigan noted that some Ohlone continue to practice their Native religion, Kuksu, while others practice a hybrid of Christianity and Kuksu. This also applies to many other Native Californians whose ancestors were introduced to Christianity by Euro-Americans but maintained ties to their Native cultures and religions as well. For examples of cultural and religious blending among other groups of contemporary Native Californians, see Malcolm Margolin, ed., *The Way We Lived: California Indian Stories, Songs, and Reminiscences* (Berkeley: Heyday Books and the California Historical Society, 1993), 190–192.

29. Perrigan, "Ohlone Descendant and Devout Catholic Tells Painful Truths." Galvan sits on the board of The Serra Cause, an organization that has worked to have Serra canonized by the Catholic Church. He participated in a Mass as the pope formally proclaimed Serra's canonization. Cindy Wooden, "Pope Canonizes Junipero Serra, Proclaims joy of Mission Spirit," *Catholic San Francisco* September 25, 2015. http://www.catholic-sf.org/ns.php?newsid=30&id=63879.

30. Michael Galvan, "No Veneration for Serra," in *The Missions of California: A Legacy*

*of Genocide,* ed. Rupert Costo and Jeannette Henry Costo (San Francisco: Indian Historian Press, 1987), 168–170. Michael Galvan is the brother of Andrew Galvan.

31. Steven W. Hackel, *Children of Coyote, Missionaries of Saint Francis: Indian-Spanish Relations in Colonial California, 1769–1850* (Chapel Hill: University of North Carolina Press, 2005), 322–330.

32. The statues of Serra at several Spanish California sites have been vandalized in the wake of controversy that followed the pope's declaration of Serra as a saint. The statue at the Monterey Presidio was decapitated in mid-October 2015 and protestors wrote "Saint of Genocide" on the headstone of Serra in the days after his canonization.

33. Betty Goerke, "Bishop Quinn Apologizes to the Coast Miwok," *Acorn* 39 (spring 2008): 1, 7. Bishop Francis Quinn was retired at the time of his apology. He worked for years among the Navajo in Arizona. This experience gave him personal connections and knowledge of the richness of Native spirituality and culture.

34. Ibid.

35. Patrick Dwire, "Healing Historical Wounds," *Good Times,* January 9, 2013, http://www.gtweekly.com/index.php/santa-cruz-news/santa-cruz-local-news/4472-healing-historical-wounds.html.

36. Jim Yardley and William Neuman, "In Bolivia, Pope Francis Apologizes for Church's 'Grave Sins,'" *New York Times,* July 10, 2015, A4.

37. Janice Ramos as quoted in Claudia Jurmain and William McCawley, *O, My Ancestor: Recognition and Renewal for the Gabrielino-Tongva People of the Los Angeles Area* (Berkeley: Heyday Books, 2009), 137.

38. Jurmain and McCawley, *O, My Ancestor,* 89; Cindi Alvitre, as quoted in Jurmain and McCawley, *O, My Ancestor,* 136.

39. Ibid., 136.

40. Desirée Martinez, as quoted in Jurmain and McCawley, *O, My Ancestor,* 187.

41. Zevi Gutfreund, "Standing Up to Sugar Cubes: The Contest over Ethnic Identity in California's Fourth-Grade Mission Curriculum," *Southern California Quarterly* 92 (summer 2010): 161-197.

42. Ibid., 192. Alternative projects that present students with multiple perspectives through primary sources analysis and engaging in hands-on activities emerged in many classrooms; yet many other teachers continue to use the mission-model project in a way that promotes the romanticized mission myth in popular histories of California.

# Select Bibliography

**Primary Sources**

Boscana, Geronimo. *Chinigchinich*. 1933. Reprint. Banning, CA: Malki Museum Press, 1978.

Crespí, Juan. *A Description of Distant Roads: Original Journals of the First Expedition into California, 1769–1770*, edited and translated by Alan K. Brown. San Diego: San Diego State University Press, 2001.

Geiger, Maynard, ed. and trans. *Letter of Luis Jayme, O.F.M. San Diego, October 17, 1772*. Los Angeles: Dawson's Book Shop, 1970.

Jackson, Helen Hunt. *A Century of Dishonor: A Sketch of the United States Government's Dealings with Some of the Indian Tribes*. New York: Harper and Brothers, 1881.

---. *Ramona: A Story*. Boston: Roberts Brothers, 1884.

---. *Glimpses of California and the Missions*. Boston: Little, Brown, and Company, 1907.

James, George Wharton. *In and Out of the Old Missions of California*. Boston: Little, Brown, and Company, 1906.

---. *Through Ramona's Country*. Boston: Little, Brown, and Company, 1909.

Kenneally, Finbar, ed. *Writings of Fermín Francisco de Lasuén*. 2 Vols. Washington, DC: Academy of American Franciscan History, 1965.

Kotzebue, Otto von. *A New Voyage Round the World, in the Years 1823, 24, 25, and 26*. Vol. II. London: Henry Colburn and Richard Bentley, 1830.

Mann, F. A. "La Purisima Concepcion Missions [*sic*] at Lompoc, California: A Historical Memorial." 1912. Pamphlet. Huntington Library, San Marino, California,

Margolin, Malcolm, ed. *Life in a California Mission: The Journals of Jean François De La Pérouse, Monterey in 1786*. Berkeley: Heyday Books, 1989.

McGroarty, John S. *California: Its History and Romance*. Los Angeles: Grafton Publishing Company, 1911.

---. *History of Southern California*. 1914. Reprint, Fresno: California History Books, 1979.

---. *Mission Memories*. Los Angeles: Neuner Corporation, 1929.

Palou, Francisco. *Historical Memoirs of New California*. 4 Vols. Edited and translated by Herbert Eugene Bolton. New York: Russell & Russell, 1926.

Reed, Mai Richie. *Mai Richie Reed Diaries, 1907–1908*. Unpublished diaries. Huntington Library, San Marino, CA.

Tibesar, Antonine, ed. *Writings of Junípero Serra*. 4 Vols. Washington DC: Academy of American Franciscan History, 1955–1966.

Warner, J.J., Benjamin Hayes, and J.P. Widney. *An Historical Sketch of Los Angeles County: From the Spanish Occupancy, by the Founding of Mission San Gabriel Arcángel, September 8, 1771, to July 4, 1876.* Los Angeles: Mirror Printing, Ruling and Binding House, 1876.

## Secondary Sources

Anderson, Kat. *Tending the Wild: Native American Knowledge and the Management of California's Natural Resources.* Berkeley: University of California Press, 2005.

Allen, Paul F. "Tourists in Southern California, 1875–1903." Master's thesis. Claremont Colleges, Claremont, California, 1940.

Aron, Stephen. "Lessons in Conquest: Towards a Greater Western History." *Pacific Historical Review* 63 (May 1994): 125-147.

Avila, Eric. *Popular Culture in the Age of White Flight: Fear and Fantasy in Suburban Los Angeles.* Berkeley: University of California Press, 2004.

Bancroft, Hubert Howe. *History of California.* 6 vols. San Francisco: The History Company, 1884–1890.

Basso, Keith. *Wisdom Sits in Places: Landscape and Language Among the Western Apache.* Albuquerque: University of New Mexico Press, 1996.

Bannon, John Francis ed. *Bolton and the Spanish Borderlands.* Norman: University of Oklahoma Press, 1964.

Bean, Lowell J. *Mukat's People: The Cahuilla of Southern California.* Berkeley: University of California Press, 1972.

Bean, Lowell J. and Thomas F. King, eds. *'Antap: California Indian Political and Economic Organization.* Ramona, CA: Ballena Press, 1974.

Beebe, Rose Marie and Robert M. Senkewicz, eds. *Lands of Promise and Despair: Chronicles of Early California, 1535–1864.* Santa Clara, CA: Santa Clara University, in conjunction with Heyday Books, 2001.

Biolsi, Thomas and Larry J. Zimmerman, eds. *Indians and Anthropologists: Vine Deloria Jr. and the Critique of Anthropology.* Tucson: University of Arizona Press, 1997.

Bingham, Edwin R. *Charles F. Lummis: Editor of the Southwest.* San Marino, CA: Huntington Library, 2006.

Blackburn, Thomas C. and Kat Anderson, eds. *Before the Wilderness: Environmental Management by Native Californians.* Menlo Park: Ballena Press, 1993.

Bolton, Herbert E. *The Spanish Borderlands: A Chronicle of Old Florida and the Southwest.* New Haven, CT: Yale University Press, 1921.

---. "Defensive Spanish Exploration and the Significance of Borderlands." In *Bolton and the Spanish Borderland*, edited by John Francis Bannon, 32–64. 1930. Reprint, Norman: University of Oklahoma Press, 1964.

Bouvier, Virginia. *Women and the Conquest of California, 1542-1840: Codes of Silence.* Tucson: University of Arizona Press, 2001.

Bremer, Thomas S. "Tourists and Religion at Temple Square and Mission San Juan

Capistrano." Special Issue. *Journal of American Folklore* 113 (autumn 2000): 422-435.

Carrico, Richard L. "Sociopolitical Aspects of the 1775 Revolt at Mission San Diego de Alcala: an Ethnohistorical Approach." *The Journal of San Diego History* 43 (Summer 1997).

---. *Strangers in a Stolen Land: Indians of San Diego County from Prehistory to the New Deal.* San Diego: Sunbelt Publications, 2008.

Castañeda, Antonia I. "Sexual Violence in the Politics and Policies of Conquest." *Building With our Hands: New Directions in Chicana Studies*, edited by Adela de la Torre and Beatríz M. Pesquera, 15–33. Berkeley, University of California Press, 1993.

Castillo, Edward D., ed. *Native American Perspectives on the Hispanic Colonization of Alta California.* Spanish Borderlands Sourcebook 26. New York: Garland Publishing, 1991.

---. "Gender Status Decline, Resistance, and Accommodation among Female Neophytes in the Missions of California: A San Gabriel Case Study." *American Indian Culture and Research Journal* 8 (1994): 67–93.

---. "Blood Came from Their Mouths: Tongva and Chumash Responses to the Pandemic of 1801." *American Indian Culture and Research Journal* 23 (summer 1999): 47–61.

Chan, Sucheng. "A People of Exceptional Character: Ethnic Diversity, Nativism, and Racism in the California Gold Rush." Special Issue. *California History* 79 (2000): 44–85.

Cook, Sherburne F. *The Conflict Between the California Indians and White Civilization.* 1943. Reprint, Berkeley: University of California Press, 1976.

Cooper, Karen Coody. *Spirited Encounters: American Indians Protest Museum Policies and Practices.* Lanham, MI: Alta Mira Press, 2008.

Costo, Rupert and Jeannette Henry Costo, eds. *The Missions of California: A Legacy of Genocide.* San Francisco: Indian Historian Press, 1987.

Crosby, Alfred W. *The Columbian Exchange: Biological and Cultural Consequences of 1492.* Westport, CT: Praeger, 2003.

Culver, Lawrence. *The Frontier of Leisure: Southern California and the Shaping of Modern America.* New York: Oxford University Press, 2010.

Dartt-Newton, Deana and Jon M. Erlandso. "Little Choice for the Chumash: Colonialism Cattle, and Coercion in the California Missions." Special Issue. *American Indian Quarterly* 30 (2006): 416–430.

DeLyser, Dydia. "Ramona Memories: Fiction, Tourist Practices, and Placing the Past in Southern California." *Annals of the Association of American Geographers* 93 (December 2003): 886–908.

---. *Ramona Memories: Tourism and the Shaping of Southern California.* Minneapolis: University of Minnesota Press, 2005.

Delay, Brian. *War of a Thousand Deserts: Indian Raids and the U.S.-Mexican War.* New Haven, CT: Yale University Press, 2008.

Deverell, William. *White Washed Adobe: The Rise of Los Angeles and the Remaking of Its Mexican Past.* Berkeley: University of California Press, 2005.

Dixon, Roland B. and Alfred L. Kroeber "The Native Languages of California." *American Anthropologist* 5 (1903): 1–26.

Dudley, Gordon. Charles F. Lummis: Crusader in Corduroy. Los Angeles: Cultural Assets Press, 1972.

Engelhardt, Zephyrin. *The Franciscans in California.* Harbor Springs, MI: Holy Childhood Indian School, 1897.

---. *The Missions and Missionaries of California.* 4 Vols. San Francisco: James H. Berry Company, 1908–1915.

---. *The Missions and Missionaries of California: San Diego Mission.* San Francisco: The James H. Barry Company, 1920.

---. *San Gabriel Mission and the Beginning of Los Angeles.* Chicago: Franciscan Herald Press, 1927.

Engstrand, Iris H.W. "Seekers of the 'Northern Mystery': European Exploration of California and the Pacific." In *Contested Eden: California Before the Gold Rush,* edited by Ramon A. Gutierrez and Richard J. Orsi, 78–110. Berkeley: University of California Press, 1998.

Gaither, Edmund Barry. "'Hey! That's Mine!': Thoughts on Pluralism and American Museums." In *Museums and Communities: The Politics of Public Culture,* edited by Ivan Karp, Christine Mullen Kreamer, and Steven D. Levine, 56–64. Washington, DC: Smithsonian Institution Press, 1992.

Geiger, Maynard. *The Indians of Mission Santa Bárbara.* 2nd ed. Santa Barbara: Franciscan Friars, 2010.

Gerhard, Peter. *The Northern Frontier of New Spain.* Rev. ed. Norman: University of Oklahoma Press, 1993.

Gonzales, Nathan. "Riverside, Tourism, and the Indian: Frank A. Miller and the Creation of Sherman Institute." *Southern California Quarterly* 84 (2002): 194–221.

Guest, Francis F. "An Examination of the Thesis of S.F. Cook on the Forced Conversion of Indians in the California Missions." *Southern California Quarterly* 61 (1979): 1–77.

---. "Cultural Perspectives on California Mission Life." *Southern California Quarterly* 65 (1983): 1–65.

---. "An Inquiry into the Role of the Discipline in the California Missions." *Southern California Quarterly* 71 (1989): 1–68.

Guinn, James Miller. *A History of California and an Extended History of Los Angeles and Environs: Also Containing Biographies of Well-known Citizens of the Past and Present.* Los Angeles: Historic Records Company, 1915.

Gulliford, Andrew. "Bones of Contention: The Repatriation of Native American Human Remains." *The Public Historian* 18 (Autumn 1996): 119–143.

Gutierrez, Ramon A. and Richard J. Orsi, eds. *Contested Eden: California Before the Gold Rush.* Berkeley: University of California Press, 1998.

Haas, Lisbeth. *Conquest and Historical Identities in California: 1769–1936.* Berkeley:

University of California Press, 1995.

---. *Indigenous Scholar: Writings on Luiseño Language and Colonial History, c. 1840*. Berkeley: University of California Press, 2011.

---. *Saints and Citizens: Indigenous Histories of Colonial Missions and Mexican California*. Berkeley: University of California Press, 2014.

Hackel, Steven W. "The Staff of Leadership: Indian Authority in the Missions of Alta California." *William and Mary Quarterly* 54 (April 1997): 347–376.

---. "Sources of Rebellion: Indian Testimony and the Mission San Gabriel Uprising of 1785." *Ethnohistory* 50 (2003): 643–669.

---. *Children of Coyote, Missionaries of Saint Francis: Indian-Spanish Relations in Colonia California, 1769–1850*. Chapel Hill: University of North Carolina Press, 2005.

Hackel, Steven W., ed. *Alta California: Peoples in Motion, Identities in Formation, 1769–1850*. Berkeley: University of California Press, published for the Huntington-USC Institute on California and the West, 2010.

Halpin, Joseph. "Musical Activities and Ceremonies at Mission Santa Clara de Asís." *California Historical Quarterly* 50 (1971): 35–42.

Heizer, Robert F., ed. *The Indians of Los Angeles County: Hugo Reid's Letters of 1852*. Highland Park: Southwest Museum, 1968.

Heizer, Robert F., ed. *Handbook of North American Indians*. Vol. 8, California. Washington, DC: Smithsonian Institute Press, 1978.

Hurtado, Albert. *Indian Survival on the California Frontier*. New Haven, CT: Yale University Press, 1988.

Jackson, Robert H. and Edward D. Castillo. *Indians, Franciscans, and Spanish Colonization: The Impact of the Mission System on the California Indians*. Albuquerque: University of New Mexico Press, 1995.

Jennings, Francis. *The Invasion of America: Indians, Colonialism, and the Cant of Conquest*. Chapel Hill: University of North Carolina Press, 1975.

Jordan, Terry G. *North American Cattle-Ranching Frontiers: Origins, Diffusion, and Differentiation*. Albuquerque: University of New Mexico Press, 1993.

Kelleher, Michael. "Images of the Past: Historical Authenticity and Inauthenticity from Disney to Times Square." *CRM: The Journal of Heritage Stewardship* 1 (Summer 2004): 6–19.

Kessell, John L. *Kiva, Cross, and Crown: The Pecos Indians and New Mexico, 1540-1840*. Albuquerque: University of New Mexico Press, 1987.

---. *Spain in the Southwest*. Norman: University of Oklahoma Press, 2002.

Kimbro, Edna E. and Julia G. Costello. *The California Missions: History, Art, and Preservation*. Los Angeles: The Getty Conservation Institute, 2009.

Knudtson, Peter M. *Wintun Indians of California and their Neighbors*. Happy Camp, CA: Naturegraph Publishers, 1977.

Krech, Shepard and Barbara A. Hail, eds. *Collecting Native America, 1870-1960*. Washington, DC: Smithsonian Institution Press, 1999.

Krech, Shepard. *The Ecological Indian: Myth and History*. New York: W.W. Norton and Company, 1999.

Kroeber, Alfred L. "Shoshonean Dialects of California." *American Archeology and Ethnology* 4 (February 1907): 140–145.

---. *Handbook of the Indians of California*. Washington, DC: Government Printing Office, 1928.

Kropp, Phoebe. *California Vieja: Culture and Memory in a Modern American Place*. Berkeley: University of California Press, 2006.

Lavenda, Robert, H. "Festivals and the Creation of Public Culture: Whose Voice(s)?" In *Museums and Communities: The Politics of Public Culture*, edited by Ivan Karp, Christine Mullen Kreamer, and Steven D. Levine, 76–104. Washington, DC: Smithsonian Institution Press, 1992.

Lightfoot, Kent G. *Indians, Missionaries, and Merchants: The Legacy of Colonial Encounters on the California Frontiers*. Berkeley: University of California Press, 2005.

Lindsay, Brendan C. *Murder State: California's Native American Genocide, 1846–1873*. Lincoln: University of Nebraska Press, 2012.

Longstreth, Richard W., ed. *Cultural Landscapes: Balancing Nature and Heritage in Preservation Practice*. Minneapolis: University of Minnesota Press, 2008.

Lonnberg, Allen. "The Digger Indian Stereotype in California." Journal of California and Great Basin Anthropology 3 (1981): 215–223.

Margolin, Malcolm, ed. *The Way We Lived: California Indian Stories, Songs, and Reminiscences*. Berkeley: Heyday Books and the California Historical Society, 1993.

Maurer, Evan M. "Presenting the American Indian: From Europe to America." In *The Changing Presentation of the American Indian*, edited by Ann Kawasaki, 15–28. Washington, DC: National Museum of the American Indian, 2000.

McCawley, William. *The First Angelinos: The Gabrielino Indians of Los Angeles*. Banning, CA: Malki Museum Press, 1996.

McGroarty, John S. *California: Its History and Romance*. Los Angeles: Grafton Publishing Company, 1911.

---. *History of Southern California*. 1914. Reprint, Fresno: California History Books, 1979.

---. *Mission Memories*. Los Angeles: Neuner Corporation, 1929.

McWilliams, Cary. *North from Mexico: The Spanish-Speaking People of the United States*. New York: Praeger, 1948.

Mihesuah, Devon A., ed. *Repatriation Reader: Who Owns American Indian Remains?* Lincoln: University of Nebraska Press, 2000.

Milliken, Randall. *A Time of Little Choice: The Disintegration of Tribal Culture in the San Francisco Bay Area, 1769–1810*. Menlo Park, CA: Ballena Press, 1995.

Miskwish, Michael Connolly. *Kumeyaay: A History Textbook*. El Cajon, CA: Sycuan Press, 2007.

Nash, Gary B. *Red, White, and Black: The People of Early North America*. Englewood, NJ: Prentice-Hall, 1974.

Nieto-Phillips, John M. *The Language of Blood: The Making of Spanish-American Identity in New Mexico, 1880–1930s*. Albuquerque: University of New Mexico Press, 2004.

Norton, Jack. *Genocide in Northwestern California: When Our Worlds Cried.* San Francisco: Indian Historian Press, 1979.Nunis, Doyce B. Jr. and Edward D. Castillo. "California Mission Indians: Two Perspectives." *California History* 70 (1991): 206–215.

Panich, Lee and Tsim Schneider, eds. *Indigenous Landscapes and Spanish Missions: New Perspectives from Archeology and Ethnohistory.* Tucson: University of Arizona Press, 2014.

Phillips, George Harwood. "Indians in Los Angeles, 1781–1875: Economic Integration, Social Disintegration." *Pacific Historical Review* 49 (August 1980): 427-451.

---. *Indians and Intruders in Central California, 1769–1849.* Norman: University of Oklahoma Press, 1993.

---. *Vineyards and Vaqueros: Indian Labor and the Economic Expansion of Southern California, 1771–1877.* Norman: Arthur H. Clark, 2010.

---. *Chiefs and Challengers: Indian Resistance and Cooperation in Southern California.* Second Edition. Norman: University of Oklahoma Press, 2014.

Randall H. McGuire, "Why Have Archeologists Thought the Real Indians Were Dead and What Can We Do about It." In *Indians and Anthropologists: Vine Deloria Jr. and the Critique of Anthropology*, edited by Thomas Biolsi and Larry J. Zimmerman, 63–91. Tucson: University of Arizona Press, 1997.

Rawls, James J. *Indians of California: The Changing Image.* Norman: University of Oklahoma Press, 1984.

---. "The California Missions as Symbol and Myth." *California History* 71 (Fall 1992): 347–352.

Sandos, James A. "From 'Boltonlands' to 'Weberlands': The Borderlands Enter American History." *American Quarterly* 46 (December 1994): 595-604.

---. "*Levantamiento!* The 1824 Chumash Uprising Reconsidered." *Southern California Quarterly* 67 (1985): 109-133.

---. "Between Crucifix and Lance: Indian-White Relations in California, 1769-1848." In *Contested Eden: California Before the Gold Rush.* Edited by Rámon A Gutiérrez and Richard J. Orsi. Berkeley: University of California Press, 1998. Pp. 196-229.

---. *Converting California: Indians and Franciscans in the Missions.*New Haven, CT: Yale University Press, 2004.

Senate, Richard. *Ghosts of the California Missions and El Camino Real.* Santa Barbara: Shoreline Press, 2011.

Shackley, Steven ed., *The Early Ethnography of the Kumeyaay.* Berkeley: Phoebe Hearst Museum of Anthropology, 2004.

Sheehan, Bernard W. *Seeds of Extinction: Jeffersonian Philanthropy and the American Indian.* New York: W.W. Norton and Company, 1973.

Shipek, Florence C. "California Indian Reactions to the Franciscans." *The Americas* 41 (April 1985): 480-492.

---. *Pushed Into the Rocks: Southern California Indian Land Tenure, 1769-1986.* Lincoln: University of Nebraska Press, 1988.

Simmons, William S. "Indian Peoples of California." *California History* 76 (summer-fall 1997): 48–77.

Simpson, Moira G. *Making Representations: Museums in the Post-Colonial Era.* New York: Routledge, 2001.

Smith, Sherry L. *Reimagining Indians: Native Americans through Anglo Eyes, 1880-1940.* New York: Oxford University Press, 2000.

Spence, Mark David. *Dispossessing the Wilderness: Indian Removal and the Making of the National Parks.* New York: Oxford University Press, 1999.

Spicer, Edward H. *Cycles of Conquest: The Impact of Spain, Mexico, and the United States on the Indians of the Southwest, 1533-1960.* Tucson: University of Arizona Press, 1962.

Starr, Kevin. *Inventing the Dream: California through the Progressive Era.* New York: Oxford University Press, 1985.

Thomas, David Hurst, ed. *Columbian Consequences.* 3 Vols. Washington, DC: Smithsonian Institution Press, 1989-1991.

Thomas, David Hurst. *Skull Wars: Kennewick Man, Archaeology, and the Battle for Native American Identity.* New York: Basic Books, 2000.

Thompson, Mark. *American Character: The Curious Life of Charles Fletcher Lummis and the Rediscovery of the Southwest.* New York: Arcade Publishing, 2001.

Trafzer, Clifford E. "Serra's Legacy: The Desecration of American Indian Burials at Mission San Diego." *American Indian Culture and Research Journal* 16 (1992): 57-75.

---. *The People of San Manuel.* Patton, CA: San Manuel Band of Mission Indians, 2002.

Trafzer, Clifford E. and Joel Hyer, eds., *"Exterminate Them!": Written Accounts of the Murder, Rape, and Enslavement of Native Americans during the California Gold Rush.* East Lansing: Michigan State University Press, 1999.

Vaughn, Chelsea K. "Locating Absence: The Forgotten Presence of Monjeríos in the Alta California Missions." *Southern California Quarterly* 93 (2011): 141-174.

---. "The Joining of Historical Pageantry and the Spanish Fantasy Past: The Meeting of Señora Josefa Yorba and Lucretia del Valle." *The Journal of San Diego History* 57 (2011): 213-235.

Voss, Barbara L. "Colonial Sex: Archeology, Structured Space, and Sexuality in Alta California's Spanish-colonial Missions." In *Archaeologies of Sexuality.* Edited by Robert A. Schmidt and Barbara L. Voss. New York: Routledge, 2000. Pp. 35-61.

Weber, David J. *The Spanish Frontier in North America.* New Haven, CT: Yale University Press, 1992.

---. "The Spanish Borderlands of North America: A Historiography." Special Issue. *OAH Magazine of History* 14 (summer 2000): 5-11.

---. *Bárbaros: Spaniards and Their Savages in the Age of Enlightenment.* New Haven, CT: Yale University Press, 2005.

Weber, Francis J., ed. *The Pride of the Missions: A Documentary History of San Gabriel Mission.* Hong Kong: Libra Press Limited, 1978.

Wilson, Darryl and Barry Joyce, eds. *Dear Christopher: Letters to Christopher Columbus by Contemporary Native Americans.* Riverside: University of California

Publications in American Indian Studies, 1992.

White, Richard. *"It's Your Misfortune and None of My Own": A New History of the American West.* Norman: University of Oklahoma Press, 1993.

# Index